CONTEMPORARY ART
FROM THE ISLAMIC WORLD

edited by
WIJDAN ALI

with the assistance of
Suhail Bisharat

Foreword by
HRH Prince El Hassan Bin Talal

Published by Scorpion Publishing Ltd, London
on behalf of
The Royal Society of Fine Arts, Amman

First published in 1989 by Scorpion Publishing Ltd,
Victoria House, Buckhurst Hill, Essex, England,
on behalf of the Royal Society of Fine Arts, Amman, Jordan.

ISBN 0 905906 80 2 (paper)
ISBN 0 905906 84 5 (cased)

General Editor: Leonard Harrow
House Editor: John Orley
Assistant Editor: Kay Larkin
Art Director: Colin Larkin
Designer: Andrew Nash
Production Assistant: Sue Pipe
Photography: Aram Darakjian
Additional photography: Paul Hancock

Main text typeset in Linotype Berkeley Old Style 10 on 12 point
Printed on 135gsm matt art
Printed and bound in England by MacLehose & Partners Ltd

Contents

Acknowledgements

The editor wishes to express her sincere gratitude to HRH Crown Prince El Hassan Bin Talal for his constant support and continuous encouragement in bringing about the exhibition and the book *Contemporary Art from the Islamic World*.

The editor wishes to thank the Islamic Educational, Scientific and Cultural Organization (ISESCO) in the person of its President, HE Mr Abdul Hadi Butalib, Mr Namir Kirdar, Dr Ahmad Chalabi, the Ford Foundation and Petra Bank for financing the publishing of this book.

Thanks are also due to those who provided the editor with assistance and information during her work on the book, particularly: HRH Prince Faysal Bin Fahad, Minister of Culture and Youth of Saudi Arabia, HE Dato Haji Mohammad Zein Bin Haji Sarudin, Minister of Religious Affairs of Brunei Darussalam, HE Mr Mohammad Bin Issa, Minister of Culture of Morocco, Mrs Azra Ahmad, Mr Jalal Uddin Ahmad, Mr Cherif Bendoda, Dr Leila Bisharat, Miss Hiba Dajani, Mr Ihsan Idilbi, Syed Ahmad Jamal, Mr Rafik Lahham, Mrs Maryam Massoudi, and last, but not least, the Ministry of Information and Culture in Jordan.

Note on Spelling

The spelling of proper names of artists and other Arabic terms in this work has been in accordance with the usual way those names are spelt in the Roman alphabet. As so many local traditions are involved this inevitably means there is no systematic transliteration employed and therefore the proper names are often spelt idiosyncratically.

List of Artists

Algeria
BAYA
KORAICHI, MAHMOUD RACHID
NIATI, HOURIA

Bangladesh
KHAN, HAMIDUZZAMAN
MASUDUL HASSAN
MAHMUDUL HAQ
MUNIRUL ISLAM
KIBRIA, MOHAMED
RAFIQUN NABI
SHAH, ABDUS SHAKOOR
TABBAA, DODI

Brunei Darussalam
BIN YAHYA, MOHAMAD NOOR ZAIRI
DURAMAN, PG HAJI MUHAMMAD BIN PG
MAHARI, PG OMAR ALI BIN PG HJ
RASHID, ABIDIN BIN HAJI

Egypt
AWAD, KAMAL AMIN
AYAD, RAGHEB
BIKAR, HUSSEIN
EFFLATOUN, INJI
GEBALI, HUSSEIN EL-
HAFIZ, FARGHALI ABDEL
HILMY, MENHATALLAH
HUSSEIN, TAHA
MOATI, MOSTAFA ABDEL
MOSTAFA, AHMAD
MOUSTAFA, RAMZI
NADA, HAMED
NASHAR, ABDEL RAHMAN
NAWAR, AHMAD
NIMER, RABAB
NIMMER, AYAD
SAROFIM, MINA
SHEHATA, FAROUK
SHIMI, AWAD AL-
TAHER, SALAH
WANLY, SEIF

Gulf
AHMAD, YUSSEF
ASHOUR, ABDEL AZIZ
BAQSAMI, SURAYA AL-
BU HAMID, JASSEM
DIA, DIA AZIZ
JAHA, YUSSEF
MOSLY, MOUNIRA
MUFIZ, ABDEL LATIF
MULLA, HASSAN AL-
QASBI, MONA
RADWI, ABDEL HALIM
SALMAN, ABDEL RASOUL

SAQR, ISSA
SONIA, ANWAR KHAMIS
SULEIMAN, ABDEL RAHMAN
YOUSIF, NASSER AL-

Iran
HADJIZADEH, GHASSEM
MEYKADEH, SIMIN
NASSIRI, ALI
SAMIMI, RAVI
TANAVOLI, PARVIZ
ZENDEROUDI, HOSSEIN

Iraq
ATTAR, SUAD
AZZAWI, DIA
BACHIR, ALA'
CHORBACHI, WASMA KHALID
DABDOUB, RAKAN
DROUBY, HAFIZ
FATTAH, ISMA'IL
GHANI, MOHAMED
HASSAN, FAIK
JADER, KHALID AL-
JUMAIE, SALEH AL-
KAKI, JAFAR
KANIKIAN, FREISH
MASSOUDY, HASSAN
MOUTASHER, MEHDI
NASIRI, RAFA AL-
RAWI, NOURI EL-
SAID, ISSAM EL-
SALIM, NIZAR
SELIM, NAZIHA
SHAKER, SAAD
SHEIKHLEY, ISMAIL

Jordan
ABDEL AZIZ, NASR
ABU SHINDI, SALEH
AMMOURA, AZIZ
AMR, KAYED
ASHOUR, JAMAL
BISHARAT, SUHAIL
DURRA, MUHANNA
DUWAIK, YASSER
HADDADIN, SAID
JABRI, ALI
KASSIS, HAFIZ
KHAMMASH, AMMAR
KHREIS, KHALID
LAHHAM, RAFIK
MIMI, FUAD
MOUSTAFA, MOHAMMED
NAJJAR, IBRAHIM
NAWASH, AHMAD
NIMRI, KURAM

OBEIDAT, DAIF ALLAH
SADDIQ, MAHMOUD
SAUDI, MONA
SAYED, TAWFIC EL-
SHAMOUN, ABDEL RAOUF
SHEHADEH, NABIL
SHOMAN, SUHA
TABBAA, SAMER
TAHA, MAHMOUD
WIJDAN
YEHIA, ADNAN
ZEID, FAHRELNISSA

Lebanon
ABBOUD. CHAFIC
ADNAN, ETEL
DOUAIHY, SALIBA
ELBACHA, AMIN
GUIRAGOSSIAN. EMMANUEL
GUIRAGOSSIAN. PAUL
KHAL, HELEN
SERAPHIME, JULIANA
TAMIM, SUHA

Libya
ERMES, ALI OMER

Malaysia
CHERS, NG BUAN
HASHIM. ISMAIL
IBRAHIM, KHALIL
JAMAL, SYED AHMAD
SHANMUGHALINGAM. NIRMALA
THIEN SHIH. LONG
YUSOF, AHMAD KHALID
ZUBIR, SHARIFA FATIMAH

Morocco
ABDEL AZIZ, ABOU ALI
AZZA, AL-HACHIMI
BELKAHIA, FARID
HARIRI, ABDULLA
MELEHI, MOHAMED
QOTBI, MAHDI
YOUSSUFI, OMAR

Pakistan
AGHA, ZUBEIDA
AKHLAQ, ZAHOORUL
DAVID, COLIN
HASSAN, MANSOORA
IKRAMULLAH, NAZ
IMAM, ALI
NAQSH, JAMIL
RASUL, GHULAM
SADEQUAIN
SAJJAD, SHAHID

SAURA, NAJMI
SHAHZADA, LAILA
SHARIF, HAJI MOHAMMAD
SHUJAULLAH, USTAD
SIDDIQUI, SHAKEEL
ZAIDI, HASSAN SHAHNAWAZ
ZARINA

Palestine
ANANI, NABIL
ARAFAT, AFAF
BADR, ISSAM
BADRAN, SAMIRA
BARAKAT, TAYSIR
BOULLATA, KAMAL
MANSOUR, SULEIMAN
NUSSEIBEH, MUNIRA
SALAMEH, SAMIR
SHAWA, LEILA
ZARU, SAMIA

Sudan
ABDAL AAL, AHMAD IBRAHIM
ABDULLA, MUHAMMAD AHMED

ADAM, SHAMS EDDIN
AWAAM, IBRAHIM EL-
BAGHDADI, BASTAWI
DIAB, RASHID
IBRAHIM, KAMALA
KHAIRY, OMER
KHALIL, MOHAMED OMER
KHATIM, ABDEL BASIT
NOOR, HUSSEIN HADI MOHAMED
OTEIBI, MOHAMED ABDULLA
RABBAH, MAJDOUB
SHIBRAIN, AHMAD MOHAMED

Syria
BURHAN, SAMI
CHURA, NASIR
HAMMAD, MAHMOUD
MOUDARRES, FATEH
NABA'A, NAZIR
ZAYYAT, ELIAS

Tunisia
ASRAM, KHALID
AZZABI, BRAHIM

BEN MEFTAH, MOHAMED
BEN SLIMAN, KHALID
DAHAK, IBRAHIM
GUERMASSI, ALI
KAMEL, RAFIK
LABBAN, HEDI
MAHDAOUI, NJA

Turkey
ABAÇ, NURI
ARBAŞ, AVNI
DINO, ABIDIN
ERBIL, DEVRIM
EREN, CEMIL
EROL, TURAN
EYÜBOĞLU, BEDRI RAHMI
GÖKÇEBAĞ, YALÇIN
MUALLA, FIKRET
TURANI, ADNAN
UYGUR, BURHAN

Yemen
FUTAIH, FUAD AL-

Foreword
HRH Prince EL Hassan Bin Talal

It gives me great pleasure to introduce the following book, edited by Her Royal Highness Princess Wijdan Ali, on the occasion of the convening of the Exhibition on Contemporary Art from the Islamic World. This exhibition is organized by the Royal Society of Fine Arts in the Hashemite Kingdom of Jordan, in collaboration with the Islamic Arts Foundation in the United Kingdom.

This book focuses on bringing together the cultural differences between the Islamic and Western traditions, which, in my opinion, would develop a pre-eminent understanding, and consequently improve relationships among the people and countries of these two civilizations.

Her Royal Highness gives a general explanation of the transition in Islamic countries from the practising of classical Islamic art forms to modern Western art, such as painting on canvas, sculptures, graphics and ceramics. Various prominent art historians have contributed to this book by outlining the artistic background of each participating country in an historical context, by reviewing the development of its contemporary art, by giving a critique of the works of the 207 participating artists, and conclude by evaluating the present art scene.

I thank the Barbican Centre of London for hosting this Exhibition as it marks the sincere intention of furthering the cultural accord between the Islamic and Western Worlds, in a spirit of mutual understanding and co-operation.

El Hassan Bin Talal
Crown Prince of the Hashemite Kingdom of Jordan

Director's Note

Suhail Bisharat

On 12 February 1980 the Jordan National Gallery of Fine Arts was officially opened by their Majesties King Hussein and Queen Noor. It was a national accomplishment made possible by the full co-operation and support of the Jordanian community.

The Jordan National Gallery of Fine Arts began with an idea, not a collection. Founded by the Royal Society of Fine Arts in 1979, it was Her Royal Highness Princess Wijdan Ali, President of the Royal Society of Fine Arts, who turned the idea into reality. With its establishment the Jordan National Gallery became the pioneer in its field, not only in Jordan but in the rest of the Arab and Islamic world. It was the first institution to promote the full spectrum of contemporary Islamic art in terms of its development, its appreciation and international recognition.

It also has built a collection of contemporary Arab and Islamic artists working on canvas, in graphics, lithographs, ceramics, stone or other sculptural material. There is a small but interesting and historically important collection of nineteenth century Orientalist paintings as well. Because it is not based on an inheritance from any major collection, the Jordan National Gallery has had to acquire piecemeal its works of art over the last ten years.

In the early years it was most fortunate to have many distinguished patrons and collectors lend support. From the Royal Family to private individuals, government bodies, the Royal Jordanian Airlines, the various banks, private as well as public institutions joined hands with Jordanian as well as Arab Islamic artists in making the Jordan National Gallery the success it is today. Today the Jordan National Gallery has gained an international reputation for the excellence and the representative character of its collection. Most of the works of both Jordanian and Islamic artists can be found in almost every imaginable medium, technique and style from the representative to the abstract. In no other single art museum can one see such a broad range of exhibits enabling one to view and experience the development of artistic expression in the region.

The Jordan National Gallery houses today over 1,000 works: oil paintings, watercolours, prints, ceramics and sculptures. The works are representative of major schools of art from the turn of the century.

Because of the increasing importance of the Gallery's collection in number and quality, it has become imperative that these works be made available to a larger public. The Royal Society of Fine Arts is also extremely active in arranging cultural exchanges, in supporting deserving artists, and in bridging cultural barriers. The Jordan National Gallery has arranged exhibitions for works of art drawn from major Western sources such as the Pompidou Centre in Paris, the Victoria and Albert Museum in London, the Harvard Semitic Museum, and the Turkish museums, as well as from many international galleries and museums of the Arab Islamic world.

The Gallery's main function is to collect, record, document, publish and exhibit works by contemporary Arab and Islamic artists of excellence. Exhibitions selected from the Jordan National Gallery have been sent for display in Istanbul, Ankara, Warsaw, Krakow and Paris. It is a non-profit organization and the Gallery is dependent on financial gifts or the individual donations of works by artists themselves. Its success depends essentially upon the appreciation, understanding and generosity of the public at large, whether from within the region or from distant countries.

This exhibition celebrates the tenth anniversary of the Royal Society of Fine Arts. It is drawn from the Gallery's permanent collection. It does not represent a historical survey, but it does represent the richness and importance of contemporary Islamic art.

The Jordan National Gallery is unique among the museums of the Arab world. No other museum contains a permanent collection that spans the same geographical compass but also maintains the continuing effort to document and record artists and art movements from all the Islamic countries.

The selection on exhibit at the Barbican Centre expresses different national schools and stylistic trends from twenty-three countries. We pay tribute to all these artists whose works are exhibited and are no longer with us.

Both the Board of Trustees and myself are pleased to share this exhibition with the public. It is hoped that a better understanding of the Arab and Islamic world through art will add a new dimension to the cultural collaboration between East and West.

Introduction
Wijdan Ali

The Islamic world today covers all of North and Central Africa, the Middle East, including Turkey, Iran and Pakistan and most of Southeast Asia. Great empires have risen and fallen on these lands, leaving behind them sequences of Islamic civilization, with its universality and unity in its diversity.

After the apex of the empires had fallen, colonial rule followed, sometimes lasting for centuries, and led to a period of artistic lethargy and cultural stagnation. Artists lost those attentive patrons who had lavished their support on the arts. The occupation of the Islamic lands by foreign colonizers not only undermined their economic self-sufficiency but also debilitated their arts. Western aesthetics and culture overpowered indigenous traditional art.

Since the beginning of the twentieth century, before and after gaining independence, most Islamic countries went through an intellectual and political rebirth, which affected their artistic development and created a cultural resurrection among their intellectuals. One of the main areas that benefited from this renaissance was fine arts. Yet, the renaissance in modern Islamic painting and sculpture that occurred was to adhere to Western aesthetics and norms, causing a loss of cultural identity which created a schizophrenic sense of guilt within the modern Islamic artist: his education and training became totally Western while his beliefs and convictions remained conventional. This, by no means, is tied to the misconception of a ban on figurative painting in Islam which most Westerners and some Muslims alike came to reiterate.

Painting In Islam

Islam's ban on creating the image of living beings comes from the traditions of the Prophet. The ban was intended to deter converts to the new religion from reverting to atheism and the worship of idols. Idols were worshipped by most inhabitants of the Arabian Peninsula before the advent of Islam. Figurative painting and the sculpture of living beings was, and is, banned in places of worship so that they would not distract worshippers from their prayers and spiritual meditation or become an instrument in the hands of kings and rulers to elevate themselves to saintly positions. The Dome of the Rock in Jerusalem and the Great Umayyad Mosque in Damascus, both built during the first century of Islam, contain superb examples of mosaic murals depicting cities, rivers, waterfalls, trees and flowers. If human paintings and statues were excluded from the mosque they nevertheless remained part of the decorative arts of secular buildings. The early Umayyad palaces in Jordan and Syria, and later the Abassid palaces of Samarra in Iraq, witnessed the early bloom of Islamic pictorial art. Figurative painting also continued in manuscript illustration. Two schools of painting, Baghdad and Mosul, flourished in Iraq during the thirteenth century. Each school had its own rules and style. Later Moghul, Safavid and Ottoman miniatures reached a peak of perfection in India, Iran and Turkey.

Islamic art focuses on the spiritual representation of objects and beings, not their material qualities. The Islamic artist thus chose two-dimensional stylization to represent his forms and totally neglected the exact imitation of nature. The art of abstraction in Islamic art was not born from any lack of skill on the artist's part, but from his rejection of materialism and its ephemeral qualities. His quest was one for the eternal representation of the spirit. Nature, humans and objects, in Islamic painting, are represented by their spiritual, not their physical and material qualities. The spiritual rejection of the material gave birth to the stylized and abstract ornamentation of the arabesque.

At the outset Islam borrowed a great deal from other artistic traditions that it came in contact with such as Byzantine, Sassanian, Buddhist, Chinese and others. It attained diversity within unity, in a world where the closest and most direct line between two points was sailing around a continent. Today, as the world becomes smaller international trends and styles move rapidly within the exchange of knowledge and technology among nations. Art everywhere has shed its limited and limiting traits and is heading towards universalism.

Modern Islamic Art

Despite the vast distances that separate some of the countries of the Islamic world and their diverse backgrounds, all share many common traits in the development of their contemporary art.

1 The training of all modern Islamic artists, whether at home or abroad, is Western-oriented and follows Western norms, aesthetics and rules.

2 Most Islamic artists share a common search for their artistic identity, in a way that will allow them to combine their Eastern origins with their Western education and way of life. At the Saqqah-Khaneh in Tehran or the Tunis School, at La Chimère Group in Cairo or the Baghdad Group, the quest is the same and continues a relentless effort to achieve assimilation and synthesis between traditional heritage and Western modernity.

3 Almost all modern Islamic artists, even those in the most progressive countries, have a problem communicating with their own societies. Art and artists are alienated from the public. In general, art is regarded as no more than a hobby for the idle to practise and a luxury for the rich to enjoy. This accounts for the limited number of Islamic artists who are able to live off their art. Governments too have yet to support and patronize the arts in a substantial way.

There are notable disparities between countries of the Islamic world, not only in their standard of living but also in the development of the modern art movement in each country. The prosperity of a country or its per capita income, by no means reflects its cultural and artistic progress.

This book accompanies the exhibition of 'Contemporary Art from the Islamic World'. Together they form part of an endeavour to show the progress and evolution of plastic arts in most regions of the Islamic world. Jordan's Royal Society of Fine Arts and the Islamic Arts Foundation in London through the book and the exhibition, bring a message of peace, beauty and love from the Islamic East to the West in an effort to close a cultural gap that has led to blurred vision on both sides.

Hopefully, 'Contemporary Art from the Islamic World' will be a two way bridge that will carry the flow of inspiration, trends, styles and ideas between Islamic and Western cultures.

Algeria
Benamar Mediene

Introduction

Any consideration of modern Arab-Muslim art must have an element of bitterness followed by a long line of questioning. It is worth noting that in the four-volume, 6,800 page encyclopaedia *La Pleiade*, edited by Gallimard under the direction of Bernard Dorival, only six pages are devoted to modern plastic art in the Arab and Muslim countries of the Orient and in Maghrib. Israel, Iran and Pakistan are also included in this region. Six pages in which a handful of artists' names are lost in an incoherent history, lacking cultural depth and continuity.

Any aesthetic ordering gives way to a collection of indistinct anecdotes. They appear from nowhere and stand alone within the haze of names, each of them remaining on the periphery of society, suspended above social reality. This ordering is only seen as continual if it is the result of copying and reproduction rather than as a result of the work done by the Arab-Muslim artists of Western aesthetics which I consider to be at the geometrical crux of universal art. Jacques Berque was right to reverse the relationship between art and the universal: 'Mais du reste pourquoi sanctionner par des constats d'existence ou de carence la présomption que les genres seraient universels, alors que seuls le sont les appels auxquels ils répondent, et fort diversement d'âge en âge et de société en société?'

Dorival accounts for the poverty of the plastic arts in the Islamic countries by emphasising the importance of religious and political taboos which inhibit and even prevent the spirit of creativity. The feeling of bitterness that I mentioned earlier is in fact rather ambivalent since it is based half on reality and half on prejudice, as suggested by Dorival whose knowledge is indisputable.

An historical analysis of Arab art (such as Dorival's) is conducted from a 'height' and is consequently lead to make the following assertions: the religious and political taboos control, infringe, censor and manipulate artistic expression, removing it from its true function or even replacing it. But these taboos do not prevent artistic expression since art affirms its existence by standing against moral, religious and political principles and dogmas and by using its own language and making its own way through the body of society, i.e., through communication and culture.

This type of analysis has another implication: that of guaranteeing something that has merely been postulated about the Muslim world and the organic relations it has between art and religious ethics and between religious ethics and the political norm. Here, weight and nuance are added. For even if the art and the artist in the Arab-Muslim countries are set apart, threatened with silence, exile or compromise they are still able to express themselves in certain restricted areas and what they say, and how, may then be expanded upon.

If not, how else would we have heard about the Egyptians Ramsis Younan, Georges Henein, Hamad Abdullah, Fouad Kemal, etc., who founded the surrealist group 'Art and Freedom' from 1939 onwards? During its existence the group transgressed all the traditionally sacred and powerful values and expressed them instead through subversive artistic activities. The artists wanted 'to introduce a new vocabulary into the Arabic language that would convey some of the changes in the cultural world.'

'Art and Freedom': two central ideas that are dialectically complementary – each one encouraging and throwing light on the other in the continual movement of creation. If this was not so, how would we understand that the Iraqis Jawad Salim and Faiq Hassan were at the same time grasping the essence of twentieth century modern art without folding under the influence of Picasso and Matisse – though realising their valuable contribution – and creating a modern dynamic stance without dialogizing their peoples' past and present?

In the 1950s the Iraqi sculptors and the group 'Modern Art of Baghdad' created by Jawad Salim put forward a manifesto based on the duality of 'the singular and the universal'. It was a particular problem at a time when the over-estimation of past classicism corresponded to a present situation of lack, a situation moving negatively in relation to 'a people crying out to be heard, a people on a quest for truth and beauty.' In Iraq, as in Egypt, the idea of 'Art and Freedom' was at the heart of the quest.

In independent Algeria during the 1960s, each fountain pen, each camera and each paintbrush was directed towards paying homage to its heroes. According to the artists, the form did not matter as long as the people grasped the meaning. The most popular means of expression in pictorial art revolved around the cult of the 'hero', the restoration of the past, the lives of the people, nationalisations and the socialist commercial sphere, etc.

The National Union of Plastic Artists (UNAP) became the most important forum for artists and at the same time it promoted themes and dimensions of works. Although this movement (UNAP) occupied the centre stage in the 1960s, it was not the only one in existence. Outside of the UNAP, many other painters were working on their own areas of study. Issiakhem, Khadda, Baya, Mesil, Ali-Khodja, Yélles, Martinez, Samson, Louail, Temmam, Ranem, Bouzid, Aksouh, etc, tried to bring back 'L'Ecole Nationale des Beaux Arts d'Alger'. Like their counterparts in Egypt, Iraq, Tunisia and Morocco, the Algerians faced the same problem of the relationship between national and international art; how can one be an individual, a romantic, a creator and still retain a means of communication with the public at large? How can a modernist avoid being labelled an outsider? How can one react to the depths of one's being, one's conscience and sub-conscience and one's fantasies without being seen as a pervert, a plagiarist or a fanatic obsessed with the Western world?

In the fifteen years after independence, the Brownian movement within the UNAP introduced controls for the Algerian galleries and selected various artists for exhibitions abroad. In 1967 a group of painters led by Mesil founded the 'Aouchem' movement (Berber word for 'tattooing') supported by a theoretical manifesto. Their aim was to get away from the heavy and time-consuming debates on the universal and the authentic. 'Aouchem' or tattooing signified a return to Berber-Algerian culture and its ancestry; a revival and reappraisal of all that had been forbidden and suppressed under colonialism and religious doctrine. It stood firmly opposed to 'gratuitous Western abstraction' and extolled the virtues of the true symbols and totems that say something about the world we live in.

Such passionate feeling for this half revolutionary, half nostalgic movement helps to convey the confusion among Algerian painters in the first few years of independence. There was a feeling of identity crisis both on an historical-ethnic level and on an aesthetic level. In fact, those who signed the manifesto ended up reviving the problems that they wished to lay to rest; by lifting obstacles they created obstacles; by setting themselves guidelines they imposed restrictions upon themselves.

In the 1970s a new generation of painters appeared: Silem, Zerouki, Bourdine, Ouadahi, Mokrani, Bellakh, Bisker, Benyahia . . . Some passed through UNAP, others were tutees of masters such as Issiakhem, Khadda, or Martinez. They offered originality and the promise of enrichment in Algerian plastic art. Liberated from external political and religious constraints, they were permitted a freedom of expression.

It is true that success in art, or at least, the capitalist conception and appreciation of art, is assessed and measured in the galleries of London, Paris, New York and Tokyo. It is true that no Arab artist has ever reached the level of the great masters in these capital cities. It is also true that art is still not considered to be a major subject in Arab countries. Finally, it is true that any historical, critical and intellectual work based on art is still insufficient, superficial and inaccurate.

This probably explains why Dorival devoted only six pages of his encyclopaedia to modern art in the Arab Muslim nations, two pages to Israel and five lines on Algeria!

In the Maghrib, aesthetic analysis is almost non-existent. Intellectually it does not exist except in snatches of literary commentary. Analyses are half finished and often limited, lacking in depth and historical accuracy. Aestheticism remains in suspension.

In universities and research departments an artistic object is either ignored and treated with disinterest or else mistrusted and seen as unimportant on the scale of social priorities. The intelligentsia is on the fringe of society. The artist walks the fine line between society and oblivion.

The cultural institutions – schools, mass media, publishers and artistic associations – control and influence ideas and minds. The progression of modernism is commanded as an army would be. Theoretical and philosophical work, i.e., thoughts that are impossible to veto, are nevertheless kept in line. The major concept in Algeria is 'unity of thought'. Supported by political dogma, it weakens the capacity for individual thought and destroys the spirit of creativity. For any of the nations wishing to keep up with modern times, it is almost impossible not to examine and copy the foreign (i.e. Western) role models.

Algeria 1950

Issiakhem was both a presenter and a prophet. He was to painting what Kateb, Feraoun, Dib, Mameri, Hammani, Haddad, and Djebbar were to the novel, what Lacheraf, Sahli were to the essay and what Aba, Senac, Amrani, Greki and Hadj Ali were to poetry.

The fifties were a time when tormented Algeria resolved to settle her accounts on every front. Prophets and speakers, using art as a political mouthpiece, announced a widening of the path towards universality.

The historical net began to tighten as the Algerian artists consolidated their efforts. The painters: Issiakhem, Khadda, Temmam, Ali-Khodja, Guermaz, Louail, Baya, Yélles, Mesli, Benanteur, Samson, Aksouh; the writers: Kateb, Feraoun, Dib, Mameri, Hammani, Haddad, and Djebbar; the essayist Lacheraf; and the poets: Aba, Senac, Amrani, Greki . . . were the loudhailers whose words had a piercing effect on the Algerian people.

They were not mystic visionaries nor political soothsayers. They merely wanted to convey a message: the destruction of Algeria had only been superficial. Although her cultural foundations had been severely shaken, Algeria would rise again, transformed according to the eternal movement of life.

Ignoring the arrogance of the censors, they strived to be heard. To be heard not in part but in full. To be heard not in certain houses in certain areas, but everywhere. The message was: The Painting and the Book. There was a feeling of urgency, a need to paint and to write in the face of their ever-present occupier and usurper.

In the fifties violence was a prominent feature in Algeria, becoming more and more banal in its daily repetition. The people felt that their history had been stolen from them, that their country had been inhabited by strangers. As for the painter he was driven to smashing through the barriers and restrictions in order to catch a glimpse of the hinterland again. After all, perspective only has meaning when one can see everything.

In the centenary celebrations of July 1930 (when Issiakhem was only two and Kateb was a one-year-old) French Algeria was bursting with self-importance. It was an egotistical ceremony on the part of the coloniser who, thinking he was in possession of the body of the Algerian, was in fact only in possession of its shadow. The coloniser was blind – not recognising and even negating the very presence of the Algerian, blind in his exercise of force, subjection and murder, blind in his ignorance.

Colonialism took over. The territory was possessed. The people had nothing left to prove, nothing left of its identity. The West was proud of its missionaries, approved of them, blessed them, and sent in the troops when the slightest attempt was made to undermine their position of high morality.

Painting from Algeria or Algerian Painting?

Issiakhem and Kateb were two outrageous artists who met in 1951. On the one hand they called for an end to the preoccupation that Algerian art had with aesthetic 'passéisme', and with the exotic and the folkloric. On the other hand they called for the end of 'L'Ecole d'Alger' that reeked of colonial ideology.

From Louis Bertrand to Albert Camus (via Randau, Carré, Dinet, Aubry and Audisio) the philosophers of the time worked to represent and convey the structure of intellectual colonialism. From Dinet's spiritualism, Randau's positive humanism and Camus' existentialism to Bertrand's mystic latinism, variation thrived in the intellectual circles. The Algerian people, however, were seen as a more passive reality, as a piece of set fiction whose destiny has been decided in advance. To onlookers, the colonial world gave the appearance of order and reason.

The Algerian artist was lost behind the protocol, lost behind the facade of the Société des Beaux Arts (founded in 1851), the Algerian Museum of 1900, etc., where the latest celebrities and styles were seen. When present, the Algerian artist was not 'exposing' his art, he was merely exhibiting it.

When Youssef ben Haffaf exhibited his ceramics and his wood and copper engravings in Algeria, Paris and Lyon at the beginning of the 1920s, he was received more as an artisan than an artist. As for his work, it was not appreciated for its aesthetic value but for its value as a symbol and microcosm of his native status.

When Mohammed Racim, the celebrated miniaturist and calligrapher, exhibited in June 1935 at the 35th Salon of Algerian artists, his portrait of the head of the Academie d'Alger was given precedence over his theme and technique.

By the end of the nineteenth century when the impressionists Albert Lebourg and Albert Marquet were painting on walls, roofs and mosques, Algerian painting was holding a delicate balance between two aesthetic poles: that of romantic and sensualist orientalism (à la Delacroix and à la Fromentin). This style was sometimes spiritualistic (Dinet, Carré) and sometimes profane and descriptive (Bascoulès, van Biesbrock, Saraillon, Chevalier, Antoni, Flasschoen, Lino, Descamps . . .). That of neo-classicism (à la David). This style was revived by Emile Aubry (Prix de Rome 1907) in his biblical and allegorical scenes.

Influential philosophers had their views on the Arab-Berber mentality. Augustin Berque: '. . . the Berber is not a dreamer. He has no lyrical imagination. His approach never extends beyond the cold contact with objects. The Berber artist is still an artisan.' A. Gayet, Arab art historian: '. . . He is indifferent to the shapes and colours that would provoke emotion from the rest of us . . . How is his perception so different from ours? . . . The Arab soul no longer belongs to our race . . .'

Algerian painting continued to ignore or reject out of hand the Modernism used by Picasso and Braque, Matisse and Max Ernst, Paul Klee and Kandinsky to revive primitive art. By the end of the

1930s it had reached a point of deadlock and stagnation. Variations on the themes of orientalism and neo-classicism became grotesque and degenerated into weakened forms of folklore and the syrupy representations of 'passéisme'.

The members of the 'Villa Abdellatif', Cuavy, Bascoulès, Antoni, Berasconi, Assus, de Maisonseul, Galliero, sponsored by Albert Marquet, involved themselves in Algerian culture and in Impressionism. They rejected exoticism and other styles and uses of colour that made the spectator feel as if he was the 'owner' of the object.

At the beginning of the 1940s, Sauveur Galliero and Jean de Maisonseul dissociated themselves from the neo-impressionists of the 'Villa Abdellatif'. To these two artists, art was a quest for authenticity and universality. It was in a realm above national and individual problems and went beyond superficial materiality. To them art could only be abstract art. As Mondrian said, 'the *chose* is more important than the *rapport*'.

The authenticity and universality movement has no sense unless it completely avoids social contradictions and other undermining factors that are inevitable in a growing country like Algeria. Yet it was this movement that dominated 'L'Ecole d'Alger' in its first exhibition on 17 December 1953.

How could Marquet's 'possession of objects' and Galliero's 'universality and authenticity' be realised in a country whose history had been confiscated, whose imagination had been wiped clean and whose people had been treated as objects rather than as subjects?

How did Algerian painters of the time appear and distinguish themselves? Each artist has a different background.

The brothers Omar and Mohammed Racim came from bourgeois Algiers. Others like Mameri were forced into exile in Morocco and Spain. For most (calligraphers, ceramic and copper artists their art was required for its practical and/or decorative value. An artistic object was only useful if it could be sold. Life was different for Omar and Mohammed Racim, Temmam and Ranem. Calligraphy brought them closer to abstract art. It was not merely a simple form of ornamentation and illustration as Georges Marçais seemed to suggest; it was a skill of great importance. The 'letter' and the 'word' were symbols – profane symbols of spiritualism and religion. Hence there was a need to create one's own area of expression by turning away from the here and now in order to delve into the past again as the Racim brothers, Mameri, Hemche, Temmam or Ranem had done.

It was a tumultuous time for Algerian life and Algerian art. It was a time for putting an end to ambivalent and ambiguous expression. The isolated, hesitant artists of the past were no more. The new representatives brought new excitement together with the realisation that universal art could only be possible if every man, his territory, his history and his future were fully recognised and respected.

Algerian Painters in Paris

In 1953 Issiakhem arrived in Paris. His cultural and theoretical knowledge had been severely retarded by colonialism. By contrast, the Mexicans Atl, Diego Rivera and David Siqueiros, who had arrived in Paris at the beginning of the century, took with them considerable experience and a long tradition of imaginative painting, inspired by their predecessors and ancestors.

Their main intention was to speed up the collapse of the old academic empire in Mexico – an empire already under threat by modern artists such as José Posada. By attacking artistic institutions in this way they were also launching an assault on Mexico's entire political system. In their actions the Mexican reformers highlighted the dialectical relationship between an agitated populist revolutionary movement and a thriving Western artistic movement.

They arrived in Paris at a very exciting time – Modernism had just wrenched itself away from the Greek and Roman influences of the Renaissance period. It was also the time when Picasso, Matisse, Ernst, etc., began to distinguish themselves.

The two principle phases of Modernism were Cubism and Surrealism. African and Oceanic sculpture were welcomed by Modernism for its aesthetic simplicity, its ability to express a magical and iconic quality that Western art had seemed unable to capture.

When he arrived in Paris, Issiakhem met up with other painters from the Maghreb (Guermaz, Khadda, Mesli, Yellès, Benanteur, Ali-Khodja; the Moroccans: Cherkaoui, Gherbaoui; the Tunisians: Hedi Turki, Sehili, Gorgi). Few in number, scattered over the capital city and poorly equipped, they were perplexed by the huge gaps in their artistic knowledge. But the biggest danger, a danger that had eluded the Mexicans, was the influence of Western ideas on their sculpture and their cultural symbols. The danger was enhanced by a lull in the traditional/modern debate. The call for symbols of Berber, Arab and Muslim culture remained an essentially nostalgic issue because, on the one hand, their social base had been fractured by colonialism, and on the other hand, the Arab artists' knowledge of their aesthetic history was incomplete because it had been interpreted by the reductive vision of the orientalists. Also, in the religious domain, the Koran and the Sunna had not been fully translated.

Mohammed Khadda, Abdullah Benanteur and Ahmed Cherkaoui were the first of the Maghribians to interpret and interiorise Arab calligraphy in the way that Klee, Kandinsky, Matisse and Mondrian had done before them with their 'empire de signes'.

Like his fellow artists from Maghrib, Issiakhem led a life of double exile in Paris, that of 'qui je suis' and that of a painter seeking to express himself through the language of his art. For him, exile was a state of totality. Painting a picture was not a true means of displaying his identity since the picture was finalised for and in itself. He was superfluous. He was haunted by the question, 'What manner of painter am I?', and he knew that the answer lay not in his claims for cultural identity but in his use of art as a universal concept, i.e., each line, each colour had to apply to every civilisation, to every spectator. Kateb Yacine achieved this with the publication of *Nedjma* in 1956.

In Paris in the 1950s, the schools began to break free from artistic restraints. Issiakhem's sharp eye witnessed the coming together of abstract expressionism and other forms of modern art, action painting, etc. This is what I refer to as the aesthetic melting pot. A melting pot where styles meet and merge, where individual letters and signs are lost in a violent blaze of colour and expression.

According to Artaud the opinion was commonly held that the artist was haunted by the fear of the void. When he drew line after line on the canvas, it was not merely intended for the appreciation of the spectator, it was to satisfy the artist's own 'need to fill the void'. To fill the void was to find the path that led away from the abyss to the 'land of painters'.

Two Major Painters

Baya

Baya's style was based on the dreams and imagination of the child. Her form was constant, her expression repetitious. Using one theme she introduced shade and nuance.

It is the dream that comes to life in Baya's work. A dream that has been prolonged into the time of wakefulness. The artist cannot, does not, want to remain silent nor does she wish to contain or check any outburst or overflowing. Baya is present in her painting. She is standing in a field with the wind kissing her cheek, at one with nature in a magical time and setting.

Unable to read or understand the alphabet and without the ability to explain her work in theoretical discourse, she stands at the heart of surrealism. André Breton: '. . . here is Baya . . .

showing what a united, harmonious and loving world of youth can be.' Pablo Picasso was more direct. He took Baya by the hand and led her to his country home at Vallauris to watch her knead the clay and bring to life the magic of youth.

'Infancy is the golden age of questions and man can never find the answers to them', wrote Henri Michaux. Baya still lived in her infancy, inhibited by nothing and exercising her deep desire to speak out and communicate in an Algeria that had been reduced to silence.

An orphan at the age of five, Baya directed her grief and her solitude towards a world of birds and animals, a world of delicate dark-eyed women, a world of citares and mandolins. Her work had a Mediterranean feel – the gentle Saharan breeze accompanying the sensual rhythm of andalou music.

Between 1952 and 1967 Baya stopped painting. These years were spent bearing children at Blida. In 1967 she picked up her paintbrush and watercolours again. Censoring had stopped. On the eve of her sixtieth year she began to paint again, capturing on canvas some of the great mysteries of the universe.

Baya was born to paint just as Michelangelo was born to sculpt and Rimbaud and Kateb Yacine were born to write.

Khadda

Khadda, born in 1930 (the centenary year of colonialisation) occupies a central position in Algerian painting. To my eyes this central position is one of a semaphore rather than a citadel. A semaphore conveys the idea of a movement and a message. By using such a sign, the semaphore can express a conventional truth, i.e., a truth that carries no connotations.

Khadda's statements of truth are metaphorical. His approach is semiotic. His signs are inscribed on the canvas and engraved into the wood. The realisation of the sign is only the beginning, its destiny is never decided.

Khadda uses many alphabets and many forms of writing. To him writing is creating, it is the 'valuing of values' as Brayet suggested. The tamazight alphabet with its cabal style, the Arabic calligraphy, the magical lines of tattooing and totems . . . all are gathered together to produce a single total vision.

In his two works on canvas, *Dit de clerc* and *Saisons fiancées*, he expresses the universality of man and his history. *Dit de clerc* is based on an ochre background, its theme being the fear of silence, the fear of a time when man will think no more. *Saisons fiancées* is painted in blue and black Chinese inks, the colours colliding to produce an earthquake effect. The canvas is only on the surface but it opens up a host of questions and possibilities. Not even the artist's hand can finalise the picture; its fate is undecided. The seasons in *Saisons fiancées* are cyclical by nature – there is no beginning and no end.

The idea of engagement/betrothal serves to nullify the cycle and to suggest a marriage. It is man's discovery of freedom that is the issue in Khadda's work. Like Klee he could paint it in a dark room with his eyes closed. Khadda is always saying – always signalling – the fact that life is there for us and that life is within us.

See colour p. 49 for plate of the following artist's work:

BAYA

MAHMOUD RACHID KORAICHI
Algeria, b. 1947

Koraichi studied art at the Higher Institute of Fine Arts in Algeria and at various schools, including the Superior National School of Arts in Paris. His works seem to struggle to free themselves of their canvas boundaries. He is sure of the strong lines he uses and employs calligraphy in an abstract symbolic manner so that his alphabets turn into symbols for revolution and protest. He avoids colour, especially in his graphics, and depends on a dramatic contrast of black with white. By so doing he avoids distraction from the seriousness of the message he transmits. He is an artist who has been successful in portraying national problems through a linear calligraphic style outside the boundaries of classical symbolism.

Untitled
Etching
76 x 56 cm
1980

HOURIA NIATI
Algeria, b. 1949

Houria Niati studied art at the Camden Art Centre for a year before going to Croydon College of Art. She is among the foremost Arab women painters, an extremely talented and totally committed artist. Since moving to London in 1977, Niati has managed to carve a niche for herself in the very competitive London art world. Her highly expressive canvases, filled with dreamlike figures, deal with man's destiny, pleasure and pain in an unpretentious, childish manner which brings to mind his innocent beginnings and simple end. Unaffected by success and favourable critiques, she continues to strive modestly and self-effacingly towards higher peaks of excellence. Niati epitomizes the best in modern Islamic art.

The Expectation May Be Tomorrow
Oil and pastel
110 x 80 cm
1988

Bangladesh

Dil Afroze Quader

In a country where 80% of the population is Muslim, the art heritage of Bangladesh has been peculiarly eclectic. It has reflected the intermingling of the cultures of all who have passed through this richly fertile, largest delta of the world. The Hindu mingled with the Buddhist and Islamic to create a peculiarly Bangladeshi ethos.

The vast resources of the sculptural figural tradition of the Hindu and Buddhist conquerors have influenced figural art representation. This is borne out by the figurines excavated at Mohasthangarh, the terracotta plaques and stone sculptures at Paharpur and Mainamoti.

From the Pala dynasty of the eighth century AD down to the nineteenth century, Bengal has a clearly discernible folk art tradition of drawing, painting and wood-cut making. There were the mythological painting on scrolls of incidents from the Ramayana and other religious books, and finally the pata paintings done in bold economic strokes on pottery. Although very little of the ancient arts has survived the humid weather and the hands of vandals and art smugglers, what little there is bears witness to the artistic temperament and skill of the Bangladeshis through the ages.

Folk artists used such perishable surfaces as palm leaf paper, scroll cloth, earthenware, and the walls and floors of mud houses for expression of experiences which were traditionally lyrical. They displayed a very competent manipulative skill and control over their media which was entirely handmade. The vast brick walls of Bengali architecture naturally invited floral decorations. Nothing survives except a small fragment at Nalanda.

Influence of Islamic Art

The influence of Muslim art in Bangladesh was never extensively overt perhaps because there was not the widespread patronage of local artists by the Muslim conquerors to foster and disseminate a total idea of Muslim art tradition. The strong local indigenous art tradition could not be replaced but only embellished by the new incoming tradition of Muslim art. As such it did not penetrate to the practising artists to be developed and established as a potent influence beyond its impact on architecture. The most distinctive feature of this architecture is the employment of burnt bricks made from the rich alluvial soil, thin and solid enough to be flexibly used for arch, dome, vault and even decorative media, such as terracotta and glazed tiles, in the construction of mosques and important buildings.

Calligraphy

To give artistic form to the Arabic words of the Holy Koran, calligraphy developed in the Islamic world with beauty and accuracy into an archetypal art form showing a wide stylistic variety. The Bengali script however is very different from the flowing Arabic script and does not lend itself easily to such artistic rendering. Calligraphy thus was never a popularly practised art form in Bangladesh. Historically, before the emergence of Bengali as the popular language of the area, calligraphy was used for the embellishment of manuscripts, buildings, coins, fabrics and objects of all conceivable kinds. The local artists developed a form of calligraphy known as the Tughra style for their purposes. On the basis of various styles and subtlety of letter arrangements, the Tughra of Bangladesh has been divided into several categories based on the delineation between the letters with curvatures of various shapes. Sometimes the intricacies defy easy reading but retain the delicacy of the visual impact. Modern Bangladesh has a few artists practising calligraphy. They are Saiful Islam, Abu Taher, Murtaza Bashir and Shamsul Islam Nizami.

During British rule in India (1757–1947), art suffered a complete eclipse. Towards the beginning of the present century art was institutionalised. Art schools were set up on the British model to impart education on the lines of the classical British art tradition of stylized landscapes and formal painting in oil and watercolour. The indigenous old Indian and later Islamic art traditions lost favour and gave way to soulless imitations produced by people performing in styles and media foreign to them.

Some genuine native traditions survived, e.g. *potua* painting (scrolls used by itinerant story tellers) and *kalighat* paintings (cheap and swift washed-on watercolour compositions on any subject matter), but they suffered the stigma of being thought inferior and common.

As the Indian sub-continent concertedly sought independence, a group of the intelligentsia led a search for our values and identity and a rediscovery of our traditions. Sculpture as a living modern art began again in 1930. In the forefront of these Revivalists was the famous Tagore family of Calcutta. Rabindranath Tagore won the Nobel Prize for Literature in 1913 and received a knighthood in 1915 which he returned in 1919 in protest. He was an artist as well, and under his encouragement his nephew, Abanindranath, and the latter's students began the reintroduction and reinterpretation of Bengali cultural traditions into art. He argued that national independence meant nothing if it were not preceded by social and cultural renewal from within.

The Art Movement in Bangladesh

The beginning of the modern artistic tradition of Bangladesh took place in 1948, just after the independence of India and the creation of Pakistan of which it was initially a province. Five painters who felt the need for such an institution became the founders of the Art Institute at Dhaka. Bred among the beauty of rural Bangladeshi landscapes the emotion of their work was fired with the zeal of newly achieved independence.

The contemporary artists of Bangladesh may be grouped into the following three generations, each succeeding generation moving further away from British Indian training and nearer to the discovery of their own identity:

1 the first generation responsible for setting up the first art institute at Dhaka in 1948. They were students of the Calcutta Art School of the British Indian Period.
2 the second generation are the students of the first generation, trained at tertiary level at the Art Institute at Dhaka, followed by training abroad. A significant group of talented artists belong to this group which brought together Western modernism and their own traditional outlook to formulate the avantgarde art of Bangladesh. Some of them are working as freelance artists but many are teaching at different art centres in the country.
3 the third or the present generation are students of the first two. Thrown more upon the country's own resources the direction for this generation is yet to emerge.

Prominent Artists

As pioneers in a newly emerging country, first as part of Pakistan then as Bangladesh, artists have struggled to clear a path for others to follow. A few of the names whose dedicated contribution to the art movement deserves mention are:

Zainul Abedin: Pioneer of the art movement, he is the founder of the present Institute of Fine Arts. His drawing and sketches of the man-made Bengal famine of 1943 made him famous at 29. His formal education took place in Calcutta, West Bengal and in the UK. Travelling extensively he met Picasso, Rivera and Segiros, all of whom he admired. But he always said that it is the nature and the people of Bangladesh that inspired him. Like the rivers his art is characterised by powerful lyrical lines; like the rural people his art is simple and sensitive, portraying the human struggle for existence in powerful expressionist black lines.

He established the folk art museum at Sonargaon.

Anwarul Huq: A founder teacher of the Institute of Fine Arts, he was deeply influenced by Western mannerism. He took pleasure in doing still life, figurative painting and portraiture, displaying a warmth of colour and subtlety of drawing.

Quamrul Hassan: Born and trained in Calcutta, West Bengal, he was however an artist of the people and landscape of Bangladesh. His art was based on elements of folklore, pata painting. His earlier phase was devoted to watercolours of jewel-like clarity. Later he resorted to compositions in wood-cut and posters to reflect urban social and moral degradation as well as the varied aspects of rural life.

S. M. Sultan: Trained in Calcutta, Sultan is a well-travelled man who now leads the life of an ascetic. He is realistic in his approach and depicts the life of the toiling mass in bold lines bringing out the power and beauty of the human physiognomy. He stresses the farmers' unlimited capacity for toil and suffering, the intensity of their struggle with life.

Mohammad Kibria: He is regarded as an earlier member of the second generation who trained in Calcutta. He began as a romantic painter of the people, in a geometric, semi-abstract style but matured into a purely abstract artist in the 1960s after his training in Japan. He works in oil, etching and lithographs for very abstract representation of the texture, colour and lines he sees around him.

Influence of Western Art

Since the first Arts Institute was built on the colonial British model of Calcutta Art College and conducted by people trained there and in countries of the West, the emphasis and major focus of teaching was Western art and this influence was palpably present in the art of the first generation. However, being steeped in the rural culture of the country, the artists have exploited the local scenario, the joys and sorrows of the common people and interpreted the hopes and aspirations of the peasant with his bullocks, the boatmen, the fishermen among the intricate patterns of their nets, the tribal woman, the snake charmer, etc., in universal terms.

Two of the foremost painters of the first generation, Zainul Abedin and Quamrul Hassan, under the influence of the Bengali Revivalists, made consistent efforts to develop a style that would be truly nationalistic and modern. For this they invoked the style of Jamini Roy of the Bengal School of Painting and combined it with the folk art tradition of Bangladesh to develop a modern nationalistic style. Although both the artists evolved their own unique personal style, they could not induce a sufficiently large following among their students to mark the beginning of a significant new trend.

The second generation gained distance from British Indian art. Among them a significant group have the talent and the necessary exposure to Western modernism to be able to merge the East and the West in their art. The last four decades have witnessed the gradual transition from the traditional European academic naturalism of British Indian art to the latest styles of international modern artistic techniques.

The influence of international art produced some forceful artists who could mould the trends to their needs. But in the main it produced imitators and led to a gradual alienation of the artist from his public, from his roots. Then came the War of Liberation in 1971 which created Bangladesh. It shook the social paradigm of the country and altered the characteristics of Bangladesh art in form and content. A new vigour became visible, a strength founded on new national hopes and aspirations.

Art School/College

At the primary and secondary levels there are no institutions devoted entirely to the teaching of art. At the tertiary level art education is rendered in the following institutions:

1 Government Institute of Art, Dhaka – 1948
2 Chittagong Art College – 1974
3 Rajshahi Art College – 1978
4 Khulna Art College – 1983

Apart from these, there is a Department of Fine Arts in Chittagong University, opened in 1968.

Shilpokola Academy

Established in 1974, Shilpokola Academy is the principal organiser of art activities in the country. It arranges national and international art exhibitions, holds seminars and symposia on art, organises one-man shows, young artists' exhibitions, collectors' exhibitions, mobile exhibitions and art publications of books, monographs, journals and catalogues. It has organised visits and exhibition of Bangladeshi artists and their work abroad.

National Art Gallery

This was established in 1975 and is housed within the Shilpokola Academy precincts. At present it has a collection of over 300 art works of Bangladeshi artists of repute and some works from the USSR and Philippines.

Art Exhibition/Art Activities

The Shilpokola Academy has arranged three Asian Art Exhibitions at Dhaka, in 1981, 1983 and 1986. It is now busy organising the fourth. Artists from 15 Asian, African and Pacific countries have participated and competed for the awards. The exhibitions bring together artistic endeavours from various cultural backgrounds through which mutual understanding and balanced co-ordination will grow and develop between the countries. Such activities give opportunity for exposure to rising artists who can experience first hand the varied expressions (in different cultural backgrounds) of contemporary human feelings through different art media. As the chairman of the jury (who is from Japan) has commented 'Asian artists are looking back home and are drawing from their past in their march ahead. Sharing experiences among themselves they are looking inward, giving up the isolation of the past.'

The Alliance Française de Dhaka has through the years been a regular patron of art in the country, organising on its premises various shows of painting, sculpture and photography by local artists.

The German Cultural Institute has taken an occasional step or two in this direction of nurturing the growth of local talents, through artists' solo exhibitions.

The Institute of Fine Arts has been the most regular sponsor of art activities and exhibitions in the country. Throughout the year there are regular exhibitions of amateur and professional artists in its gallery. Apart from this the annual exhibition of students' work is a festive time for students and teachers when most classrooms are converted into galleries by willing participants. Prizes are awarded on the basis of merit for work in various media.

The Institute runs a class for children at weekends and organises very popular competitions on national and religious occasions. The young participants from all over the country turn out excellent work as they sit engrossed in their creation on the open verandas of the Institute.

There are other private organisations which organise competitions now and then in which there is also wide participation.

State of Contemporary Art

For their reflection of national values and frank social depiction and criticism, the artists of Bangladesh have always received honour if not financial patronage from their countrymen. Zainul Abedin, who is regarded as the founder of the art movement of the country, enjoyed great honour and prestige during his lifetime and is a figure of veneration after his death. He was a National Professor of Bangladesh and was awarded an honorary D.Lit degree by Delhi University, India.

Our artists have visited many countries with group and solo exhibitions. They have participated in international exhibitions in Latin America, Europe and Asian Biennials and Triennials. Rafiqun Nabi, Mohammad Kibria, Farida Zaman, Abdus Sattar and Abdul Baset are some of the artists who have won prizes in the German Democratic Republic, Yugoslavia, Pakistan, India and other countries. In 1985 Quamrul Hassan's painting, *Three Daughters*, was the subject of a stamp issued in Yugoslavia. The art of Bangladesh has received mention in the journals of Europe, Australia, the Soviet Union and India. It is felt, however, that there has not been enough exposure and communication between the art and artists of Bangladesh and that of other Islamic countries for greater mutual understanding and appreciation.

Conclusion

The direction that the present generation gives to art will reflect the true Bangladeshi ethos and character. Based on the teachings of Western art, modified by the interpretation of the second generation, infused with nationalistic feeling engendered by independence, this generation should be capable of the artistic interpretation of a dimension typical of the people of this part of the world.

Art in Bangladesh has become abstract, in line with modern art, where reality to the artist is the reality of an inner necessity. The artist in the present-day world tries to transform the subject from its everyday appearance to one conceived by him for a greater expressive end. We notice that in modern art an object normally identifiable by its precise form is unimportant: what has become really important is the way it is seen by the artist and interpreted in his own terms and dimensions. An artist in Bangladesh must be rooted firmly in his own culture in order to paint the richness of knowledge, of understanding in the fullness of the senses, of the world that immediately surrounds him.

See colour pp. 50–54 for plates of the following artists' work:

HAMIDUZZAMAN KHAN
MASUDUL HASSAN
MUNIRUL ISLAM
MOHAMMAD KIBRIA
RAFIQUN NABI

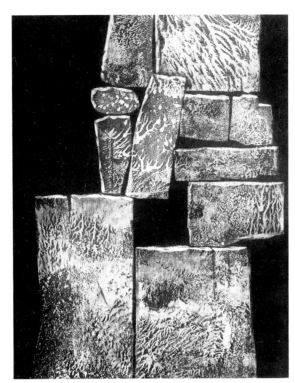

MAHMUDAL HAQ
Bangladesh, b. 1945
Mahmudal Haq successfully moves towards a fusion of painting and printmaking. He concentrates on middle tone colours, creating harmony in a number of astounding grades and textures. In some works a dense layer of black fills his entire space, and then, as with a carpenter's chisel, he digs out his desired objects, reaching maximum tonal qualities. Mahmudal Haq is a vibrant, promising cubist. He started his career as a painter and later shifted to printmaking, especially etchings, with emphasis on 'mezzotint' techniques. He gained his fine arts degree from Dhaka University in 1968. He was awarded the Monbusho Scholarship and studied at Tsukuba Scholarship University Japan in 1984.

Stone on Stone
Etching
36 x 48 cm
1984

ABDUS SHAKOOR SHAH
Bangladesh, b. 1946
Abdus Shakoor Shah is one of the young promising artists in Bangladesh. He received his Bachelor of Fine Arts Degree in drawing and painting from the Institute of Fine Arts at Dhaka University. He later studied painting at the Department of Fine Arts at Chittagong University. Shah is very concerned with the human problems, in all their aspects, that face the Third World. In his paintings, whether in inks or gouaches, human figures, young and old, join together staring from a thick, black background. Shah's message is clear; he leaves the viewer responsible for the details.

Third World
Ink, gouache
80 x 104 cm
1986

DODI TABBAA
Bangladesh, b. 1952

Dodi Tabbaa received her BA degree in graphic design from the Punjab University and subsequently she gained a Bachelor of Fine Arts degree in commercial art and marketing from the Ruskin School in Oxford. She also trained in textile design. Dodi Tabbaa is a self-taught artist, and has chosen to paint in her own personal style inspired by fantasy and the unreal. Whether in acrylic, collage or watercolours, Dodi has managed to juxtapose different shapes and elements, creating strong patterns against a personal choice of unusual colours. Her works reflect simple charm, balance and harmony.

The Shadow Theatre
Mixed media
93 x 105 cm
1986

Brunei Darussalam

Haji Matussin bin Omar

Although there is no art gallery yet established in Brunei Darussalam, this does not discourage local artists from producing works of art. The increasing number of art exhibitions and competitions held each year proves that art in Brunei Darussalam is still thriving.

To compare the standard of art in Brunei Darussalam and the competence of our artists needed for international stature is difficult. With a rough sketch, one could say art in Brunei is behind the international standard. But this is not all true because there are Brunei artists who have the ability needed for international stature. This argument is not merely based on pride, but also on facts. There are matured and budding artists, but only a few are capable of producing artworks with versatility and sophistication. A question should be asked: why are these artists not in the front line, promoting their art by producing and displaying their works? Almost all the active artists in Brunei work for the government as designers, or artists in departments such as Broadcasting and Information, the Language and Literature Bureau, Brunei Museums, or as art teachers or lecturers. They are committed to their official duties, this gives them limited time to pursue their own artistic inclinations. It also locks up the artists' talent and expression that could otherwise be shared with the public.

Since Brunei Darussalam has no art schools, art is taught in primary and secondary schools and up to advanced level only. In the late 1950s the Education Department employed a number of art teachers from abroad mainly from Singapore and Malaysia (then the Malay Peninsula). The teachers introduced new concepts in art. Talented students were encouraged to work on canvas and use oil paints. Collage was introduced and the students experimented working in sea-shells, stones, coconut shells, wood, twigs, etc. Reproduction of the works of modern artists, such as Vincent Van Gogh, Pablo Picasso, Paul Cézanne, Paul Gauguin and the French Impressionists, were introduced. A number of students were influenced by the works of modern artists, and they started to use bright colours, mixed colours on canvas, and even applied the colours straight from the tubes or used palette knives. However, their enthusiasm did not last long. Most preferred to do portraits or landscapes. They realised that artists who produced a true likeness in portraits were very much admired and they also knew that landscapes and portraits were always in great demand.

In 1962 a number of local art teachers were sent abroad to pursue their art education, and in 1964 students talented in art and with good advanced level education were selected to go abroad to study art. However, not all young art enthusiasts managed to go abroad. Those who were not able to go overseas trained themselves to keep their enthusiasm alive. Those who went abroad came back bringing with them Western orientated art concepts and experience. They were more matured in the philosophy of art and enthusiastic about new artistic forms; blending together Western art concepts with traditional subjects. Today, there are not less than forty graduates from the United Kingdom holding art certificates, diplomas and degrees in painting, graphic design and sculpture.

Among the local artists, one prominent figure who has contributed a lot to the development of art in many areas is Pengiran Asmalee or better known as Asmalee. While still at school the young Asmalee was commissioned by the Royal Palace to do two sets of paintings. One was presented to His Royal Highness The Duke of Edinburgh and the other to His Majesty The First Paramount King of Malaysia when the two royal visitors came to Brunei in 1959. For this contribution he was awarded 'The Best Artist of the Year'. The Sultan at the time, His Royal Highness Sultan Omar Ali Saifuddien, presented him with a box of oil paints and a set of technical drawing instruments.

He was still at school when he did a number of posters measuring 60 feet by 20 feet for the national language campaign. His works attracted Dato Jamil, then the head of Language and Literature Bureau. He offered young Asmalee a job as an artist, and he became the department's illustrator. Asmalee contributed a lot to the nation. He was involved in refining the state's crest and the Brunei Malay Regiment's crest. He was also asked to design some of the state's decorations. In 1966 Asmalee was awarded with a scholarship for two years to study fine art at St. Martin's School of Art in London. On his return from the United Kingdom in 1967, starting with 18 artists, he founded the Brunei Artists' Association. Today the Association has about 150 members. The huge mural depicting the life and culture of the people of Brunei Darussalam, outside the building of the Language and Literature Bureau, is a tourist attraction. Asmalee painted a great number of portraits including His Majesty the Sultan, the late Sultan Haji mar Ali Saifuddien Sa'adul Khairi Waddien and other members of the royal family. He is also a fine graphic designer and because of his talent he was asked to design the Royal Coat of Arms. One important task given to him was to design a crown for Pengiran Muda Mahkota (Crown Prince). His other contributions include designing stamps. Asmalee was nominated as ASEAN Awardee for Visual Art for 1987. The award was presented by Her Majesty Queen Chakri Sirindhorn in Bangkok, Thailand. Asmalee is not only known for his art works but is also well known as a comedian, actor, director and producer of television programmes. He is the present Director of the Welfare, Youth and Sports Department.

Other artists like Pengiran Omar Pengiran Sabtu and Pengiran Ibrahim Haji Abu Bakar are well known for their batik works. Pengiran Omar, the chief exhibition officer at the Historical Centre, prefers figure drawings, landscapes and portraits. His work is popular and he often manages to sell them during art exhibitions. Pengiran Ibrahim, a curriculum officer in charge of art and handicraft, considers himself a modern artist who likes semi-abstracts and loves to include verses of poetry in his bright coloured batik works. He also works in ceramic, copper tooling and oil paints.

Awang Sitai and Osman Mohammad both work as chief designers at The Broadcasting Department. Awang Sitai who started as an impressionist is now moving towards surrealism, while Osman Mohammad loves to paint portraits and landscapes. Both artists went to the United Kingdom to study art. Osman holds a degree in 3D majoring in theatre design, while Awang Sitai holds a degree in fine arts majoring in painting.

Abdul Rahim Haji Ahmad, the chief taxidermist, and Zainal Haji Daud, a museum education services officer, are two museum staff with promising talent in art. Abdul Rahim has been involved in the preparation of the dioramas for the Natural History Gallery of Brunei Museum. Indonesian painters like Affandi and Basuki are his favourite artists. He also likes Rembrandt's and Turner's works. Zainal Haji Daud, a self-taught painter, prefers to work with acrylic in an impressionist style. Padzil Haji Ahmad, an appointed artist at The Brunei Museum, is another self-taught painter who has done more than 150 works since he joined the department. He is a portrait painter and his favourite landscapes are the water villages.

Haji Matayir Amin, a scenic artist with the Information Department, is another promising painter in art circles. He is a traditionalist and realist. He produced a few abstract works and shows ambitions to explore new forms but chooses to paint in a traditional way. He feels that the brief history of Brunei pictorial art is too short to evolve a national style but he perceives some distinct early elements. Haji Matayir is an artist who enjoys great popularity, he has had commissions by many organisations, including Royal Brunei Airlines and the Ministry of Development. His works are bought by many art collectors within the country including the Royal Family.

Zakaria Haji Hamid is a lecturer at the University of Brunei and a prolific artist. A graduate of the Norwich School of Art in England, he is mostly interested in doing abstract works based on nature and finding a personal distinct style of his own.

In 1985, the ASEAN Committee on Culture and Information (COCI) organized a travelling exhibition to Brunei Darussalam which made a great impact on the general public and artists alike. About 240 works of art were displayed for a month at the Brunei Museum; most of the works depicted modern art schools and trends. When the exhibition was opened there was a mixed reaction, part of the public liked the works but many had their reservations. However, a number of local artists were inspired by the exhibition and a few art collectors were interested in buying the work although none were for sale.

Despite the public's resistance to new ideas and concepts in art, budding artists in Brunei have started to explore new vistas. Eventually, with the spread of art education, the public will come to accept contemporary and modern artistic norms which will encourage artists to leave their popular classical styles and venture into new prospects.

See colour pp. 55–56 for plates of the following artists' work:

MOHAMAD NOOR ZAIRI BIN YAHYA
PG HAJI MUHAMMAD BIN PG DURAMAN

PG OMAR ALI BIN PG HJ MAHARI
Brunei Darussalam, b. 1962
Mahari is a young and promising artist. He uses watercolours to paint some of the most interesting land and cityscapes of Brunei. He derives his inspiration from nature which he expresses in a sensitive and luminous way. Mahari attended the Berakas English School in Brunei where he passed his ordinary level examination in 1980. His works on Masjid Omar Ali Saiffuddin are soft and captivating, paying attention to details and balance.

Omar Ali Saif Eddin Mosque
Watercolour on paper
35 x 36 cm
1988

ABIDIN BIN HAJI RASHID
Brunei Darussalam, b. 1966
Rashid is a very young and
promising artist. He attended the
Awang Semaun Secondary School
in Brunei where he gained his
General Certificate of Education in
1987. While still studying, Rashid
distinguished himself by being
awarded first prize for the
Antidrugs Campaign Poster
Competition; he also won first prize
in a commemoration of the Silver
Jubilee in 1987. He draws his
inspiration from nature. He is a
realist in style and uses
watercolours with fine brushes to
depict his landscapes in a precise
and charming manner.

Untitled
Watercolour on paper
43 x 54 cm
1987

Egypt
*Mohammad Taha Hussein**

Egypt is the cultural meeting point of three great continents; their rich civilizations regularly pour into the country and influence its artistic and cultural traditions. For more than five thousand years, the lives of its people have revolved around the temple, the church and the mosque of Ancient Egyptian, Coptic and Islamic civilizations; each cultural legacy has left its mark on the heterogeneous artistic trends of Egypt today.

Napoleon's entrance into Alexandria in 1798 suddenly exposed Egypt to European culture and Western norms in the sciences and the arts. The French too were captivated by the Egyptian way of life and overwhelmed by the Pharaonic, Coptic and Islamic monuments they encountered. After the departure of the army, a number of French artists stayed on to record native scenes of everyday life, the souks, hammams, palaces, cemeteries, mosques and monuments. They adopted the local dress and adapted to the domestic ways of the Egyptians. Later these painters came to be known as the 'Orientalists' and their style influenced modern Egyptian painting.

The Ottoman, French and British invasions of Egypt all left their mark on its cultural, political and economic structure at the beginning of the twentieth century. During the nineteenth century Egypt sent missions to Europe and the government invited teachers from England, France and Italy to come and establish schools in the country. This exchange gave birth to a European school of art that can be best defined as academic, falling back on Renaissance traditions.

The modern art movement in Egypt started with the advent of the twentieth century. It came at a time when personal creativity in both music and literature was at its peak and religious men wrote books and articles in defence of the arts. Among them was the great religious reformer, Imam Sheikh Mohamed Abdou, who published a study in favour of painting and sculpture.

The Birth of the Egyptian Modern Art Movement

The Egyptian modern art movement passed through many stages. It began with the generation of Pioneer artists who joined in the tide of nationalism that called for independence from foreign influence. An art school was established alongside Egypt's project for a university. On 12 May 1908, Prince Youssef Kamal, a great patron of the arts, in a gesture of extensive largesse, opened the School of Fine Arts in Cairo. He financed the School for almost 20 years thereafter and instruction was provided free to talented Egyptian youth, with no prerequisite but the desire to learn. As there were no accomplished local artists, the school employed foreign artists to teach in its four departments. Painting lessons were given by Fourschella and Frederic Bonot from France and Juan Antes from Spain. Colonne taught decoration, while Laplagne was the director and supervised the section on sculpture. Students rushed from all over the country to join the new school. The first students constituted the nucleus of the pioneer generation of artists. They included the father of modern sculpture, Mahmoud Mokhtar (1891–1934) and a pupil of Laplagne, the painters Mohammad Nagy (1888–1956), Mahmoud Said (1897–1964), Ragheb Ayad (1892–1982) and Youssef Kamal (1891–1972) and the sculptor Habib Gorgi (1892–1965).

* The editor has added to the original article information taken from Lilliane Karnouk's *Modern Egyptian Art: The Emergence of a National Style*, Cairo, 1988.

The great talent of these early artists became evident in the 1920s. Their successful amalgamation of ancient traditions with contemporary trends, and reshaping them within an Egyptian mould, took the first step towards the birth of a national school of art. At the time there was no sign of continuity with Egypt's Arab traditions. The new Egypt, it was believed, would emerge out of a dominant Pharaonic-Mediterranean past; Islam was viewed as only a phase in Egypt's historic evolution.

Artistic Groups and Associations

The first major exhibition of Egyptian artists in Cairo took place in 1919. One of the main factors in the development and continuity of Egyptian modern art has been the formation of artistic groups which eventually were to play an important part in the art movement. The following are among the most prominent of these groups.

The Society of Fine Arts was founded in 1921 and did not last long. It held its first exhibition in Cairo in 1925. Among its members were Mohammad Hassan, Ahmad Youssef (1891–1970), Said Sadr (1907–1985) and Ibrahim Jaber (1901–1971). 'La Chimère' group was founded in 1927 by a number of pioneer artists surrounding the sculptor Mahmoud Mokhtar. Among the members were many foreign artists as well as Mahmoud Said, Ragheb Ayad and Mohammad Nagy. 'La Chimère' held its first exhibition in 1928 but broke up when Mokhtar left for Paris in 1930 to prepare for his exhibition there. After breaking up, its members dispersed, to meet again at the 'Salon du Caire' which was the only major annual exhibition that the Society of the Friends of Art, founded in 1923, held.

During this same period a new group emerged; its members were graduates of the Teachers Training School. It was the Society of Artistic Propaganda headed by their teacher Habib Gorgi (1892–1965) and independent of graduates of the School of Fine Arts. The group held its first exhibition in which Habib Gorgi, Nagib Assad, Labib Ayoub, Shafik Rizk and Hussain Youssef Amin took part. Gorgi was a painter and an educator who started an interesting educational experiment to demonstrate that every child was a natural artist whose creativity spontaneously developed into an original talent, provided that the child was encouraged and shown the appropriate technique. In his school, children who came from peasant families were left alone to mould their clay without direct instruction or critical feedback. This same school was expanded and developed into a tapestry school by Gorgi's son-in-law, the architect Ramsis Wissa Wassef (1890–1970). Its student artists were taken from the children and youth of Harraniya village in Giza, on the outskirts of Cairo, and the school became a centre of Folk Arts. Today it is world renowned for its naive, handwoven tapestries that depict daily village life and landscapes.

Between 1935 and 1945 artists found themselves caught in the middle of the confusion of global war and political breakdown at home. New avant-garde groups were formed who reacted against the Society of the Friends of Art and regarded it as the epitome of sterile academic training. Among those groups was the 'Art and Freedom' group organized by George Hunain. It started as a reaction against Fascist art and published a manifesto entitled *For a Revolutionary Independent Art* which was signed by thirty-seven members, including Ramses Younan, Fouad Kamel, Kamel Telmissani, Anwar Kamel and Kamal Mallakh. The members condemned the oppressive measures of Fascism and its art censorship and stressed the importance of the individual imagination as the greatest revolutionary force. The group held an exhibition in 1940 which included the works of Mahmoud Said, Ramses Younan, Fouad Kamel and Aida Shihata.

In the early fifties Mohamed Nagy formed the 'Atelier Group' with two chapters, one in Cairo and another in Alexandria, and Hamed Said established the School of Artistic Studies. For his faculty members he chose young graduates of colleges of fine and applied arts who were interested in studying nature and copying it truthfully, recording monuments and subjects with an analytical philosophy.

In the seventies, a group of artists comprised of Ahmad Nawar (b. 1942), Moustafa Razzaz (b. 1944), Abdel Rahman Nashar (b. 1932) and Ali Abdel Hafeed (b. 1944) formed the Axis Group.

Other unions and associations were formed by various groups, among them the National Society of Fine Arts and the Union of Arts and Crafts. But, the one to crown the modern art movement in Egypt was the Union of Egyptian Plastic Artists, founded in 1978. It included all painters and sculptors and in 1980 its twin, the Union of Designers of Applied Arts, was established.

Art and the State

The first art training school in Egypt was the School of Arts and Decoration opened by the government in 1835. It had sections for decoration, decorative metalwork, textile, wood carving and carpentry. Later on it became the College of Applied Arts from which a number of pioneer designers and artists graduated; among them were Said el-Sadr (1908–1985), Ahmed Osman (1907–1965), Mansour Faraj (b. 1907) and Abdul Aziz Fahim (b. 1908). In 1899 the Khadive Teachers School was opened which later developed into the Sultanniya Teachers School and finally became the Higher Institute for Teachers; a few of its graduates formed artistic groups and were leaders in the modern art movement; among them were Hussain Youssef Amin (b. 1906), Hamed Said (b. 1892), Shafik Rizk (b. 1908) and others. After this school came the establishment, in 1908, of the School of Fine Arts by Prince Youssef Kamal.

In 1939 the government opened the first art institute for girls, under the direction of the artist Zainab Abdou (b. 1906). In 1947 it became a Higher Institute for Art Teachers. In 1970 it became the College of Art Education for boys and girls. Among the artists and art educators who graduated after 1947 were Mahmoud Afifi (1894–1958), Mahmoud Basyouni (b. 1919), Hamdi Khamis (b. 1919), Moustafa Arnaouti (1919–1975), Abdul Ghani Shal (b. 1916), Zeinab Abdel Hamid (b. 1917), Laila Sulaiman (b. 1932) and other leaders of the Egyptian modern art movement.

In 1952 the Egyptian Revolution ended the monarchy. Five years later a new College of Fine Arts was established by the State in Alexandria. The dean of the new college was the sculptor Ahmed Osman, while among the faculty were Hamed Nada (b. 1924), Gamal Saguinni (1917–1977), Salah Abdel Karim, Sidki Gabakhangi (b. 1907), Ahmed Raif (b. 1924) and Maryam Abdul Alim (b. 1930).

In the 1980s training in the arts has started to move outside the metropolitan cultural centres of Cairo and Alexandria. In 1982, for example, the Ministry of Higher Education founded a new art college in Minia, a provincial city south of Cairo on the Nile, under the direction of the graphic artist Ahmad Nawar.

Since 1927 there has been a Committee for Fine Arts which later became a Directorate of Fine Arts and finally in 1956 a Higher Council for the Patronage of the Arts. In 1927 the government founded the Egyptian Academy in Rome. It has since developed to become a prestigious venue where creative Egyptian artists can show their works in Europe, far from the commercialism of art galleries.

The first Egyptian to win an art scholarship was Mahmoud Mokhtar in 1911. As soon as he graduated from the School of Fine Arts, and in recognition of his great talent, he was sent by the founder of the School, Prince Youssef Kamal, to the Ecole Nationale Des Beaux Arts in Paris to study sculpture. In 1912 the painter Ali Ahwani went on his own and was followed by Youssef

Kamal and Ragheb Ayad who both went to Rome. Since 1917 the Egyptian government has been sending young artists to train in the West and after the 1952 Revolution it started sending them to academies in countries of the Eastern bloc as well as to the West. When they came back, the graduates would teach at the various art colleges and institutes.

Art and the Egyptian Parliament

The Egyptian Parliament had played an important role in the development of modern art. In 1924 King Fouad agreed to have the Exhibition of Contemporary Art put under his patronage. This gave the movement a new impetus and made Parliament approve several laws guaranteeing freedom of expression and giving the arts official protection. It recommended that special attention be paid to the visual arts and in 1927 a decree approved plans for the establishment of the first Museum of Modern Art; it opened in 1931. A committee was formed to acquire works of art and build a collection comprised of paintings and sculpture by Egyptian and modern European artists. The latter were largely French Impressionists and Post-Impressionists, such as Monet, Manet, Rodin and others. In 1935 the Museum's first catalogue, some 224 pages in all, was published.

There are nearly thirty private and government museums in Egypt, with the Museum of Modern Art in Cairo at the lead. The Municipal Museum in Alexandria plays an important role as host to the Alexandria Biennale for Mediterranean countries. There are also exhibition halls that belong to the National Centre for Arts where exhibitions are regularly held for Egyptian and foreign artists. Among these are the Nile Exhibition Hall, the largest in the country, the Art Centres of Zamalek and Gezira and the Mohammad Mahmoud Khalil Museum. For both native and foreign artists, they constitute the most important venues in the country for exhibitions of the highest standard.

Outside Cairo and Alexandria, all the governorates in Egypt have exhibition halls within the Palaces of People's Culture. There artists from the immediate area are given the opportunity to exhibit their work.

Continuity and The Early Trend: 1911–1936

The Egyptian modern art movement actually started with the establishment of the first private art school by Prince Youssef Kamal. The Pioneer generation made up of the first graduates of this School. Their work showed distinct artistic traits that ran parallel to the national spirit of the time. Mahmoud Mokhtar interpreted, through his sculptures, the strife of his people against colonialism and exalted his country's national heroes. He was the first artist to use granite, a material widely used in the past by the ancient Egyptians. He was also the first to make his statues represent an idea rather than the image of a king or ruler. Since the beginning of the century, Egyptian artists have been obsessed with a search for an Egyptian artistic personality. Ragheb Ayad's preoccupation was to personify mass consciousness through the inherited values of ancient painting traditions. He turned to the Egyptian rural landscape – Nile boats, irrigation wheels and water buffaloes – to paint oil panels whose composition recall ancient Egyptian wall frescoes. Mahmoud Said's opulent and sensuous canvases depicted scenes of everyday life: fishermen, street vendors, and the voluptuous beauty of city and peasant women. Mohammad Nagy, an avid traveller whose travels had taken him to Europe, South America and Africa, succeeded in bridging the gap with his ancestors through his impressionistic style that embodied static strength and tamed rebellion. His occupation with mural painting in public places led him to do his most important nationalistic works such as his painting of the Egyptian people with its many different sects, symbolized in the middle by a Muslim sheikh and a Christian priest exchanging a crescent and a cross, and standing for the country's spiritual and religious unity. Mahmoud Mokhtar, Mahmoud Said and Mohammad Nagy managed to slip out of the grip of the Western academic school that ran counter to the Egyptian reality. Through their art, they were able to give examples of the authenticity of Egyptian nationalism and to portray the people's spirit, thus laying the foundation for a distinctive Egyptian modern art movement.

During the same period art revues and periodicals began to appear, with the genesis of Egypt's first artistic groups, such as La Chimère. Simultaneously, intellectuals began to debate whether Egypt was Pharaonic or Arab. Advocates of each of the two theories borrowed heavily from their traditional heritage. Egyptian architect, Moustapha Fahmi, attempted to create a contemporary Egyptian style in architecture while architect and artist Hassan Fathi (b. 1900) called for a return to local village architecture to solve the problems of housing in an overpopulated country.

The genius of the Pioneer artists in the twenties is manifest by their success at joining together the styles inspired by their ancient heritage with contemporary trends, and reshaping the whole into an indigenous Egyptian mould. This constituted the first steps on the road towards a national artistic character.

The Period after 1936

In 1937 Kamel Telmissani made a declaration entitled the Declaration of the Post-Orientalists. It explained the state of the arts prior to this date and described the direction that should follow in the future. It emphasized the need to break away from the influence of foreign artists and to build a unique Egyptian artistic personality. The declaration came right after the end of British Mandate in 1936 when there was a demand for a free Egyptian Parliament with free elections.

Between 1938 and 1946 artists like Fouad Kamel (1919–1971), Kamel Telmissani (1917–1970) and Ramses Younan (1909–1967) departed from the Pioneers' style to adopt Surrealism. This they followed until 1955, when each went his separate way. In 1944 Hussain Youssef Amin (b. 1906) called for the Group of Contemporary Art to be founded. He was the man behind the spectacular development of Egyptian art that began in 1946. As an artist he was a caring, intense teacher who followed the progress of his pupils from secondary school through art school. He worked with students who came from backgrounds totally excluded from the established mainstream of art and culture, and made them create spontaneously, without being influenced by either West or East. He believed that the work of art gave nationality its character and allowed it to be discovered and understood by others. If art was executed by simple folk, people from modest backgrounds, isolated by their own underdevelopment, then it was likely to convey a revolutionary aesthetic, a message with profound social implications. The exhibition of his students in the Group of Contemporary Art opened in 1944 and created a cultural and political explosion. Artists like Kamel Telmissani, Kamal Mallakh (1919–1986), Samir Rafii (b. 1924), Maher Raif (b. 1924), Hamed Nada (b. 1924) and Abdul Hadi Jazzar (1925–1965) joined the Group. Their aim was to employ authentic Egyptian traditions in their art, by applying popular symbols and folk philosophy, in order to counter Orientalist and imported trends. The works of the Group epitomised their rejection of prevailing superficiality. If compared to the then widespread, shallow and romantic aesthetics, we find that some had expressed an intentional distortion and unsightliness.

The Group continued to represent a front of artistic rejectionism up to the time of the Revolution in 1952, which brought about a basic upheaval that affected all classes of Egyptian society, and directly affected the country's culture in general and its modern art in particular.

The Period after the 1952 Revolution

A: 1952–1958

Right after 1952, artists found themselves in a new state of freedom which gave them the responsibility of expressing the slogans of the Revolution that happened to coincide with the same ideals they had tried to promote earlier. A new group appeared whose concern was to express the national personality through symbolism. They emphasised the aesthetics of the new Egyptian reality, which for the first time in Egypt's history managed to break away from foreign rule, local nepotism and privileged society. This trend impersonated the artistic and political aspirations of the time and was concerned with subjects pertaining to the reality of the Egyptian peasantry and manual labour. Hamid Oweis (b. 1918), Kamel Moustapha (1907–1980), Abdel Kader Rizk (sculptor) (1908–1970), Sayid Abdel Rasul (b. 1917) and Tahya Halim (b. 1920) depicted this new trend with subjects taken from the popular and rural classes: their weddings, souks and markets, folk dances and traditions. Their aim was to replace European aesthetics with indigenous ones. Their work was met with official and popular appreciation and this helped them lay the ground for an authentic, popular school.

B: 1958–1967

Although these two periods followed one right on the other and their leaders had similar aims, there was still a great difference between those artists who worked before 1958 and those who came later. In the first period, the ideas of heritage and traditional legacy were still vague and complicated, while the issue of modernization had just emerged in the artistic arena.

After 1958, the concept of combining heritage with modernity involved the preparation for a national artistic character totally liberated from all kinds of intrusive artistic influence. One group of artists resorted to their local surroundings and the Egyptian village and countryside where basic beliefs in religion and folk traditions ruled and people still considered the Nile a life-giving force. This group, in many ways, continued what their predecessors had started. Artists like Gamal Saguinni (sculptor), Ahmed Abdel Wahab (b. 1932), Adam Hunain (b. 1929), Hassan Sulaiman (b. 1929), Anwar Abdel Mawla (1920–1966), Salah Taher (b. 1917), Laila Sulaiman (b. 1932), Saleh Rida (b. 1932), Gamal Mahmoud (1929–1979), Youssef Sayida (b. 1924), Omar Nagdi (b. 1932), George Bahgoury (b. 1929), Inji Efflatoun (b. 1920), Zeinab Abdel Hamid (b. 1920), Gazbiya Sirri (b. 1925) and Alexandrian artists Moustapha Abdel Mu'ti, Mahmoud Abdallah and Said Adwi were all seeking to celebrate, through their works, the basic components of Egyptian personality. They were joined from the Pioneers' generation by Mahmoud Said, Mohammad Nagy, Ragheb Ayad, Said Sadr and Mansour Faraj.

A second group of artists resorted to ancient Egyptian artistic traditions in order to identify and express an Egyptian personality. Among this group were Tahya Halim (b. 1920), Abdel Wahab Mursi (b. 1930), Kamal Khalifa (1926–1966), Rifat Ahmad (b. 1930) and Mahmoud Rashidi (b. 1937). A third group turned to the prevalent aesthetics of Islamic art and embarked on a new experiment: the awakening to Islamic aesthetic values by artists. Islamic art, in itself, is a balanced art with versatile components that can be utilized in endless formations, based on recognized artistic conjectures and constructional design principles. Its basic starting point is a dot and its ultimate form is a circle. Its most significant characteristic is that it can form an independent entity detached from the strictures of faith.

On the other hand, during the same period and until the early seventies, a group of artists followed the West in their artistic formation and expression. In spite of their differing styles and media, which some might consider reactionary, this group was able to establish a certain dialogue between themselves and the public. Among them were Mounir Kanaan (b. 1919) who worked with abstract collages, Hamdi Khamis an artist-teacher whose works show the strong contrast of free black shapes on a white background, Moustafa Arnaouti (1919–1981) who was a follower of the neo-classical style, Ratib Siddiq (b. 1918), Mohamed Sabri (b. 1919) and Sabri Raghib (b. 1920) known for his impressionistic portraits. They also included the Alexandria Experimental Group headed by Seif Wanly (1906–1979) a prolific artist who left behind as his legacy some 10,000 oils, drawings and watercolours; there was also Farghali Abdel Hafiz (b. 1941), Ali Nabil Wahba (b. 1940), Rida Zaher (b. 1939) and Nabil Hussaini (b. 1939).

The art movement of the sixties benefited from the aftermath of the Revolution and its achievements, both in the international arena and at home. The most significant outcome of the new schools of this period was the formation of geometrical abstract art and constructional art that borrowed components and principles from Islamic elements of the arabesque; while the art of calligraphy spread, either incorporated within other constructional forms or on its own.

A period of stagnation in the art movement followed Egypt's defeat in the Five-Days War with Israel in 1967. This slump lasted until 1973, when a period of intense activity began among the established artists and the new generation. Fresh talent appeared in various fields; in graphics, Ahmad Nawar, Hussein Gebali (b. 1937), Farouk Shehata (b. 1939) and Maryam Abdul Alim; in sculpture, Farouk Ibrahim (b. 1937), Salah Abdel Karim, Ahmed Abdel Wahab (b. 1932), Samir Nashid (b. 1933) and Sabri Nashid (b. 1938); in painting, Zakaria Zaini (b. 1932), Sabri Mansour (b. 1939), Moustafa Razzaz (b. 1940), Abdel Salam Eid (b. 1940), Adli Rizkallah (b. 1940) and Sarwat Bahr (b. 1939); in ceramics, Zainab Salem (b. 1946), Fathia Maatouk, Mahrous Abubakr (b. 1940) and Muhidine Hussain (b. 1937).

The modern art movement in Egypt expanded in response to the increase in exhibition halls, both inside and outside Cairo, the greater activity of its foreign cultural centres, the establishment of the Cairo Biennale in 1982 to complement the Alexandria Biennale, and the opening of a new Arts Centre at the heart of the new Opera House. As the art movement thrived a new group of young talented artists came on the scene, among them Hazim Fathallah (b. 1942), Awad Shimi (b. 1955), Magdi Abdel Aziz (b. 1950), Abubakr Nawawi (b. 1953), Abdel Khaleq Hussain (b. 1953) and Hazim Taha Hussain (b. 1961). They combine different international and domestic styles, taking pride in their heritage and fusing it with modernity without any chauvinism or partiality.

Today in Egypt, calligraphy merges with expressionist abstraction, constructional geometric forms with the abstract geometrical school, Neo-realism with Fauvism, a melange of styles, norms and traditions, all progressing in parallel lines with international art movements and in conjunction with the spirit of modern Egyptian society.

See colour pp. 57–65 for plates of the following artists' work:

KAMAL AMIN AWAD
INJI EFFLATOUN
HUSSEIN EL-GEBALI
MENHATALLAH HILMY
MOSTAFA ABDEL MOTI
HAMED NADA
RABAB NIMER
SALAH TAHER
SEIF WANLY

RAGHEB AYAD
Egypt, 1892–1980
Ayad was one of the first contemporary Egyptian artists. He studied at the Cairo Faculty of Fine Arts when it opened in 1908 and in Rome. Upon his return he was appointed head of the Applied Arts Department and was later made director of Egypt's Museum of Modern Art. Ayad persistently tried to free himself from the Western influences which were penetrating Egyptian artistic circles. His canvases are crowded with activity, bursting with strong emotions. His water-wheels, peasants along the Nile and cows are all executed in a vertical representational manner that reflects ancient Egyptian wall frescoes. His precise lines and balanced colours reveal a sincere artist, and his last works reflect simply, but movingly, his deep religious beliefs.

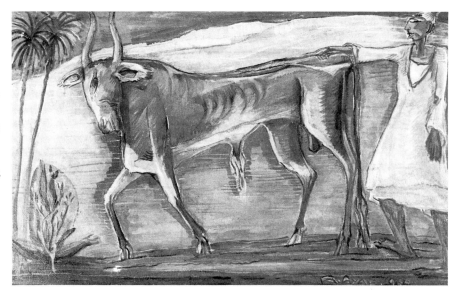

In the Field
Oil on wood
60 x 100 cm
1960

HUSSEIN BIKAR
Egypt, b. 1913
Hussein is among the pioneering artists in the Egyptian contemporary scene. He is an art critic and a musician as well as a poet. His paintings are well composed and free of any decorative influence. He is a sensitive painter with a simple, clear style. Two stages mark Bikar's development after freeing himself from academic influences: the first is his research into the fusion of colours, and the second is his austere constructionism. Since 1959 he has devoted himself to journalistic art and is one of the founding members of the Wax Museum. He recorded in detail the history of Abu Simbel Temple in eighty coloured drawings. His career as an art critic has earned him a distinguished reputation.

Zumuruda
Oil on board
100 x 75 cm
1975

FARGHALI ABDEL HAFIZ
Egypt, b. 1941
Farghali's works are essentially sculptural forms executed as paintings. He draws his inspiration from Egyptian themes, most importantly the Egyptian doll, which he paints or sculpts in wood or moulds life size in papier mâché. He derives his inspiration from folk art and Nubian traditions and he constantly returns to Upper Egypt for new influences. White dominates his canvases, with vibrant fresh pinks, yellows and brilliant blues reflecting the ancient Nubian environment. Born in Diroot, he graduated from the Faculty of Art Education in Cairo in 1962, and subsequently, from the Academy of Fine Arts in Italy in 1967. He is a teacher as well as a painter. For him, beauty is achieved through organic elements using mural colours and forms.

From the Egyptian Countryside
Mixed media
89 x 89 cm
1985

TAHA HUSSEIN
Egypt, b. 1929
Taha Hussein is one of the foremost Egyptian artists today. He is a painter, graphic artist, ceramicist, art critic and writer who has drawn on his country's rich history and past civilization. His works reflect a high intellectual content and a disciplined approach. He combines drawing and painting, and each of his forms is densely edged by countless small pyramids, fine lines and small circles. Calligraphic gestures echo in his work. After completing his studies in Egypt, he obtained a degree in ceramics from the High School of Design in Krefeld, West Germany, in 1959, a degree in graphic art from the Fine Arts Academy, Düsseldorf, and his doctorate in art history and archeology from the University of Cologne.

Orderly Vengeance and Tranquillity
Oil on canvas
100 x 100 cm
1983

AHMAD MOSTAFA
Egypt

Mostafa has achieved unusual dimensional qualities in his works; the viewer is faced first by optical illusion and then by meaning. His earlier career was as a figurative painter. After he attended the London Central School of Art and Design he wrote a definitive thesis on *The Proportional Script of Mohamed Ibn Ali Ibn Muglah* and became a full-time calligrapher using media such as tapestry, stained glass, painting and silkscreens. In some of his works there are recognisable figures like the horse, while other paintings are essentially abstract. He considers calligraphy both as a disciplined scientific medium and a creative process and he has earned a high reputation among calligraphers for combining the literal and the artistic.

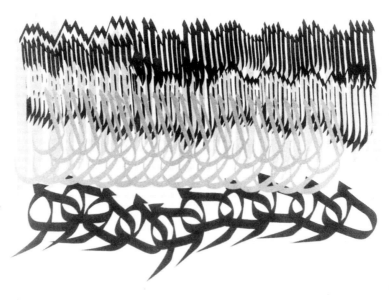

'La Ilaha Illa Hou' No God but He
Silk print
65 x 90 cm
1976

RAMZI MOUSTAFA
Egypt, by 1926

Ramzi Moustafa was best known for his work as designer and director in the Egyptian theatre. Increasingly, however, he has gained status as a painter and sculptor. Trained at the Academy of Fine Arts in Bologna, he gained his doctorate in the USA. He is now a professor at the Academy of the Arts in Cairo. Mostafa calls his paintings 'hymns' very personal letters. Their content is often the sacred name of 'Allah' enclosed in a geometric facade and continually repeated in varying colour combinations. His sculpture too often contains the sole word 'God' with repeated geometric forms in a cartouche. These all draw perhaps on the monumental granite funerary cubes of the village where he was born.

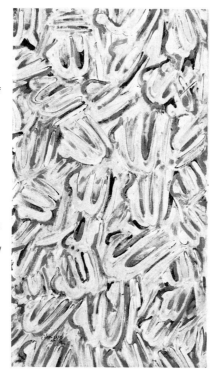

'Allah'
Oil, acrylic on canvas
85 x 153 cm
1988

ABDEL RAHMAN NASHER
Egypt, b. 1932
Nasher is among the modern Egyptian artists who consciously or unconsciously probe and search to reach the source of light, in which the artist's spirit can establish a dialogue with nature and material things. His works are organized in geometrical forms, with shafts of light falling and colliding and creating a luminous effect. He relies on space, shapes and colours in transmitting his revelations.
Nashar graduated from the Faculty of Fine Arts in Cairo, and continued his studies in Budapest where he graduated from the Budapest Art Academy in 1970. He subsequently gained his doctoral degree from Helwan University, Cairo. He is a member of the Axis Group.

Relations of Geometrical Elements
Oil on wood
95 x 95 cm
1981

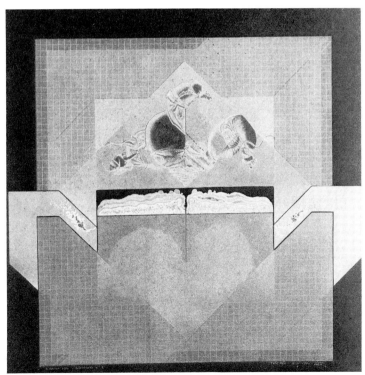

AHMAD NAWAR
Egypt, b. 1945
Nawar is both a painter and a distinguished engraver. For years he has explored the concepts of geometry and anatomy. His works are a construction of metaphysical and organic elements designed to demonstrate the human struggle. We can sense a tension between the inner world which is symbolized by human beings and the outer world represented by highly ordered geometrical surroundings. Deep, tense expressions are revealed in his engravings by densely used greys to blacks, and in his paintings by colours which shade into each other. Nawar graduated from the Faculty of Fine Arts, Cairo, and later continued his studies in Spain where he gained a diploma in graphic art and murals from the San Fernando Academy, Madrid.

Movement
Etching
55 x 59 cm
1982

AYAD NIMMER
Egypt, b. 1948
Ayad Nimmer graduated from the
College of Fine Arts in Cairo. He
lives and works in Amman. Ayad
Nimmer achieves a virtuosity in his
black and white prints and oils,
which demonstrate not only
mastery of technique but also deep
perception. In his portraits
distorted figures with blank
expressions move on the paper
with a strange hypnotism. His
paintings on the City of Salt are
monumental and expressive. Ayad
has added vitality and colour to this
ancient region.

Salt
Oil on wood
94 x 122 cm
1988

MINA SAROFIM
Egypt, b. 1923
This Egyptian artist defies
classification. He plays with the
remnants of modern Western
civilization – strips of ticker tape,
computer cards – and with an
engaging sense of the ridiculous
builds them into carefully
structured compositions. However,
his Arab upbringing is
unmistakable. The remnants
themselves are absorbed into a
sophisticated repetitive design that
resemble the delicate latticework
of an Egyptian mashrabiya. Born
and raised in cosmopolitan Cairo,
Sarofim spent much of his adult life
in Paris after completing his studies
at the Sorbonne. Sarofim makes no
claim to being an artist and likes to
speak of himself as 'having fun with
art'. A former diplomat, Sarofim
was a collector of Western and
Egyptian modern art long before he
began to paint.

The Scene
Mixed Media
70 x 50 cm
1984

FAROUK SHEHATA
Egypt, b. 1937
Born in famous Alexandria, Shehata graduated from the city's College of Fine Arts in 1962 and became Dean of the College in 1963. He subsequently travelled to Germany on a scholarship where he received his doctorate. Both in his graphic silkscreens and etchings, Shehata is a master of technique and is one of Egypt's accomplished engravers. He has skilful control over bright hues, shading and the outlines of shadowy figures and is recognized for his black and white series. His works reveal expressionist and abstract influences.
Notwithstanding his active life in Germany and Egypt, Shehata continues to experiment and explore, finding new forms of artistic synthesis.

Sadness
Print
52 x 36 cm
1975

AWAD AL-SHIMI
Egypt, b. 1949
Al-Shimi is one of Egypt's more accomplished engravers. He is a graphic art teacher at the Faculty of Fine Arts in Cairo where he completed his doctoral degree. His engravings combine exotic interiors and materials with intruding lines that cut diagonally across the work with bands of colour or lattice work. In 1983 Awad executed a set of forty zinc plates that were devoted to the 'Singing Slave'. These engravings are filled with a romantic yearning, a physical beauty, and yet one is left with the sense that the artist's ultimate objective is to investigate the relationship between sharp geometrical lines and the sumptuous rounded lines created by cloth as it falls across the curves of a female figure.

Odalesque
Print
50 x 63 cm
1985

The Gulf Countries
Wijdan Ali

In most parts of Africa and Asia, artistic roots go back to a time when people expressed their creativity in handicrafts. Besides being functional, crafts were meant to add colour and joy to the drudgery of everyday life. In the Arabian Peninsula, the most common crafts were embroidery, weaving, making jewellery in silver and gold, woodwork and decorative paintings on boats, walls and the doors of houses and mosques. The inspiration for colour and subjects came from the environment and the impression it left on the people, sparking a spontaneous interaction between the artisan, his surroundings and his media. The end results were pictures of a studied naivete, devoid of all superficiality and executed in basic primary colours.

The Arabian Gulf Co-operation Council is an economic and political union that comprises the United Arab Emirates, Bahrain, the Kingdom of Saudi Arabia, the Sultanate of Oman, Qatar and Kuwait. All members are oil producing countries in the Arabian Peninsula who share a common historical, political and cultural background.

The Teaching of Art

The beginnings of modern art in the Gulf go back to the decade of the fifties. In the thirties and forties a modern educational system began to replace the traditional system of learning (*kuttab*), where a group of young children used to congregate in one room at their tutor's house to memorize the Koran and learn discipline and good manners. Within one decade, the modern system of education had replaced the traditional way of learning.

When the modern school building replaced the *kuttab* it assumed additional roles beyond basic education. It became a community centre for social and cultural activities. Public gatherings, athletic events, plays and art exhibitions were held in schools and in some countries, the school was even the place to hold wedding celebrations and public bazaars.

These varied activities produced a dynamic interaction, born spontaneously, between society and the school which catered to the needs and ambitions of the people. For children, the school replaced the local piazza where they used to spend most of their time in play and creativity. Among other things, the schoolroom became an arena for their artistic activities where they found proper guidance and were taught the principles of drawing within the curriculum of the Ministry of Education. Because of the lack of qualified local artists, Egyptian, Iraqi and Palestinian teachers were employed to teach at the government schools. They were instrumental in moulding the talent of the first generation of artists in the 1950s. The first painters in Kuwait were: Mojab Dosari, Ayoub Hussein, Khalifa Kattan, Ahmad Zakaria Ansari, Tariq Fakhry, Qassim Yaqout, Jawad Jassim, Mohammad Damghi, Abdallah Kassar; in Bahrain: Abdul Aziz bin Mohammad al-Khalifa, Ahmad Qassim Sinni, Abdul Karim Orayid, Youssef Qassim, Aziz Zabari, Salah Madani, Youssef Ahmad Hussein, Salman Dallal, Rashid Arifi, Rashid Swar, Nasser Youssef, Abdallah Mahriqi, Abdel Karim Bosta, Jalil Orayid and Hussein Sinni; in Saudi Arabia: Abdel Halim Radwi, Jamil Mirza and Ahmad Dashash. They painted landscapes and portraits in a primitive style that loosely followed basic academic principles of drawing and painting. Some also copied well-known works by European Renaissance painters.

Kuwait was the first country to send students abroad on art scholarships. Mojab Dosari went to England in 1945 after receiving his initial training in art in Egypt, while Ahmad Qassim Sinni was the first Bahraini to be sent to England to study art in 1952. Abdel Halim Radwi was given a scholarship to Italy by the Saudi government in 1961. In 1965, Jassim Zaini was the first Qatari to go to Baghdad and from the United Arab Emirates Mohammad Youssef, Hamad Sweidi, Mohammad Idrous, Ubeid Srour and Ibrahim Moustafa were sent to Cairo, Baghdad and Damascus. Since then the number of students to study and train in art, whether in other Arab countries or in the West, has constantly multiplied.

In Oman the fine arts movement only started in 1980, at present drawing is taught at Sultan Qaboos University by an Egyptian teacher and advanced training in fine art does not exist.

Art Patronage

The most important factor instrumental in the development of the modern art movement in these countries has been government's official patronage of the arts after the discovery of oil and with the ensuing economic boom. In addition to art classes and art scholarships offered by the Ministries of Education, the Ministries of Information and Culture have also played an important role. They have provided exhibition halls for artists, participated in Arab and international biennales and exhibitions and published art books, catalogues and periodicals.

Artistic Organizations and Societies

Artistic societies such as the Emirates Society of Fine Arts (founded 1980), the Modern Art Society in Bahrain (1969), the Saudi Arabian Society for Culture and Arts (1973), the House of Saudi Arts, the Kuwaiti Society of Fine Arts (1967), the Kuwaiti National Council for Culture, Arts and Letters (1973) and the Qatar Society of Fine Arts (1980), among others, have been important in the development of the modern art movement in Gulf countries. Some of these societies belong to the government while others are private. All, however, are supported by the State and have been instrumental in encouraging artists. They hold exhibitions at home and abroad, establish ties with other Arab and international artistic institutions, start art collections of local artists, give out awards and prizes in the fine arts to local and Arab artists and spread artistic awareness among the public. In their own way, these societies and councils have replaced artists' unions in the West.

A new phenomenon to appear in the Arab world was the creation of the Free Atelier in Kuwait in 1960. The idea was instigated by Hamid Hamda, an inspector of art education, who proposed the establishment of a centre for art amateurs, under the supervision of the Department of Education (later to become the Ministry of Education), that would cater for national and resident artists. It would provide instructors, the necessary art materials and a studio where the artists could take lessons in painting, sculpture and graphics, in a free atmosphere, outside the restrictions of the regular classroom. The Department took up Hamda's suggestion and the Free Atelier for Fine Arts was born. It had morning and evening classes, thus enabling amateurs, students and professionals alike to attend. The Atelier, which was intended as a base for a college of fine arts, became a great success in spite of the fact that it did not offer a certificate and at the beginning only accepted male students. In 1972 it was removed from the patronage of the Ministry of Education and put under the Ministry of Information. It was moved to new premises in the house of al-Ghanim, a traditional Kuwaiti house with two exhibition halls, a library, several studios for painting, ceramics and graphics as well as kilns for bronze casting and ceramic firing. Abdallah Kassar was appointed its curator.

The enormous success of the Free Atelier surpassed the expectations of its founders and patrons. It provided the opportunity for Kuwaiti artists to have a strong base for practical and theoretical training in art, as well as a forum to exhibit their work. In 1980 the Free Atelier in Doha, Qatar and the Omani Atelier of Plastic Arts in Muscat, Oman, were established on the same lines as the one in Kuwait.

The second new phenomenon, also starting in Kuwait, was to have full-time artists supported by the state who would dedicate all their time to their artistic pursuits. Issa Saqr was the first such artist in 1961, and was followed by Khalifa Kattan, Badr Qattami and Abdallah Kassar. Other countries like Qatar followed suit.

Kuwait National Museum

In 1983 the Kuwait National Museum was opened. It has two wings: the first is Dar al-Athar al-Islamia and houses the fabulous, personal collection of Islamic art belonging to Sheikh Nasser and Sheikha Hossa al-Sabah; the second houses archaeological artifacts found in Kuwait which date back to the third and second millenium BC. The museum also has an ethnographic section and a small section for Kuwaiti modern art, including painting and sculpture. The importance of the National Museum to Kuwaiti and other Gulf artists, lies not only in part of it being dedicated to the exhibition of their works, but also in the contents of Dar al-Athar al-Islamia and the Sabah collection. It is a unique collection that covers all periods of Islamic culture, providing local and Arab artists, among others, with a rare opportunity to become acquainted with the development of their rich civilization; they gain first hand knowledge of its different objects. The impact of this institution on modern art in the Gulf countries may not show immediately but in the long run, especially with the special programmes for adults and children that the museum holds regularly, some kind of a local school of art will develop, inspired by its own cultural heritage.

Painting

In spite of the absence of local schools of paintings in the Gulf countries, one trait is common among most of their artists and that is subject matter. Regardless of style, most paintings, whether city or landscapes, still life or portraits, realist or surrealist, abstract or calligraphic, unite in their choice of subjects taken from scenes of local everyday life and the indigenous culture. Mojab Dosari (Kuwait) was the first painter to insist on and propagate this kind of choice of subject matter.

The subjects that mostly influenced painters from the Gulf were the sea, the desert, and their own societies. For them, the sea with its treasures has been a source of livelihood ever since man existed in that land. Through it, he could travel to faraway places, engage in commerce and discover new lands. It was also his protector, putting distance between him and possible danger. Long before oil was discovered, it provided him with wealth, livelihood, liberty and beauty. The desert, with its Bedouin nomads, had always been an inherent part of the Arabian Peninsula's history. Its cruel and harsh nature has taught its people patience and hardiness. It has nurtured in them the love for poetry and sharpened their sense of beauty and tranquillity. In it grow their cultural, social and historical roots. Finally, societies in the counties of the Gulf, as in other Muslim and Arab countries, have been exposed to the winds of change. They are conservative societies that have kept most of their traditions and customs, yet the ties of their cultural continuity are weakening, particularly after the discovery of oil which brought sudden and overwhelming affluence and a staggering exposure to Western civilization. The Gulf artist has preserved, on canvas, his cultural traditions, recording for posterity those practices that may vanish or change with time.

BAYA
Algeria, b. 1931
Baya has had to struggle to
become the artist she is today.
She was only sixteen when her
precocious genius was
recognised in Paris. Baya is
self-taught and paints a
childlike world of fairy tales, yet
there is nothing childlike in the
careful symmetry and rich
colouration of her canvases.
She uses traditional textile
motifs and tones to envelop
suggestive female figures and
adds traditional pottery with
floral designs filled with fruit
and symbolic fishes to stress
fecundity. There is a fresh
simplicity that charms and
soothes the viewer's eye. She
takes us into concealed
gardens not only of traditional
houses, but in the subconscious
of our dreams. Her works have
been called a search for
'Paradise Lost'.

Untitled
Watercolour/paper
75 x 100 cm
1980

HAMIDUZZAMAN KHAN
Bangladesh, b. 1946
Hamiduzzaman's distinction
lies in the fact that in spite of
being greatly influenced by
Rodin's work he has developed
and established a distinctive
personal expression of his own,
without any signs of imitation.
Hamiduzzaman started his
artistic career in drawing. This
has helped him a great deal in
his sculptural work, which is
precise and minimal. He is
currently an assistant
professor in the Institute of
Fine Arts, University of Dhaka.

Untitled
Ink drawing
50 x 34 cm
1981

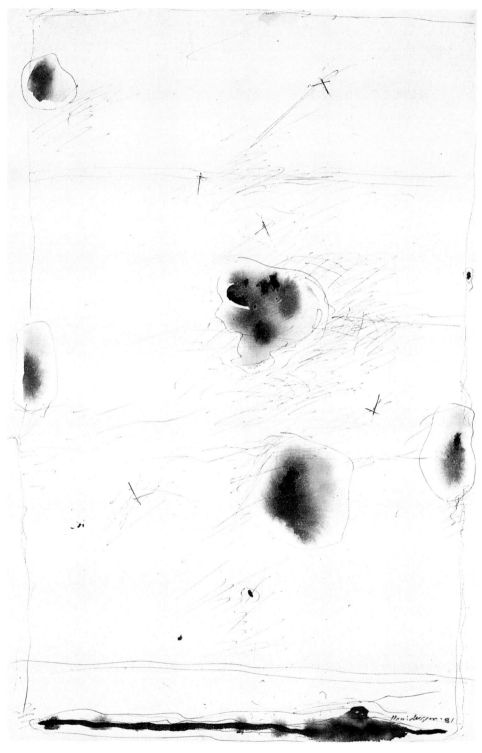

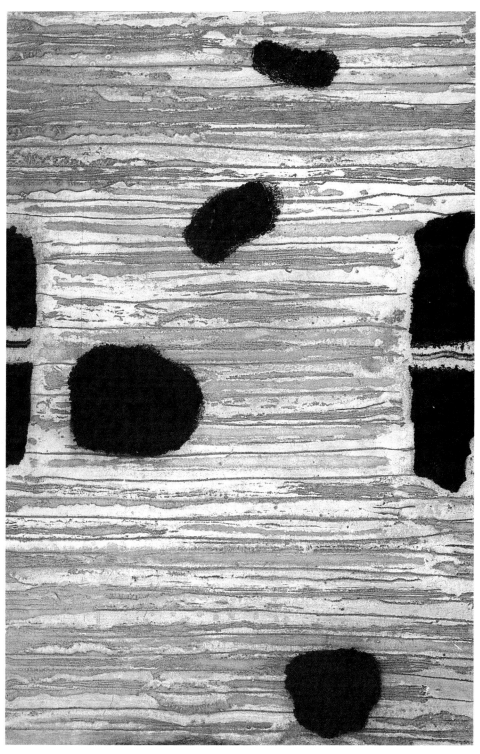

MOHAMMAD KIBRIA
Bangladesh, b. 1929
Mohammad Kibria was born in Birbhum, India. He received his art training at the College of Art and Crafts, where he graduated in Fine Arts. Subsequently he travelled to Japan where he furthered his studies at the Tokyo University of Fine Arts in 1962. Kibria now lives and works in Dhaka. He is a painter, a graphic artist and a teacher. He is among the foremost artists of today. His work reflects a tremendous sense of skill in its simplicity and balanced approach, along with a deep intellectual content.

Untitled
Pencil and ink
45 x 30 cm
1984

MASUDUL HASSAN
Bangladesh, b. 1960
Masudul Hassan is a young and
promising artist. He uses oil,
watercolours, mixed media and
pastels. The shifting styles in
his paintings are a means of
exploring new forms of
expression portraying a range
of environments and emotions.
There is almost a romantic
aspect to his work. In some
paintings bright and optimistic
colours invade his canvas; in
others, dark, mysterious
colours reflect a sense of
pessimism. Hassan trained at
the Bangladesh College of Arts
and Crafts in Dhaka. He
obtained his Bachelor of Fine
Arts from the same college and
he also attended the graphic
print workshop given by
Mahmudal Haq. He has
distinguished himself with a
long mural painting, *Life of
Bangladesh*, which measures
1900 sq ft.

Woman
Oil on canvas
81 x 82 cm
1988

MUNIRUL ISLAM
Bangladesh, b. 1943
Born in Islampur, Munirul Islam
grew up and studied in
Bangladesh. His formal art
education was at Dhaka Art
College, and he worked at the
same college as a teacher. He
gained a scholarship from the
Ministry of Foreign Affairs in
Spain, where he continued his
art studies and mural paintings.
Munirul Islam is a distinguished
artist. His fine graphic prints
reflect discipline and an
unlimited imagination. His
mastery of graphics and his
abundant source of energy
have established him as one of
the outstanding graphic artists
of today.

The Last Journey
Etching
40 x 35 cm
1978

RAFIQUN NABI
Bangladesh, b. 1943
Nabi is a painter, graphic artist, cartoonist and illustrator of children's books, working in oils, watercolour, wood cut, print pastel and drawing. He is regarded as one of the most talented artists in Bangladesh. Early realistic works soon shifted to impressionism and gradually to abstraction; all reveal a deep rooted attachment to his native land. He has succeeded in blending the techniques of the Bengal School of Painting with those of the modern West. His humanism and social consciousness are revealed in his cartoons, which mix resentment and anger with humour. Nabi graduated from the Government Institute of Fine Arts' Department of Drawing and Painting in Dhaka; he also specialized in graphic art at the Athens School of Fine Arts.

Composition
Woodcut print
73 x 47 cm
1986

PG HAJI MUHAMMAD BIN PG DURAMAN

Brunei Darussalam, b. 1946
Duraman is a self-taught artist. He has attended courses in fine art in Malaysia, in graphic and commercial art in Singapore and in art and design at Croydon College, London. Since his return to Brunei, Duraman has been actively involved in designing logos, book covers, magazines and posters. Duraman expresses his works in a semi-cubistic geometrical style with emphasis on light effects. He has been appointed the special designer for the royal family crowns, jewellery decoration and medals. He was the first to design a stamp in Brunei and among those who formed the Brunei Art Association for the development of art in Brunei Darussalam.

Untitled
Oil on·carton
44 x 83 cm
Undated

MOHAMAD NOOR ZAIRI BIN
YAHYA
Brunei Darussalam, b. 1961
After finishing his secondary
schooling in Brunei, Bin Yahya
attended a course at the
Guildford County College of
Technology in Britain and
gained his diploma in design
and printing. He furthered his
artistic studies by attending a
course at the Croydon College
of Art and he received his
higher national diploma in
1985. Upon his return to
Brunei, Bin Yahya rapidly
became a full-time artist. His
watercolours are simple and
sensitive depicting many
scenes of Brunei, especially the
crowded dwellings along the
waterfront with the mosque
rising in the background. He
has participated in many group
exhibitions and is actively
involved in the Brunei Art
Association.

Untitled
Watercolour on paper
40 x 63 cm
1986

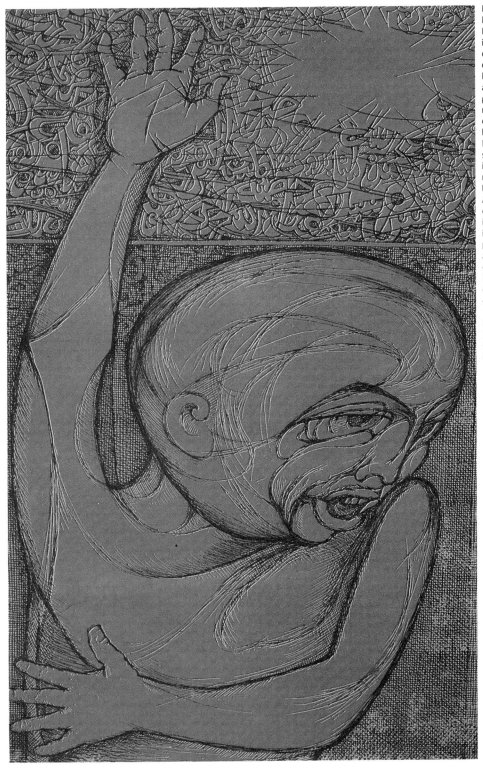

KAMAL AMIN AWAD
Egypt, 1923–1980
Kamal Awad gained his diploma
in graphic art from the College
of Fine Arts, Cairo, and was one
of the first students to do so.
He was subsequently
appointed as an assistant in the
graphic art department. His
remarkable talent and
continuous innovations gained
him a scholarship to study in
Italy and France, where he
spent some years specializing
in lithography. After he
returned to Egypt, he immersed
himself in teaching and printing.
Awad's work reflects a great
deal of social comment and
intellectual thought. It
integrates a high degree of
precision and professionalism
and has earned him awards and
distinctions in many countries.
He is recognized as a major
contributor to the development
of graphic art in Egypt.

Untitled
Etching
45 x 30 cm
Undated

INJI EFFLATOUN
Egypt

Inji Efflatoun has a distinctive, mature style. The background is a simple white, overlaid with rounded brushstrokes which build into a fullness where human figures intertwine almost inseparably with the crops they are tending. While most of her work has been of her native Egypt, fruitsellers with their wicker baskets and women in the fields, she has also painted the villages and peasants of Yugoslavia with the same kind of 'tapestry-on-canvas' technique. If she paints gondolas majestically on the Nile, there is social commentary not far below the surface. The river's current merges with its flow of lines into the very sides of the boat, and then into the facial and body muscles of the labouring sailors themselves.

Farmer's Roof
Oil on canvas
60 x 75 cm
1984

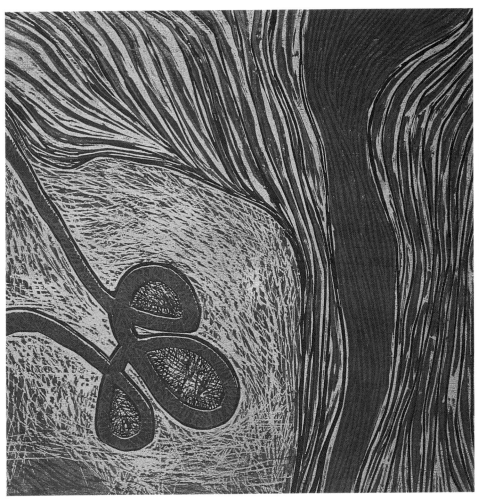

HUSSEIN EL-GEBALI
Egypt, b. 1934

El-Gebali is a master of graphic art. His achievement and sensitivity make him one of the most important Egyptian lithographers. Calligraphic elements are reconstructed into formations composed, like Egyptian architecture, of pyramids, sun circles and planes. His subtle use of colour balances and counterbalances these architectural formations. He has produced huge woodcuts and lithographs which reveal tremendous feelings of motion, and has used textile art in which contemporary graphics interact with the ancient Egyptian skill of weaving. El-Gebali graduated in 1958 from the Faculty of Fine Arts in Cairo. He also studied at the Institute of Fine Arts, Urbino, Italy, before gaining a scholarship for art research in the Netherlands. He now teaches in Cairo.

Symphony of Arabic Calligraphy
Wood print
70 x 70 cm
1982

MENHATALLAH HILMY
Egypt
In Hilmy's work the geometric influences of Islamic art can be seen. Her abstract compositions explore the possibilities to be achieved in recurring patterns and colours. An interplay of lines guides the viewer's eye to the centre from where a struggling being strives to emerge. Her inspiration is derived from ancient Egyptian as well as Islamic art. She creates soft lines and sensitive tones of colour, resulting in an atmosphere of mystery.

The Corridor
Etching
35 x 26 cm
1979

MOSTAFA ABDEL MOTI
Egypt, b. 1938
Moti is an Alexandrian and a
founder of 'The Experimentalist
Society'. He graduated in
photography from the Faculty
of Fine Arts at Alexandria in
1962 and later gained his
doctorate and then a diploma in
murals from the Academy of
San Fernando, Madrid, in
1977. In his works, circles,
triangles and squares are
obvious and essential
elements. It is by the single
variation of these elements
that Moti recreates a lyrical
human condition. His approach
is an intellectual one. His
peculiar forms exhibit a
discipline that reflects and
expands on the human
condition as well as creating an
abstract world to mirror his
own experience and culture.

Untitled
Oil on canvas on wood
100 x 100 cm
1988

HAMED NADA
Egypt, b. 1924
Hamed Nada is one of the first
Egyptian painters to use folk
themes: popular superstitions,
primitive art, human figures,
the cat, the fish and village
legends as well as ancient
Egyptian motifs. His works
reflect a direct statement of his
experiences, full of vigour and
originality combined with bold
colours, rhythms and design.
He graduated from the Royal
Academy of Fine Arts in 1951,
and later specialized in mural
painting. In spite of his
exposure to Western culture,
Nada has remained close to his
native sources. He remains one
who continues to explore and
express while leaving the
viewer to interpret and
question his world of dreams
and legends.

Folk Tale
Oil on wood
120 x 110 cm
1989

RABAB NIMER
Egypt
Rabab Nimer graduated from the Faculty of Fine Arts in Alexandria in 1963. She subsequently continued at the San Fernando Academy, Madrid, where she gained her doctorate. Rabab has experimented in her search for a new means of expressing her intellectual and imaginative sensibilities. Her canvas appears crowded with unusual faces whose enigmatic expressions reflect strange moods and thoughts. The observer is left to decipher these forms for himself and to be provoked into a dialogue with these strange, yet human faces.

Untitled
Oil on wood
98 x 124 cm
1985

SALAH TAHER
Egypt, b. 1912

Salah Taher was a student of the famous pioneer Egyptian painter Ahmad Sabry. Taher's paintings reveal diverse tendencies which mark a new spirit of liberation. In his figurative landscapes his compositions begin semi-abstract, but gradually move towards abstraction. He is an impulsive dialectician of movement. Taher has found a new aesthetic vision in which he achieves a certain measure of equilibrium and harmony. Taher has held a number of important appointments during his life. In 1944 he was appointed the director of the Museum of Modern Art, then he served in the Cabinet of the Ministry of Culture and in 1962 was appointed the director of the Opera House. Today he is active on the Supreme Council for Culture.

Untitled
Oil on carton
30 x 40 cm
1982

SEIF WANLY
Egypt, 1906–1979
Seif Wanly is known for his imaginative stage designs. His paintings of dancers, musicians, singers and actors in various ballets and opera performances are impressive. He was among the first Egyptians to establish a workshop for young artists and amateurs. He is closely associated with his brother Adham. They both painted in their free time, and have spent some time in Nubia recording its scenic beauty. Wanly has painted a large number of works in gouaches, watercolour, sketches and oils, which are now in a museum in Alexandria. He represents a bridge between the early classical pioneers and modernists. He has distinguished himself as a master and has left an impact on the modern Egyptian scene.

The Sketch Model
Oil on carton
66 x 47 cm
Undated

ABDEL AZIZ ASHOUR
Saudi Arabia, b. 1962
Born in Jeddah, Ashour
attended a training course in
Fine Arts and later trained as a
calligrapher. He relies on a
variety of Islamic decorative
forms and calligraphical
elements. He is more
concerned with the overall
pictorial result than the literal
relations of the forms. His
choice of colour is very personal
and fertile greens to yellows –
desert colours – dominate his
canvases. He is a promising
artist.

Composition No. 1
Oil on canvas
85 x 98 cm
1987

SURAYA AL-BAQSAMI
Kuwait, b. 1952

Suraya al-Baqsami is among the few Kuwaiti artists who has had to struggle to establish herself. She studied art at the Fine Arts College in Cairo and subsequently travelled to the Soviet Union where she gained her master's degree in graphic art, book illustration and designs. Later she moved to Senegal, completing a course in silkscreen printing, ceramics and drawing on silk and batik. Al-Baqsami is immersed in her traditional heritage, drawing her inspiration from early Islamic miniatures and manuscripts. Whether in oils, watercolours, etchings or silkscreens, she expresses her concern about the human individual in a simple, unpretentious manner. Her work recalls the old school of Baghdad or the miniatures of Yehia al-Wasiti.

Cemetery from the East
Watercolour
45 x 49 cm
1989

JASSEM BU HAMID
Kuwait, b. 1946

Jassem bu Hamid discovered at university that his future was in art and consequently went on to study at the College of Fine Arts and complete his artistic education at the National High School of Fine Arts in Paris in 1976. He has been a full-time artist at the Free Atelier since 1977. In his early works his style was surrealist but he gradually freed himself from its influence and indulged in figurative realism, drawing on his immediate environment. He came now under the influence of new realism, in which he could get closer to nature than the camera. His sculptures are based on modern trends. He uses various materials such as bronze, marble, wood, aluminium and stone.

Sheep Herder
Sprayed paints on canvas
49 x 49 cm
1988

YUSSEF JAHA
Saudi Arabia, b. 1954
Jaha gained his diploma in Art
Education. He is mainly
interested in painting
landscapes in a romantic style.
His colours are dark and thick,
and his use of large
brushstrokes are indicative of
his expansive works simplifying
his subject yet at the same time
creating a dynamic effect.

'Al Hada'
Oil on canvas
78 x 88 cm
1987

HASSAN AL-MULLA
Qatar, b. 1952

Al-Mulla shifts between figuration and surrealistic trends. His pictures combine Arabic letters, human figures and landscapes expressed in symbolic representations. He has an abundant store of emotions, thoughts and events which are combined together and expressed spontaneously in his paintings. The letters in al-Mulla's work are almost accidental, and he assembles his painting from different sources, building up as he goes along. His recent works are essentially concerned with his immediate environment, the sea, the land and the people. Al-Mulla graduated from the Academy of Fine Arts in Baghdad in 1975, and is an active member of the Gulf States Arts Council.

Intersection
Acrylic on canvas
89 x 115 cm
1988

ABDEL HALIM RADWI
Saudi Arabia, b. 1939
Radwi gained his art degree
from the Rome Fine Arts
Academy and his doctorate
from the Fine Arts Academy in
Spain. He is a painter and a
sculptor. Radwi draws his
inspiration from his country's
culture and folklore. He has
completed a large tapestry
based on one of his paintings
which is hanging alongside the
work of other artists at
Jeddah's King Abdul Aziz
International Airport. His
compositions, in which he
paints folk-dances, daily
scenes, mashrabiyas, birds and
covered houses, are cheerful.
His colours are personal and at
times there is a lack of concern
with the proportions of his
figures. Radwi has actively
encouraged present-day Saudi
Arabian artists to draw on their
rich heritage as a source of
inspiration.

Folkloric Dance
Oil on canvas
70 x 90 cm
1987

ABDEL RASUL SALMAN
Kuwait, b. 1946
Salman is an innovator and
never ceases to experiment,
drawing on the rich resources
of his cultural heritage. He
graduated with a diploma from
the Teachers' Institute in 1973
and later received his diploma
in calligraphy. Salman
examines the traditional
aspects of his environment. His
style shifts between romantic
realism and surrealism using
vibrant colours of blue and
purple. His works in calligraphy
are outstanding and have
earned him a distinguished
reputation. Salman has written
a number of articles on the
development of art in Kuwait
and the Arab Islamic world.

God the Glorious
Oil on canvas
100 x 100 cm
1978

ANWAR KHAMIS SONIA
Oman, b. 1948
Sonia draws his inspiration
from his immediate
environment, and he expresses
whether in oils or watercolours
his visual experience of the sea,
the people, the houses and
daily scenes. He was born in
Bahrain, but grew up in Oman
where he lives and works. He
attended a training course in
drawing and painting in Britain
in 1982. His works reflect
simplicity and are charming and
honest.

Old Door
Watercolour
45 x 30 cm
1988

ABDEL RAHMAN SULEIMAN
Saudi Arabia, b. 1954
Born in al-Hasa, he gained his
teacher's diploma in 1974. He
is one of the promising second
generation of young artists in
Saudi Arabia. He is a writer as
well as a painter and editor of
the *Al-Yom* newspaper.
Suleiman is conscious of his
Islamic heritage and in his
works he draws on decorative
Islamic motifs and Islamic
architecture in a realistic style.
In a previous phase of his work
Suleiman moved towards
symbolism, which provided a
rich and diverse source for his
inspiration.

Event 2
Mixed media/carton
52 x 73 cm
1988

NASSER AL-YOUSIF
Bahrain, b. 1940
Al-Yousif is considered among
the founders of art
development in Bahrain. His
early works were mostly
woodcuts and engravings on
leather. In 1980, al-Yousif
encountered zinc engravings at
the Assilah Festival for Culture
and Art in Morocco, and
realized the importance of
etchings in perfecting his
artistic talents. His work
depicts the traditional way of
life in Bahrain. Although there
is considerable intellectual
content in his paintings, his
clarity of colour and warmth of
tone provide a simple charm.
He is aware of the scarcity of
raw materials for such
techniques in Bahrain and he is
also aware of the tremendous
challenge in producing a
graphic print. Yet al-Yousif
remains strong in his
endeavours as a graphic artist.

The Two Sisters
Etching
45 x 23 cm
1988

SIMIN MEYKADEH
Iran, b. 1941
Simin Meykadeh's early
training was at Tortington Park
School in Sussex, England, and
later at the University of
Minneapolis, Minnesota,
where she graduated in 1960.
A student in Barbara Pierce's
painting class, she
distinguished herself as a
painter. Her works are large
abstract shapes in subtle
earthy tones giving the viewer a
feeling of space and
monumentality. Simin is chiefly
concerned with producing a
dramatic effect by portraying
large figures and unusual
dimensions, and creating a
dialogue between her work and
the viewer.

Gregory No 2
Acrylic on paper
113 x 89 cm
Undated

HOSSEIN ZENDEROUDI
Iran, b. 1937
While many calligraphers have followed a strict tradition, Zenderoudi has been able to free himself from calligraphic rules. In his works, letters are spread across the entire space of the canvas in a simple, spontaneous yet rhythmic manner. He graduates his colours to produce a captivating and powerful effect. He is concerned with a language which possesses a universal dimension. He founded the Saqqah-Khaneh school, which derived its inspiration from folk art and Shi'ite religious iconography, and has illustrated the Koran with a series of serigraphs. He believes that creativity is basically 'a spiritual search'. Zenderoudi was born in Tehran and studied at the School of Fine Arts for Boys and the School of Decorative Arts in Tehran.

Untitled
Etching
56 x 76 cm
1986

SUAD ATTAR
Iraq, b. 1942
Born in Baghdad, Suad Attar
studied at the University of
California before obtaining a
BA in Fine Arts from Baghdad
University. She later studied
printmaking at the Wimbledon
School of Art and the Central
School of Art and Design in
London. Her work is a highly
rich mixture of dream and
reality. The emphasis is on
linear modulation and she is
concerned with minute details
balanced by the overall
pictorial design. Her gardens of
paradise filled with palm trees,
peacocks and women are
constantly repeated motifs
inspired by Assyrian and
Medieval Baghdadi painting
which provides a rich resource
for her works in oils and
graphics. She is a distinguished
artist committed to the artistic
traditions of her native country.

Blue Paradise
Oil on canvas
34 x 40 cm
1989

DIA AZZAWI
Iraq, b. 1939

Whatever his subjects may be, and many are difficult to define, Azzawi's compositions are full of vigour and reflect a series of abstract symbols. In his oils, gouaches and etchings, he has creatively unearthed a richly coloured abstract series and remarkable monumental figuration from his ancient Sumerian heritage. His work is graced with a wealth of calligraphical expression which he blends into a modern, poetic interpretation. His early training as an archaeologist at the University of Baghdad, where he graduated in 1962, and a degree in fine arts have enabled him to become a talented painter, printmaker and illustrator and have enhanced his ties with his ancient artistic heritage.

What El Nifari Said to Abdullah
Gouache on paper
110 x 77 cm
1983

RAKAN DABDOUB
Iraq, b. 1940
Born in ancient Mosul,
Dabdoub has tapped the rich
archeological sites of Iraq for
inspiration. The marble walls of
the houses and the ruined
castles of Mosul have provided
him with colour, texture and
form. Dabdoub graduated from
the Academy of Rome in 1965.
He was trained as a sculptor,
and his paintings reflect the
sculptural approach both in
structure and tactile quality. In
his paintings, Dabdoub, though
constantly reconstructing,
altering, adding, and omitting,
always focuses on one vision.
His works reflect a mystical
experience of light. They may
have many and varied
implications yet they remain
solid and forbidding. His female
figures, executed in a sculptural
manner, remind the viewer of
ancient Ishtar.

A Woman's Thought
Oil on wood
100 x 100 cm
1975

FAIK HASSAN
Iraq, b. 1914
Faik Hassan is a pioneer of
Modern Art in the Arab Islamic
world and an acknowledged
master. He studied at L'Ecole
des Beaux Arts, Paris,
graduating in 1939. His work
has followed the style of many
European schools but has
never lost its originality or its
unmistakably Iraqi origins,
even in his cubist compositions
where bedouin and peasants
still retain their allegiance to
the Tigris and Euphrates. His
expressionistic phase was
perhaps the richest because he
was able to highlight a strange
mixture of sympathy and
horror in his people. Later he
turned to Realism and
Impressionism, recording
characters and street scenes in
Baghdad with a sensitive, fresh
eye and delicate brush. His
portraits of horses and life in
the desert are equally
impressive.

The Tent
Oil on wood
60 x 90 cm
1956

SALEH AL-JUMAIE
Iraq, b. 1939
Al-Jumaie was born in Sewaira.
He graduated from the Institute
of Fine Arts, Baghdad, and
later from the College of Arts
and Crafts, California. He has
lived in San Francisco since
1980. He works in a variety of
materials: oils, watercolours
and even aluminium, which
harks back to the
coppersmith's ancient trade.
Initially his calligraphy has the
appearance of an
understandable text but as the
eye focuses, the letters turn
into something more ancient,
recalling wet Assyrian clay
tablets. Like other
contemporary Arab artists in
his own country and also in
North Africa, he has placed his
aesthetic search above verbal
expression. He has a special
control over bright hues,
shading through text and the
suggestion of shadowy figures.

The Ocean
Oil and zinc
100 x 100 cm
1981

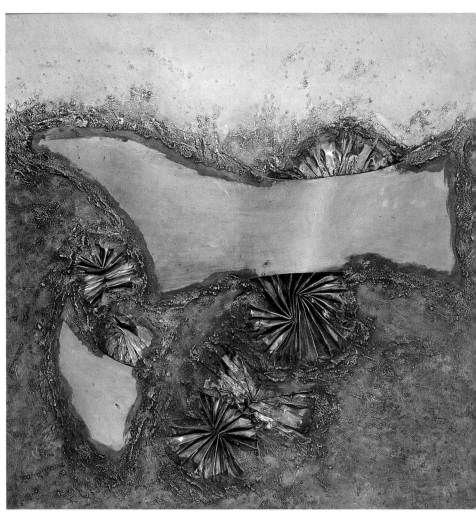

NOURI EL-RAWI
Iraq, b. 1925
Born in Rawa on the Euphrates, Rawi graduated in art from the Fine Arts Institute, Baghdad, in 1959. Rawi has turned to his native roots for inspiration. The nostalgic remembrance of old village houses nourishes his imagination. His works are poetic and lyrical. He is conscious of the changes that are taking place in his environment, yet he finds comfort in the mystery of his origins. His themes are mystical, moving between an inner self and an outer vision where his communication with nature is conducted in love and secrecy. Rawi is a founder member of the Iraqi Art Society, and has researched and published a number of articles on modern Iraqi arts.

Town
Oil on canvas
100 x 110 cm
1979

ISSAM EL-SAID
Iraq, 1939–1988
Born in Baghdad, el-Said
obtained a degree in
architecture from Corpus
Christi College, Cambridge. He
was fascinated by the geometry
of Islamic Art and in 1976
published *Geometrical
Concepts in Islamic Art*. His
calligraphic works became
especially well known in
London, where his paintings
have been on permanent
display. Although el-Said made
London his home, he
maintained close intellectual
and personal ties with the Arab
World. His murals draw on both
Arab geometry and the blues of
Turkey's wall tiles and are light,
airy and soothingly rich in
colour. The Jordan National
Gallery adopted one of these
works as the background for
the museum's emblem. El-Said
also did the groundwork for the
Islamic decoration section of
Qatar National Museum.

He is the Omnipotent
Acrylic on canvas
91 x 91 cm
1983

NIZAR SALIM
Iraq, 1925–1982
Born in Ankara, Salim was raised in Baghdad in a distinguished family of painters and intellectuals. He was educated in Baghdad at the College of Law and the Institute of Fine Arts, and was later appointed to the Ministry of Foreign Affairs. He was a writer, illustrator, art critic, cartoonist and painter. When he turned to painting he employed the skills and sharp eye of the cartoonist. His works contain a continuous commentary, marked with much compassion, and possess a sense of humour and of colour. Some of them appear to be individual character studies but in fact are Iraqi types. He published many books and will be remembered as an individual who has contributed greatly toward the development of art in Iraq.

Sudanese
Oil on canvas
52 x 45 cm
1957

NAZIHA SELIM
Iraq
Naziha Selim was born in
Turkey but grew up in Baghdad.
She studied at the Fine Arts
Institute in Baghdad, the
Institut des Beaux Arts in Paris
and, with the aid of a research
grant, in the German
Democratic Republic, where
she specialized in children's
book illustration and children's
theatre settings. She also
gained some experience in
enamelling and inlay work.
After spending seven years in
Paris, she returned to
Baghdad. She decided to free
herself from French influences
and to return to a simple naive
style in portraying the life of
Iraqi women. As well as being
an established woman artist,
she also teaches in the
Academy of Fine Arts in
Baghdad.

One Night's Dream
Oil on canvas
55 x 65 cm
1978

ISMAIL SHEIKHLEY
Iraq, b. 1927
Sheikhley was educated at the Fine Arts Institute in Baghdad, and at L'Ecole des Beaux Arts in Paris where he graduated in 1951. He was a founder member of the Primitive Group or Pioneers with Faik Hassan and also of the Iraqi Artists' Society. Sheikhley's works show a close relation to Faik Hassan's. His earlier works were predominantly scenes of Iraqi daily life, but he later turned his attention to female figures, villages and palm trees. His scenes of women are arranged in endless variations. The figures appear in groups, lacking details, and consist of masses of colour juxtaposed against impressionistic bright green or desert sun colours. There is a lyrical spirit, similar to that of Arabic poetry, in his works.

A Souk in Baghdad
Oil on canvas
65 x 80 cm
1980

NASR ABDEL AZIZ
Jordan, b. 1942
Abdel Aziz is a painter, a
teacher and television
producer. He was born in
Hebron and studied at the
College of Fine Arts in Cairo
where he graduated in 1968.
He continued his graduate
studies in the field of film
production. Abdel Aziz is a
figurative painter whose
individual style is concerned
with cultural traditions. His
paintings depict the rural life of
the peasant, and the traditional
way of life. He simplifies his
subjects with simple
geometrical lines, creating
both harmony and balance.

Untitled
Oil on wood
90 x 107 cm
1981

JAMAL ASHOUR
Jordan, b. 1958
Ashour trained at the Institute of Fine Arts in Baghdad where he received his diploma in 1980. Subsequently he travelled to Italy and gained his master's degree from the Fine Arts Academy in Florence in 1985. He returned to Amman and became a full-time artist. Ashour started as a figurative painter, preoccupied with national scenes in which he expressed his thoughts using a modern technique. The woman plays an important part in Ashour's work: he relies on a mathematical logic, $1 + 9 = 1$, which stands for one woman, nine months to form a human being, thus creating one uniform whole. His paintings reflect a deep sense of tradition yet at the same time express the liberal vision of Ashour's own intellect.

Women
Mixed media on wood
90 x 83 cm
1989

SUHAIL BISHARAT
Jordan, b. 1942

A geologist by training and an innovative self-taught artist by vocation, Suhail Bisharat has chosen to paint with coffee. A mundane medium that he has come to master and control, he utilizes all its gradations of brown, mixing it sometimes with black china ink to accentuate parts of the painting and at other times with gold to highlight a point. At first glance, Bisharat's monochromatic works give the impression of being there by accident, but looking more closely their well-studied composition betrays the artist's flight into fantasy through volatile shapes coupled with graceful lines and subtle shading. His scientific background has helped him to achieve a special technique by which he fixes his medium to the paper.

The Shining Gate
Coffee and gold on paper
41 x 66 cm
1980

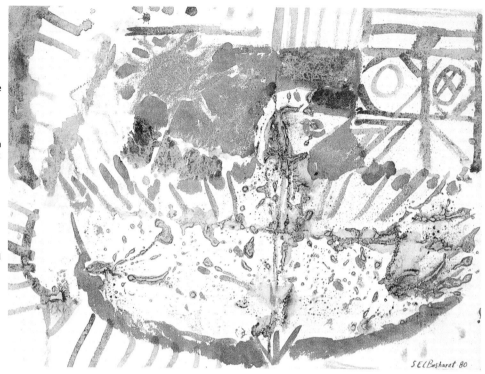

ALI JABRI
Jordan, b. 1943
Jabri is the only contemporary
Jordanian painter to spend
month after month in the
rigours of the desert, at
archaeological digs recording
his surroundings and living the
life of a Bedouin shepherd.
Jabri's roots belong to Aleppo
and the Jordanian highlands.
His schooling in Egypt and
Europe and his studies at
Stanford University have given
him an unusually intimate
knowledge of high cultures.
When he returned to Amman he
totally immersed himself in
Arab culture. Responsible for
new installations at the Jordan
Museum of Popular Traditions,
Jabri devotes himself to
museography and painting. In
both he captures with
sensitivity and skill a
threatened heritage, and
records in a personalized
realistic style the light, colour
and valour of ancient traditions
undergoing rapid
transformation.

This and following page:
Diptych
A: Ibn Tulun's Mosque
Water colour and pencil/paper
70 x 100 cm
1977

RAFIK LAHHAM
Jordan, b. 1932
Lahham has examined the rural landscape in depth and experimented on many different levels with a combination of Nabatean images, calligraphy and Islamic motifs. Born in Damascus, he now lives and works in Jordan. Lahham studied Fine Arts in Rome where he received his diploma from the ENALC Academy. He also studied sculpture at the San Jacomo Institute while in Rome. He continued his art studies at the Rochester Institute, and became president of the Jordanian Arts Associations in 1979.

From My Country
Oil on canvas
50 x 70 cm
1982

FUAD MIMI

Jordan, b. 1949

'My style is impressionistic, my aim is to create harmony between colour and subject . . . My subject is our society, our land, traditions and people.' Fuad Mimi studied television production and direction at the BBC in London, and later studied Art at St. Martin's College of Art. Mimi is widely known in Jordan as a writer, artist and television director. He sets himself high standards of perfection in all forms of production. Mimi is a quiet man who draws on the Jordanian landscape, exulting in windswept cloaks against the vast desert, the contrast of red and green in the hillsides or the intensity of the exotic lemon, orange and date trees of the fertile Jordan Valley.

Landscape 3
Oil on wood
70 x 50 cm
Undated

IBRAHIM NAJJAR
Jordan, b. 1949
Born in Jerusalem, Najjar
graduated from the Fine Arts
College of Cairo in 1976, and
completed his master's degree
at Helwan University in 1982.
He is now working on his
doctorate. Najjar's work is
concerned with the Palestinian
cause, the sacrifice and the
torture. He figuratively and
symbolically portrays on
canvas the suffering of
Palestinians, the human
desecration, in the lifeless
white and cold blues of winding,
curved sheets.

Untitled
Watercolour
35 x 28 cm
Undated

AHMAD NAWASH
Jordan, b. 1934
Nawash is one of the leading figures in Jordanian contemporary art. An uncompromising artist, his distinctive style in figuration expresses an intricate caricature of mankind's oppression by man. Nawash conveys his own tragic experience with a subtlety that embodies deep emotional suppression. Nawash received his diploma from the Bordeaux Academy of Fine Arts in France and studied graphics in Florence, Italy. His works are about fusing method and image, the visible public and private feelings. They cover a wide range of observations about places, people and emotions he has experienced. His mood can be cynical and sarcastic but his message is clear: through painting, it is possible to approach a common ground, to share an experience without falling into crude generalizations.

Opposite Direction
Oil on wood
55 x 65 cm
1984

ABDEL RAOUF SHAMOUN
Jordan, b. 1958
Shamoun is an artist, writer and art critic. He graduated from the University of Jordan with a BA. As an artist he is self-taught. Shamoun shocks with his intensely intellectual, figurative paintings in which subjects are disturbed and unbalanced in sharp contrast to the carefully balanced layout of his composition. Through his paintings he has experimented with and explored the inner struggle of contemporary society, and through his numerous articles he has contributed to the awareness of art and art appreciation. He has worked hard to put together a series of illustrations for child education. He is noted for his silent nature and hypersensitivity toward his painting.

The Passage
Oil on canvas
80 x 70 cm
1988

SUHA SHOMAN
Jordan, b. 1944
Suha Shoman is one of Jordan's
promising mature painters.
Born in Jerusalem, she made
Amman her home after studying
Law in Paris. She began to
develop her talent under the
guidance of the distinguished
painter Fahrelnissa Zeid.
Shoman's first large abstract
oils showed the influence of her
mentor, but also an emerging,
very individual style: her seas
washing around coral reefs
cause the viewer to wonder if
he is observing the
phenomenon from a satellite or
through a microscope.
Shoman's attraction to either
vast seascapes or the great
rocky outcrops above Petra
has taken her outside to paint
her strongest oils. Similar
environments have produced
some of her most sensitive
water colours, which are
contrastingly diminutive and
figurative.

The Legend of Petra
Oil on canvas
100 x 80 cm
Undated

WIJDAN
Jordan, b. 1939
Wijdan studied history and politics at Beirut University College and later art with Armando Bruno and Muhanna Durra. She was initially a diplomat in the Jordanian Foreign Service and the first woman to represent Jordan at the United Nations. Her paintings of Islamic cities and desert landscapes are distinguished by their texture. The unity and boldness of her large canvases mask an intensity of suffering through pigments combed into the shimmering expanse of landscape. Her latest experimentations are with calligraphy, utilizing the Arabic alphabet for its aesthetics and content and using the same combed texture. Wijdan is the founder and president of the Royal Society of Fine Arts and a leader in promoting artistic expression in the Arab and Islamic countries.

Calligraphy
Oil on board
40 x 50 cm
1985

FAHRELNISSA ZEID
Jordan, b. 1898

Born into a distinguished family of statesmen and intellectuals, Fahrelnissa Zeid was educated at the Istanbul Academy of Fine Arts (1920) and afterwards in Paris. Upon her return to Turkey she was among the founders of the 'D Group'. Her early realistic paintings of Istanbul interiors fitted with oriental carpets evolved into great abstract canvases where her fascination with oriental colour and shapes came to dominate. Later her work moved into the pure abstraction of the cosmos filled with shining whorls and comets. Her special strength became portraiture in a soul-searching, oriental form where the eyes are luminous and stylized and the outline of the figure simplified. She lives today in Jordan where she continues to paint with vigour and creativity.

The Bath
Oil on canvas
141 x 137 cm
1948

CHAFIC ABBOUD
Lebanon, b. 1926
Chafic Abboud abandoned his
engineering studies in 1945 to
attend the Lebanese Academy
of Fine Arts and in 1945
continued his training in Paris
where he attended the National
School of Fine Arts. He also
spent some time in Lhote
Studio. His earlier works were
strongly figurative and
possessed a great deal of
detail; his subsequent work
moved toward abstraction and
semi-abstraction where the
emphasis was placed on
colours – reds, greens, blues
and pinks. His paintings are a
synthesis of intellectual play
between harmonizing forms
and movement, resulting in a
rich luminosity.

Sea Stories
Oil on canvas
115 x 125 cm
1986

ETEL ADNAN
Lebanon, b. 1925

Poet, literary critic and painter, Etel Adnan discovered her gift for visual expression long after she had established herself as a writer, having studied literature at the Sorbonne and Harvard. As she explored new materials she learned that 'painting is a language without a language problem'. She created and recreated a single massive landscape through the seasons with oils, ceramics and tapestry. Adnan then turned to illustration of poetry and long, accordion-like folios suggestive of oriental texts. Her life, rooted in Lebanon where she is the art critic and cultural editor of *L'Orient Le Jour*, is enriched with classical Islamic traditions as well as the freedom of individual expression she fought to gain.

'Allah'
Mixed media
30 x 75 x 10 cm
1987

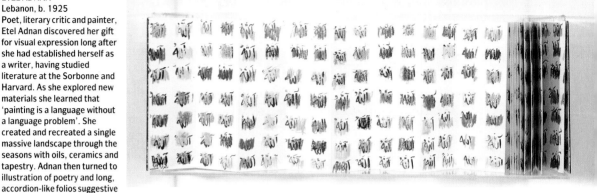

SALIBA DOUAIHY
Lebanon, b. 1912
Douaihy's paintings of the
eastern Mediterranean are
intensely individualistic yet
inseparable from his native
land. He studied under the
Lebanese master Habib Srour
before going to Paris in 1932.
After a year in Rome he
returned to Lebanon and was
commissioned to decorate the
walls and ceilings of the Diman
church, a task which proved his
creative strength and limitless
imagination. Douaihy's art is
his country, its people, and its
faces in different lights. In
1950 he left for the United
States where he continued to
experiment with light,
regarding it as a source of
fertility. His fascination with
the sun, the earth, the sky and a
particular blue became known
as 'Douaihy's style' and has
won him a distinguished
reputation among the great
artists of today.

Homage to Apollo
Acrylic on canvas
70 x 89 cm
1989

AMIN ELBACHA

Lebanon, b. 1932

Amin Elbacha graduated from the Lebanese Academy of Fine Arts in 1957. He practises in oils, watercolour, etching and mosaics. He chooses his subjects from nature, whether man, flora or fauna, interpreting them in an uncomplicated, childlike style with clear colours. Sometimes he uses flowing lines to define form and colour and at other times he uses colours to define form and space; in both cases there is tranquillity and spontaneity in his work without anger or revolt, simply a calm humanity. In his spontaneity lies his strength and from it radiate his talent and artistic sensitivity.

Composition
Oil on wood
28 x 40 cm
1962

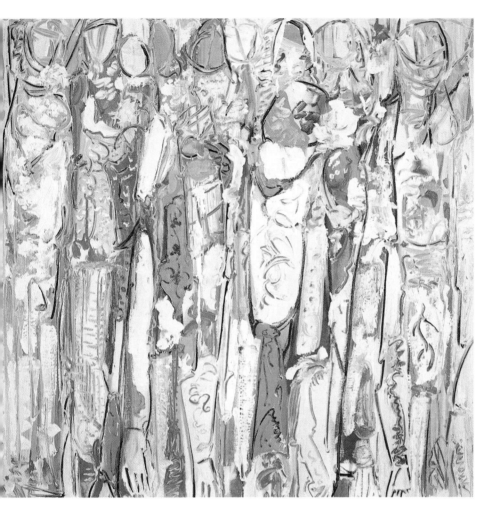

PAUL GUIRAGOSSIAN
Lebanon, b. 1926
Guiragossian's religious
upbringing has had an
influential effect on his life, and
the family is the dominant
theme in his work. In his early
career he painted daily scenes,
slums, the children of poverty,
women and mothers. His works
reveal sharp realism – thick
black lines expressing tragedy
and suffering. They are
unparalleled for their
directness, luminosity and
density of colour. His
brushstrokes are thick and
brutal, a demonstration
against misery or an expression
of joy, and faceless bodies are
transformed into columns of
colours where the attitude of
the figure dominates. He began
painting at the Yarcon Studio in
1942 and continued at Florence
Academy of Fine Arts in 1957.
He has spent many years in
Paris and the United States.

Purity
Oil on canvas
100 x 100 cm
Undated

SUHA TAMIM
Lebanon, 1936–1986
Suha's work suggests lightness
and spontaneity without
sacrificing intellectual depth.
Her almost abstract
juxtaposition of blocks of
colour reflects the impression
of an Arab city. While her
earlier works were executed in
a traditional style, she later
moved towards non-figuration,
using mixed media to reflect
her Muslim heritage. Her soft
pastel paintings of battle-
scarred Beirut are a disturbing
reminder that a fresh and neat
environment still exists behind
the ugly, ruined city which not
long ago enjoyed peace. She
graduated from the American
University of Beirut with a
master's degree in biology and
then studied at London
University. She began her
artistic career in 1968. She will
be remembered as an artist
who has added new vigour to
the reinterpretation of
traditional art.

Beirut Today
Mixed media
40 x 50 cm
Undated

ALI OMER ERMES
Libya, b. 1945
Ermes studied in England at the
Plymouth College of
Architecture before returning
to Tripoli to teach art. His
works are characterized by an
unusual combination of poetry
and calligraphy. Two years as a
consultant to the World of
Islam Festival, during which he
travelled extensively in the
East,has had a visible impact on
his work. The sweep of the
letters on his canvas and the
yellow background suggest an
oriental flair, although he also
favours an Islamic lapis lazuli.
Between his central characters
he works in vases of poetry
from Arab poets. The central
letter may be gold while tiny
black or faded tan texts may be
punctuated by red as in old
annotated versions of the
Koran.

'Shedda'
Mixed media
72 x 72 cm
1980

NG BUAN CHERS
Malaysia
Chers is a painter as well as a
lecturer. Her formal art
training was at the National
Academy of Arts in Taiwan, and
later at the Chelsea School of
Art where she obtained her
post diploma in printmaking.
Chers has had the opportunity
to be exposed to Chinese as
well as Western arts, and so
her works are a reminder of
Chinese painting. Ng Buan
Chers' sparse grey landscapes
with subtle texture and
delicate nuances evoke
meditative moods quite
removed from the lush tropical
colouristic preferences of the
majority of Malaysian artists.

'Song 1001'
Acrylic on canvas
102 x 76 cm
1984

ISMAIL HASHIM
Malaysia
Ismail Hashim is a graphic
artist as well as a leading figure
in art photography. His
bathroom series depicts
aspects of Malaysian life. He is
mainly concerned with his own
immediate environment which
is rapidly changing and, in some
cases, disappearing. He has
recorded in detail
contemporary socio-cultural
conditions in Malaysia.

The Bathroom
Hand-tinted photograph
55 x 49 cm
1988

SYED AHMAD JAMAL
Malaysia, b. 1929
Jamal's formal art training was at Birmingham School of Architecture and subsequently at Chelsea School of Art; he furthered his studies at the Institute of Education, the Art Institute of Chicago and the University of Hawaii. Jamal has been active in art since the late fifties and has concentrated his efforts on the pyramid-shaped 'Gunung Ledang' and energy series which focus on a continuous interflow of force radiating from within and without. He draws his inspiration from a rich love of the region's myths and legends yet at the same time maintains his perception of the contemporary.

'Tawaf'
Acrylic on canvas
91.5 x 91.5 cm
1986

SHARIFA FATIMAH ZUBIR
Malaysia, b. 1948
Sharifa Fatimah Zubir's formal
art training was at Mara
Institute of Technology where
she completed a course in
design and colour theories. She
continued her art studies at
Reading University where she
learnt etching techniques and
abstract acrylic painting. The
distinction she gained at
Reading earned her the John D.
Rockefeller III Fund Fellowship
which enabled her to study Fine
Arts at the Pratt Institute in
New York. She graduated in
1976. Fatimah Zubir is one of
the few Malaysian artists who
work in pure abstract forms.
She depicts growth in nature
through colour and shape and
has tremendous skill in slow
moving, soft shapes which fuse
in chromatic space. Exposure
to other cultures has given her
art a strong conviction.

Solitude
Acrylic on canvas
108 x 100 cm
1989

ABOU ALI ABDEL AZIZ
Morocco, b. 1939
Abdel Aziz was born in
Marrakesh, and his formal art
education was at Tetuan School
of Fine Arts where he studied
painting and sculpture.
Subsequently he travelled to
Spain and continued his
painting studies at Santa Isabel
in Seville in 1964. In 1967 he
completed his studies in
painting, sculpture, etching
and fresco at San Fernando
School of Fine Arts. In 1970 he
studied fresco at the
International School of Fresco
at San Cugat del Valle in
Barcelona. In his works
sculptural features are echoed
into his paintings, figures pay
tribute, and the broad
brushstrokes and subtle
sensitive colours result in a
semi abstract form.

Untitled
Acrylic
30 x 30 cm
Undated

AL-HACHIMI AZZA
Morocco, b. 1950

Azza started his formal art
education at the School of Fine
Arts in Tetouan, Morocco, in
1965. In 1969 he joined the
Royal Academy of Fine Arts in
Brussels, where he studied
painting, sculpture and
drawing, and later the Superior
School of Architecture and
Visual Art in Brussels where he
studied graphic printing
techniques, dry point linoleum
etching and woodcuts. He is
mainly concerned with
mezzotint technique and is a
master in his own right. His
works may have surrealistic
influences yet Azza captures an
immediate sense of self. His
works are technically well
executed, balanced and display
a sensitive use of colour in a
difficult technique. Hard
discipline and serious
commitment constitute Azza's
professionalism.

L'Immobilité
Etching
34 x 27 cm
1984

ABDULLA HARIRI
Morocco, b. 1949
Hariri is an imaginative,
innovative graphic artist
concerned primarily with
Arabic calligraphy. Letters and
diacriticals are used in contrast
to simplified geometrical
shapes. The letters may cross
the page in a moving mass
emphasising the difference
between flowing Arabic
calligraphy and a static Latin
alphabet, even moving from left
to right rather than from right
to left which Arabic demands.
His experiments extend into
other materials, such as paper,
acrylics, plastics and linoleum.
Hariri studied theatre design
and cinematography in
Toulouse after completing his
training in Fine Arts in
Casablanca. Subsequently he
studied design in Rome and
graphics in Poland. His home
has always been Casablanca.

Untitled
Mixed media
36 x 50 cm
1988

MOHAMED MELEHI
Morocco, b. 1936
Melehi returned to his birth place, Asilah, on the Atlantic Coast to transform its seabeaten walls with expansive murals of bright polychrome waves. He brought other artists with him and helped organise the Asilah Festival of Culture in 1978. Trained at the Academy of Fine Arts in Tetonan, then in Seville, Madrid, the Academy of Fine Arts in Rome, the Academy of Fine Arts in Paris and finally Columbia University, Melehi has been a leading force among Morocco's painters, teachers and art critics since 1964. His canvases have an undulating energy that thrusts the viewer forward along monochrome waves of colour caught off the canvas itself and a tremendous sense of freedom that is not contained by walls.

Untitled
Enamel on wood
100 x 120 cm
1981

MANSOORA HASSAN
Pakistan

Mansoora Hassan is a painter, graphic artist, printmaker and a photographer, who has led the way in oriental elements. Mansoora uses the three media with varying emphasis to create her works. A mixture of historic memory emerges combining fragments of Moorish Spain and Buddhist culture of her native Pakistan. She also used calligraphic elements from the Alhambra and Ottoman Istanbul. Mansoora Hassan graduated from the National College of Arts in Lahore in 1971 and subsequently obtained her master's degree in Fine Arts from the Pratt Institute, New York in 1976. She has conducted many workshops in printmaking, silkscreening, and photography. She has gained an international reputation and has created a world of form, fantasy and dancing figures with rhythmic colours.

The Moghul and the Dancer
Etching
47 x 62 cm
1987

ALI IMAM
Pakistan, b. 1924
Imam studied at Naypur School of Art and Sir J. J. School of Art in Bombay, then graduated from Punjab University in Lahore. Imam's style is a highly individual one. Although its base is Impressionism yet it has a distinct oriental feel. The oriental woman is the principle form in his paintings. He portrays her shyness and sensitivity with a spontaneous gesture as a bent head, cast down eyes, or a timid look. His colours are tranquil and with them he captures a fleeting moment which he freezes on canvas. Ali Imam is considered a major modern Islamic artist who has created a style that joins high modern technique and oriental characteristics.

Spinning Wheel
Oil on canvas
87 x 117 cm
1981

JAMIL NAQSH
Pakistan, b. 1937
Jamil Naqsh's power and
appeal were such that he won
recognition in his early years.
Born in Kairana, he studied art
under the guidance of his father
Abdul Basit, an accomplished
artist of the Mughal School.
This opportunity gave him an
invaluable grounding in the
application of colours and
detailed work. He subsequently
went to the Mayo School of
Arts, Lahore. His modern
themes of contemporary man
besieged by tensions created
by the industrial era are a
result of his powerful studies
and vision. His work juxtaposes
man with birds, or man
threatened with disintegration
and struggling for survival. His
technique is a combination of
traditional and modern, as
evident in his studies of human
physique.

Composition
Oil on canvas
107 x 107 cm
1980

LAILA SHAHZADA
Pakistan
Laila Shahzada is known for her canvases which bring to life the archaeological heritage of Pakistan by a metamorphosis of ancient content in the context of contemporary painting. Her new period the 'driftwood series' of whirling lines, flowing curves and throbbing rhythms create kinetic waves and fantastic figures, sometimes moulding them into Arabic script and at other times into forms that combine mythology with a reality of dreams.

Conflict
Oil on canvas
108 x 68.5 cm
Undated

USTAD SHUJAULLAH
Pakistan
A student of Haji Mohammad
Sharif, Ustad Shujaullah is the
only artist after the death of his
teacher to continue the
tradition of classical miniature
painting. Perpetuating Mughal
traditions, in the choice of
subject matter and its
execution, Shujaullah has kept
this flame alive. Unfortunately
few followed suit; nevertheless
he succeeded in becoming the
bridge between past traditions
and the present.

Woman and a Bird
Mixed media
20 x 30 cm
Undated

AFAF ARAFAT
Palestine, b. 1925
Afaf Arafat is a painter,
ceramicist and teacher. She
studied art and pottery at Bath
Academy where she graduated
in 1957. Subsequently she
continued for her master's
degree in Art at the State
University of Tennessee. Yet in
spite of her education abroad,
Afaf Arafat has remained pure,
realistic and expressionistic in
depicting scenes derived from
daily life. Her orange-pickers,
peasants in the field and nature
in different seasons are
captivating. She has a great
sense of balance and a subtle
choice of colour. In her later
works Afaf is experimenting in
watercolours where her
abilities and skill are to be
tested.

Orange Picking
Oil on canvas
60 x 90 cm
1975

SULEIMAN MANSOUR
Palestine, b. 1947

Mansour was born in Bir Zeit
where he now teaches. He has
remained in Palestine to paint
and exhibit so his knowledge of
subjugation comes from direct
experience. His subjects are
overtly expressive of his
personal political realities. One
image has become a rallying
symbol throughout the Arab
world: a solid hardworking
villager weighed down by the
cares of the world moves
ahead, carrying on his back the
globe filled with Jerusalem.
Mansour also paints more
subtle images on canvas where
the outline of a human profile is
partially concealed with one
part of the canvas prominently
displaying calligraphy in a shaft
of light. He maintains his
allegiance to his homeland
while experimenting with a
variety of media including wood
and brass.

Untitled
Oil on wood
41 x 50 cm
1980

SAMIR SALAMEH
Palestine, b. 1944
Salameh was born in Safad, Palestine, but his development as an artist has followed the long winding route of many refugees. Salameh had his first formal training in Damascus and then went on to study art in Paris but has repeatedly returned to exhibit in Damascus, Kuwait, Baghdad, Tunisia, Morocco and Egypt. Like other contemporary artists Salameh has devoted himself to penetrating the boundary between the traditional calligraphy of the *khattat* and calligraphy as a plastic art form which also carries inherent connotations of the 'Holy Word of the Koran'. A bold overlay of modern calligraphy is the only prominent sign that the work is a modern studied collage rather than a random pastiche of excerpts from ancient texts.

Arabic Calligraphy
Watercolour
70 x 100 cm
1987

SAMIA ZARU
Palestine, b. 1938
Samia Zaru is a painter and a sculptor. She has experimented with a variety of welded sculptures, geometrical and figurative images on canvas, textile collages, ropes and woven wall pieces. Her themes are the homeland, time and conflict. Her sculptures are built directly from welded and scrap metal, similarly her collage paintings make use of embroidery and textile elements juxtaposed against vibrant colours. Samia graduated from the American University of Beirut and later continued her postgraduate studies at the Corcoran Art Gallery and at the American University in Washington DC. In most of her abstract expressionist work, a direct artistic impact is felt, creating an interaction between the work of art and the viewer.

Struggle and Conflict
Oil, collage on canvas
102 x 91 cm
1985

SHAMS EDDIN ADAM
Sudan, b. 1959
Adam graduated from the
College of Fine and Applied
Arts in Khartoum in 1984. He
works with coloured inks, oils,
poster colours, water colours
and black ink. His paintings
contain all kinds of animals
which he uses to express his
thoughts and environment. He
is more interested in movement
and spontaneity in execution.
His works appear to be the
exploration of one's roots,
tracing them back to the
beginning of time.

Untitled
Oil on carton
93 x 122 cm
Undated

IBRAHIM EL-AWAAM
Sudan, b. 1935
El-Awaam studied at the American University of Cairo and subsequently at the School of Fine and Applied Arts in Khartoum. His works have an intellectual content and an aesthetic quality. He has managed to reconcile the visual and his feelings, and to express his temperament as a Sudanese, an African and to combine these with his poetic Arab nature. Calligraphy occupies an important part in Awaam's works which are not ornamental, but captivating and dramatic. He has had a profound effect on the modern contemporary art scene in Sudan. He consistently seeks and researches for new means of visual expression by drawing on his local environment or on an external universal one.

Letters from Quran
China ink on paper
30 x 40 cm
1985

BASTAWI BAGHDADI
Sudan, b. 1927
Bastawi is regarded as a
pioneering artist of Sudan.
Born in Omdurman, he studied
design at the Gordon Memorial
College, Khartoum in 1946, at
Goldsmith College, London,
where he graduated in 1949
and went on to the Pratt
Institute, New York. Bastawi
Baghdadi has earned a
distinguished reputation for his
portraits, most captivating in
their manner and style. He is
equally known for his depiction
of many aspects of Sudan with a
sharp realism and a mature
style. Bastawi is an influential
teacher who has served in
many important administrative
and teaching posts. He is a
founding member of the
Sudanese Association in 1951
and served on the National
Council for the Arts and Letters
in Sudan. Khartoum remains
his home, where he still paints.

Three Mourning Women
Oil on Burlap
75 x 95 cm
1971

KAMALA IBRAHIM
Sudan
Kamala Ibrahim's works are distinctive in their expressionistic distortion. She enlarges the proportion of the head and in the exaggeration of the shape of the mouth and nose creating deformed, mysterious humans, yet recognisably something else. Ibrahim's formal art training was at the Faculty of Fine Arts in Khartoum and she subsequently continued her art studies at the Royal College in London. In her works the viewer is probing into an enlarged, disturbing world as if looking through a magnifying glass.

Loneliness
Oil on canvas
103 x 103 cm
1987

MOHAMED OMER KHALIL
Sudan, b. 1936

Mohamed Khalil is a most
accomplished graphic artist,
painter and teacher, whose
work relies on forms and
pattern, comprising symbols,
artefacts, stamps or any kind of
motifs derived from his
Sudanese background. The
gradational colours of black
and the different contrasts of
black contribute to the
achievement of sensibility and
drama. Khalil studied and then
taught at the School of Fine and
Applied Art till 1963, and
continued his studies at the
Fine Art Academy of Florence.
He is now in the United States.
Khalil aims to be as original as
possible and avoids being
drawn by the conventional
forces so that his works reflect
a great deal of freedom and
appear in their natural, true
form.

Colombia
Etching
53 x 53 cm
Undated

SAMI BURHAN
Syria, b. 1929
Born in Aleppo, Burhan studied
graphics and sculpture in Paris
and Rome. His works deal with
calligraphy as a compositional
element. He has tremendous
skill in the use of colour tones
and colour contrast which play
an important part in his
paintings. The red burnt heat
tones that embrace his
calligraphical expression stand
in contrast to his yellow-sand
textured colours. He has a skill
in creating a translucent,
luminous glazed-like effect in
his works. He has distinguished
himself with a large piece of
sculpture that he designed for
the entrance of the King Saud
University in Riyadh.

Unity
Oil on wood
30 x 30 cm
1980

FATEH MOUDARRES
Syria, b. 1922
Moudarres is one of the
leaders of Syria's modern art
movement. He trained at the
Academy of Fine Arts in Rome
and later in Paris. A professor
of Fine Arts at Damascus
University, he has trained
generations of Syria's
students. His style is highly
personal. Moudarres called it
'surrealistic and figurative with
a strong element of absraction'.
He depicts nature and Syria's
past; faces emerge from rocks,
or blend into the hillside. His
figures are two dimensional
and square like Assyrian stone
cuttings while others float
under the topmost surface of
the canvas. He blends the
human and natural landscapes
of Syria into a timeless present.

Christ the Child of Palestine
Oil on canvas
78 x 59 cm
1989

NAZIR NABA'A
Syria, b. 1938
After his initial fine arts training in Cairo, Naba'a was posted to Deir el-Zor to teach. There he discovered the richness of Syrian popular traditions of dress and folktales as well as the landscape. Upon his return to Damascus he applied himself to political subjects, including posters. Subsequent periods in Paris took him even further into the study of decorative detail. In his subsequent work, however, the detail moves into the sub-surface while voluptuous, realistic lines lead the viewer's eyes across the surface. Nazir uses Arabic calligraphy in an embellished decorative form that draws its inspiration from Syrian wood panelling and decorated porcelain. Naba'a is professor of fine arts at the University of Damascus.

Lover of the Son
Acrylic oil on canvas
64 x 95 cm
1967

ELIAS ZAYYAT
Syria, b. 1935
Eastern iconography forms the mode of expression for Zayyat's social commentary in oils. His upbringing in Damascus and then his training in Bulgaria surrounded him with the watchful, mournful expression of iconographic art. Zayyat has perfected even the natural orange and burnt red lines of early icons. Philosophical comment in calligraphy and political symbols hide under the surface. Zayyat teaches art and printing at the University of Damascus and also restores ancient icons. The painstaking rediscovery of the art of the iconographer has contributed during his lifetime to his large canvases in oils where he frees himself from ancient traditions that limit size, content, colouration, resorting to early sources only when he chooses.

Maloula Mazar
Tempra and oil on canvas
80 x 60 cm
1989

KHALID ASRAM
Tunisia
All kinds of masks, faces, fish,
birds, eyes, animals crowd
Asram's paintings. The outlines
of one shape become the
outlines of another. These
notations contribute to an
overall design of interlocking
forms. The juxtaposition of
shapes creates a strong
decorative pattern that forcibly
flattens the forms against a
blue background. There is a
tremendous interaction of
forms. Asram continues to
experiment finding new means
of expression in which he
combines ancient tradition and
fantasy echoed in a
contemporary trend.

Untitled
Oil on canvas
90.5 x 71 cm
1985

IBRAHIM DAHAK
Tunisia, b. 1931
Dahak lives in Sidi Bou Said
above Tunisia's capital. He
moved to this artists' colony
from Gafsa. He studied at the
Academy of Fine Arts in Tunis
and also Rome. Few artists in
the Arab world cut their
engravings with such forceful
determination. His subjects are
not necessarily new but the
lines are a combination of
medieval harshness and
flowing forms. The countryside
and figures in his work come
from the heart, not from
copying illuminated
manuscripts. His work uses
colour in a dramatic fashion
with no attempt to blend hues.
The central figure has the most
striking colour reserved for it
alone: a passionate purple for a
man contorted by grief, a blood
red for a warrior taking a
stance of defiance.

Ribat in Hammamat
Oil on paper
72 x 76 cm
1987

ALI GUERMASSI
Tunisia, b. 1923

Ali Guermassi is considered
one of the pioneering artists in
Tunis today. A self-taught
artist, Guermassi has
established a personal style; it
could be described as primitive
yet he has established a
distinctive style of his own. He
uses oils to depict the charming
scenes of Tunis, the cafes, the
market scenes, the busy
streets and describe in his own
way the daily scenes of Tunis.
His paintings are simple and
easy to appreciate resulting in
a dialogue between the viewer
and the work.

Mazar Ali Basha
Oil on canvas
100 x 80 cm
Undated

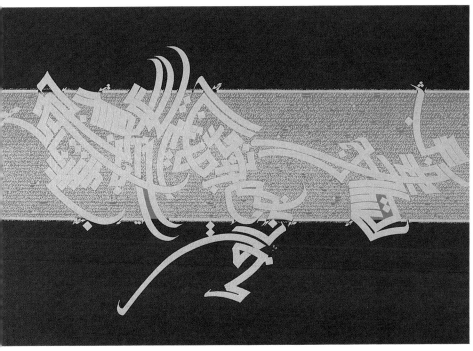

NJA MAHDAOUI
Tunisia, b. 1937
Mahdaoui studied art in La Figurie Museum in Carthage. With Mahdaoui, Arabic calligraphy assumes a nonliteral, purely visual expression. Working on parchment with china ink, Mahdaoui uses long, slender brushstrokes reminiscent of stylized flowing *tughras*, or official signatures of the Ottoman sultans. But a closer look shows that these black, smooth and sweeping lines form no name, no word whatsoever. They are pure pleasure that takes the easy, self confident flow developed over centuries and moves into a visual composition of select, pure lines over delicately shaded parchment surfaces. Mahdaoui avoids the use of religious texts, adding content from other illusions instead to express a new cultural reference that may enrich the inner historical heritage of Tunisia.

Calligraphical Composition
Screen print
27 x 37 cm
Undated

GOUIDER TRIKI
Tunisia, b. 1949
Triki belongs to the second
generation of Tunisian artists
and its first generation of
engravers, who studied under
Hedi Turki in Tunis. Triki
studied in Paris and spent time
in the studios of Lagrange and
Couteau where he learned
wood cutting and wood
engraving. He strengthened his
spiritual links with his Tunisian
roots by spending part of his
time farming the land while
working at his art. Triki's
engravings look into his
childhood in Nabeul combining
the reality of the Tunisian
townscape of domes, minarets
and blue doors with a childlike
fantasy of airplanes, animals
and bicycles; others explore
the souls behind Tunisian faces
which in their traditional
headgear make up the entire
pattern of the engraving.

Untitled
Etching
49 x 39 cm
Undated

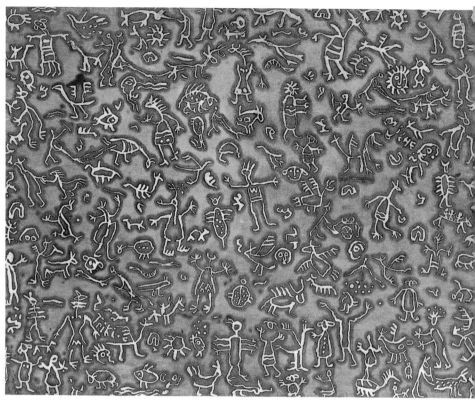

HEDI TURKI
Tunisia, b. 1922
Turki belongs to Tunisia's second generation of painters and is in the forefront of abstraction. Turki showed a remarkable talent for painting as a young boy under difficult circumstances. He took various jobs until he won a scholarship to the Academy of Fine Arts in Rome. His early work was realistic but a trip to the United States exposed him to the work of Jackson Pollock, Mark Tobey and Ben Shan. While portraits brought him early fame he is sought after today for his vertically hatched abstract canvases where light colours and shadows create a *trompe l'oeil* like that of finely striped Tunisian silk. He lives today in a traditional white washed house in Sidi Bou Said.

Espace Bleu ou Vert
Oil on canvas
81 x 100 cm
1986

NURI ABAÇ
Turkey, b. 1926
Abaç's work is unmistakably
surrealist as well as Turkish,
drawing heavily on the images
of traditional shadow puppets
Abaç has evolved a peculiarly
curved, intertwined set of
forms in his compositions
where even the modern objects
take on the undulating lines of
the shadow puppet figures.
Trained at the Academy of Fine
Arts in Istanbul, Abaç has
repeatedly returned to the folk
traditions and mythology of
Anatolia. Each composition is a
wry commentary on modern
Turkish life, drawing the
characters from the head
downwards in Ottoman
turbans and beards and
undressing them from below to
appear in modern shorts or
blue jeans. Neither above or
below are they dignified, but
amusing and thoughtprovoking.

The Shepherd
Oil on canvas
65 x 65 cm
1979

AVNI ARBAŞ
Turkey, b. 1919
Arbaş was member of the 'New Group' in Turkey during the 1940s who chose a dimly lit, dark decor for his paintings. He continued this choice of setting when he settled in France, where the natural light was conducive to studies in the perpetual dark of shadows. A student under both Lhote and Leger, Arbaş chose to keep himself free of identification with any 'school'. Despite his long years abroad, Arbaş repeatedly draws on Anatolia for his subjects. Its soil and people keep drawing him back, but in these canvases there is a grim, dark resignation. An abstract painter as well, Arbaş paints in sombre tones of browns and grays, where only a subdued streak of orange may cast light.

The Bosphorus at Night
Oil on canvas
97 x 130 cm
1981

BEDRI RAHMI EYÖBOĞLU
Turkey, 1913–1975
Eyöboğlu belonged to Turkey's
first generation of painters who
left Istanbul to discover and
paint in Anatolia. Born on the
Black Sea coast, he studied in
Istanbul and in 1931 went to
Paris to study with Lhote. Upon
his return to Istanbul, he joined
the Academy and became a
founding member of the 'D
Group'. He looked to the active
studios of Europe for
inspiration and in turn became
an influential teacher.
Eyöboğlu's explorations on
canvas moved through
calligraphy, mosaics and even
printing on textiles, where he
took the traditional crafts,
particularly local embroidery,
as his source for colours and
forms. His willingness to
experiment with mass
production made art much
more accessible to the public.

Untitled
Mixed media/board
122 x 85 cm
1963

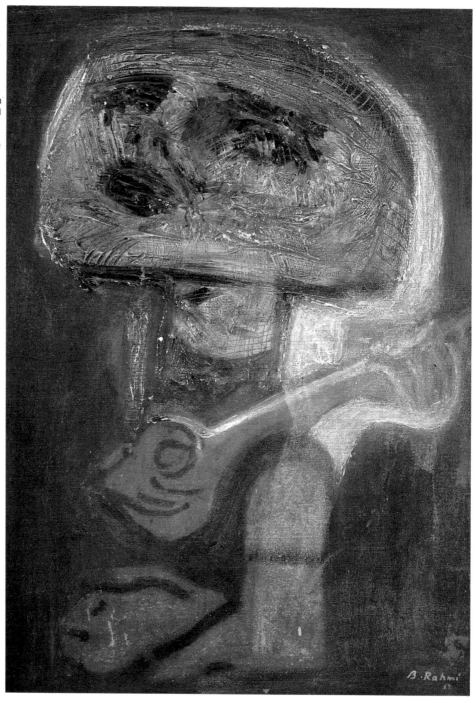

YALÇIN GÖKÇEBAĞ
Turkey, b. 1944
Gökçebağ pursues a studiedly naive style despite his formal training at the Gazi Institute. A film producer and graphic designer, Gökçebağ's canvases have the same wide-angle overview as the camera's lens. However, Gökçebağ works each small component of the canvas with exacting detail after Turkish miniatures. At times he removes all human figures from his landscapes. He comes from a small city in south-central Anatolia and has lived all his professional life in Ankara in the centre of Turkey, closer to the villages and countryside of Anatolia than cosmopolitan Istanbul. His refined naivete underscores an intention to maintain his connection with these roots, rather than move towards the intellectually effete forms of expression occasionally found in Istanbul.

Game
Oil on wood
60 x 65 cm
1980

FIKRET MUALLA
Turkey, 1903–1967
Since his lonely death in
France, Mualla's reputation as
one of Turkey's masters of this
century has soared. His life
time was spent in estrangement
from family and society first in
Turkey and then in self imposed
exile in France. Born in
Istanbul, the son of a modest
civil servant, Mualla attended
the elite Galatasaray Lycée.
Between 1920 and 1926 he
studied graphic art in Berlin.
Unable to keep a teaching job in
Turkey and suffering from
bouts of depression, Mualla
left for France in 1939, never to
return. His gouache and
watercolour paintings are filled
with the seamy and extravagant
side of Paris night life. Most
typical of his best works are
bright, sparkling colour and
fluid forms.

Untitled
Mixed media/canvas
50 x 63 cm
1959

The prevailing style in painting in the fifties and sixties was a primitive academic style that belonged to no school but pictured the subject realistically, according to the ability of the artists. Among the early Realist artists are: Jassim Zaini from Qatar and Mojab Dossari and Mohammad Damghi from Kuwait. With the increase in governmental support, in the form of scholarships, in the mid-sixties and seventies, the increase in the number of exhibitions, the easy accessibility of travel and an exposure to Western art led to a departure from rigid academic forms. Thus a new era of experimentation with the various modern Western schools began. Those experiments varied from in-depth studies to superficial imitative trials that blindly followed visual forms without indulging in the meaning and philosophy behind them. The most popular schools of painting to imitate have been the Impressionist, the Expressionist, the Abstract and the Surrealist. Among the Impressionist artists there are: Abdel Qadir Rayis and Ibrahim Mustafa from the United Arab Emirates: Ahmad Qassim Sinni, Abdel Rahim Sharif, Abdel Karim Bosta, Rashid al-Khalifa and Ahmad Nashaba from Bahrain; Mohammad Moussa Salim and Ahmad Falamban from Saudi Arabia; Anwar Khamis Sonia, Ahmad Aladawi and Rabiha Mahmoud from Oman; Mohammad Ali Abd Rabih and Issa Ghanim from Qatar and from Kuwait Jassim Bou Hamad and Jaafar Islah. Among the Expressionist artists are Abdel Qadir Rayis and Hassan Sharif from the United Arab Emirates; Zia Aziz Zia and Safia Ben Zugur from Saudi Arabia; Lal Bakhsh, Faisal Samra and Mahmoud Youssef Makki from Oman; Hassan Mulla from Qatar; Thuraya Baqsami from Kuwait and from Bahrain Mohammad Khamis, Abbas Moussawi, Ahmad Baqir and Ishaq Kohaji. Some of the Abstract painters are: Safia and Rashid Swar, Ishaq Kohaji and Abdel Latif Mofiz from Bahrain; Abdel Halim Radwi, Saleh Khatab, Ali Ghamdi, Fouad Mugharbil and Mounira Mosly from Saudi Arabia; Abdullah Taki, who was the first artist in the area to depart from academic restrictions, and Abdallah Salem from Kuwait. Surrealism became quite popular among Gulf artists. Through it they have found a style with which they could depict the frustrations of their societies and break through their social and cultural inhibitions. Among the well known Surrealist artists are: Muna Amin Khaja from the United Arab Emirates; Khalil Hassan Khalil, Mohammad Siam, Turki Dossari and Mohammad Assim Jaha from Saudi Arabia; Abdel Rasul Salman, Jassim Bou Hamad, Khazal Awad, Sami Mohammad, Abdallah Kassar, Yousseh Qattami, Salem Khoraji, and Khalifa Kattan from Kuwait and Abdallah Mahriqi from Bahrain. Among the Symbolic artists are: Ali Numan, Basil Alkazzi and Amir Abdel Rida from Kuwait; and Salman Malki from Qatar. As in other Islamic countries, Arabic calligraphy has had an obvious effect on painting in the Gulf, claiming a large following. Among the calligraphic painters who also use Islamic motifs are: Obeid Srour, Mohammad Mandi and Hisham Mazloum from the United Arab Emirates; Abdel Karim Irayid, Hussein Qassim Sinni, Mahmoud Yamani, Nasser Youssef from Bahrain; Wafiqa Sultan and Youssef Ahmad from Qatar; Mohammad Shaikh and Abdel Rasul Salman from Kuwait; and Suleiman Babjaa, Baq Shaikhoun, Ali Ruzaiza from Saudi Arabia

Sculpture

If the history of modern painting in the countries of the Gulf does not exceed four decades, the history of sculpture is even shorter. Yet the achievements of some of the sculptors from the Gulf, in particular from Kuwait, surpass the progress reached by others in painting. In spite of the lack of a tradition in sculpture, a few sculptors have managed to attain international standards in these short two decades. Among them are Issa Saqr, Jawad Jassem Shahri, Khalifa Kattan, Sami Mohammad, Khazal Awad Qaffas and Jassim Bou Hamad all from Kuwait. Their subjects deal with humanitarian matters and problems, while some of Issa Saqr's works reflect indigenous traits. Other distinguished sculptors and ceramicists are : Mohammad Youssef, Abdel Rahim Salim and

Salim Jawhar from the United Arab Emirates; Ali Mhaimid from Bahrain; and Najib Khamis Sonia and Majid Hanini from Oman. The media most artists use are: marble, stone, plaster, bronze, wood, ceramics, copper and brass.

Conclusion

The modern art movement in countries of the Gulf represents the accelerating artistic growth in a rich, developing part of the Arab world. In a period of less than four decades, artists in the Gulf have managed to travel a long way from the rudimentary art training in primary and secondary schools to a certain degree of maturity and professionalism coupled with the quest for a distinct artistic identity. Complete dependence on the state has given way to an independent, meaningful and planned policy towards well-defined aims and objectives. The artistic experience of the modern Gulf States presents a good example of healthy co-operation between an affluent, developing society and its artists. Generous patronage and material and moral support provided by the State have effectively raised the intellectual and cultural standards without censorship or the obstruction of freedom of expression. Now the artist may utilize this support to realize his artistic identity and find his way towards developing a school of art with distinctive features and characteristics of its own.

See colour pp. 66–75 for plates of the following artists' work:

ABDEL AZIZ ASHOUR
SURAYA AL-BAQSAMI
JASSEM BU HAMID
YUSSEF JAHA
HASSAN AL-MULLA
ABDEL HALIM RADWI
ABDEL RASUL SALMAN
ANWAR KHAMIS SONIA
ABDEL RAHMAN SULEIMAN
NASSER AL-YOUSIF

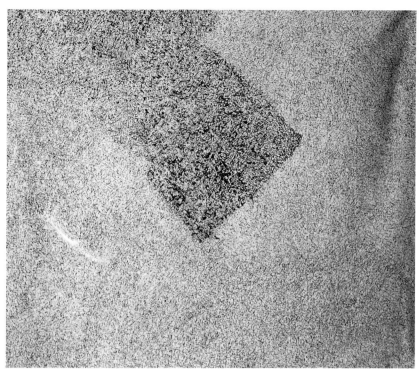

YUSSEF AHMAD
Qatar, b. 1955

Yussef Ahmad builds his paintings with Arabic calligraphy. He uses black inks on his base of natural pure linen. The letters are arranged rhythmically and systematically, and are pure abstract signs lacking any literal meaning and not conforming to any calligraphic tradition. Sometimes in his works the viewer may divine a symbolic representation that appears like a horse or a bird. He has developed a definite style of his own in which he searches for new forms of composition through calligraphy. Ahmad completed his BA at the College of Art Education, Helwan University, in 1975 and later gained his master's from Oakland City, California.

A Trial for Unity
Ink on canvas
150 x 150 cm
1982

DIA AZIZ DIA
Saudi Arabia, b. 1947

Born in Cairo, Dia Aziz Dia grew up and lives in Saudi Arabia. He gained his fine arts degree from the Academy of Fine Arts in Rome. His paintings exhibit a certain academic style and convey his concern for the tragedy of events.

Victory or Death
Oil on wood
90 x 125 cm
1988

MOUNIRA MOSLY
Saudi Arabia
Mounira Mosly was born in
Mecca. She graduated from the
College of Fine Arts, Cairo, in
1972, subsequently gaining a
diploma in graphic arts in
California. Mosly is a painter, a
graphic artist and a teacher.
She has also designed and
illustrated books, published
articles on art and studied
children's art. She was the
founder of the Dammam Art
Gallery. Mosly creates her own
world; her works reveal a
series of symbols and outbursts
of emotions and colours. She is
among the few Saudi women
artists who have been able to
free themselves from academic
influences. Monira Mosly takes
as her theme the vanishing
customs and rituals of the past
she treasures the past so that
future generations can benefit
from it.

Circle within Circles
Mixed media/burlap
43 x 100 cm
1988

ABDEL LATIF MUFIZ
Bahrain, b. 1950
Mufiz graduated from the Fine Arts
Academy in Baghdad University
and specialized in art education.
Mufiz's early style was semi-realist
to impressionist. He gradually
shifted from semi-abstract to
abstract. He uses his mixed media
and ink in a rapid, spontaneous
fashion, almost like action painting,
to demonstrate his deep and
disturbing thoughts. His colours are
bright and his brushstrokes are thin
and dense. He is constantly
searching for new methods and
techniques.

David
Acrylic on paper
75 x 65 cm
1988

MONA QASBI
Saudi Arabia, b. 1959
Mona Qasbi is a promising young artist from Saudi Arabia. Born in Jeddah, she received her art training at King Abdal Aziz University where she gained her degree from the College of Arts. Like many artists who have used Arabic alphabets and calligraphy, she is more spiritually inspired than literal. Her works are closely related to miniature paintings, although there is a lack of emphasis and depth. She uses gold with a black background and calligraphical elements.

Al Kaaba Gate
Mixed media on glass
80 x 80 cm
1987

ISSA SAQR
Kuwait, b. 1940
Issa Saqr was a student of the Egyptian sculptor Shawqi Dasouqi, who taught him ceramics. He was one of the first Kuwaiti artists to gain admission to the Free Atelier. He obtained a scholarship to study in Egypt under the famous sculptor Jamal Sequini and was one of the founders of the Kuwaiti Formative Society for the Arts in 1967. Between 1981 and 1983 he gained experience in bronze casting at the Johnson Institute, New Jersey, USA. Issa Saqr is very attached to his roots and to the events of daily life. He started out as a ceramicist but soon found that sculpture, less fragile than ceramics in its susceptibility to heat and colour control, was more appealing.

The Silent Voice
Copper
50 x 62 cm
Undated

Iran
Kameran Diba

Iran's culture since Sassanian times has influenced, in one way or another, the Indian Subcontinent, Turkey and all of the Middle East, including North Africa and al-Andalus in the Iberian Peninsula. During the Shi'ite Safavid Dynasty in the sixteenth century art in all its forms flourished in Iran; great artists like Bihzad worked in the Royal Ateliers on important manuscripts, producing great masterpieces. In the seventeenth century poetic scenes depicting lovers against a background of nature appeared in fresco paintings and manuscript drawings.

During the Qajar Dynasty, in the late eighteenth and nineteenth centuries, contacts with Russia and Western Europe began to influence Iranian art. Certain innovations appeared, in the use of materials such as oil paints and in the manner of execution by using gradation instead of applying colour on a totally flat area. Manuscript drawing and lacquer painting were popular as well as two-dimensional, large-scale European-style oil paintings. Portraits, in particular, became popular.

The Early Years

Towards the end of the nineteenth century and during the early twentieth century, Iranians, including students, began to travel more frequently to Europe. Among these students was Mohammad Gaffari or Kamal ul-Molk (1852–1940), the last court painter of the Qajar shahs and the one to introduce academic realism into Iran. He came at a time when Iranians were being gradually exposed to the marvels of new technology, and when photography had just appeared. In his paintings, he broke with the formal stereotype style of his day to adopt a naturalistic manner that competed with the camera in its rendering of fine detail. He introduced a basic change in outlook by looking at nature objectively and by sparing no effort to record the minutest details of everything he observed. He was the artist as master draughtsman and supreme colourist. But the new Western style Kamal ul-Molk and his disciples adopted was already on its way out in Europe.

Abul-Hassan Khan Gaffari was another eminent Qajar painter who visited Italy in the mid-nineteenth century to study European painting techniques in the museums of Rome and Florence. The style he adopted from the European masters affected only his own work while Kamal ul-Molk created a fundamental change in the Iranian norms of painting and art appreciation. The traditional media of miniature manuscript illustration and lacquer-work were replaced by Western-style easel painting, as the artist's primary medium of expression. Kamal ul-Molk established a school of fine arts, Madrasa-ye Sanaye-e Mostazrafa, in Tehran in 1911 and was its director until his retirement in 1928. This school exerted a major influence in the promotion of Western-style academic painting. Through the school, he trained and launched a host of disciples who propagated and popularized the new style at the expense of traditional painting. All through the twenties, thirties and even forties when Cubism, Surrealism, Expressionism and Abstractionism were rampant in Europe, the so called 'modern' artists of Iran were those working with oils and watercolours. They painted academic renderings of Iranian subjects: family gatherings, street scenes, the countryside and floral still life. Other less serious artists made copies of Central European landscapes: snow-capped mountains, scenic lakes and châteaux with green pastures in the foreground. In spite of the severe decline in the traditional arts, they survived into the early decades of the twentieth century and folk art flourished.

Murals and oil paintings were used to decorate local coffee houses, and as a result came to be known as *Qahwa-Khana* or 'coffee-house' paintings. Their subjects were taken from the *Shahnama* and accounts of the Shi'ite martyrs. Votive art, such as those employed in shrines and Saqqah-Khaneh, banners, standards and symbols of martyrdom displayed in Shi'ite passion plays and processions, provided another level of artistic expression for popular artists and would provide a rich source of iconography for later painters and sculptors.

In 1934, Tehran University was established, and in 1938 its School of Fine Arts opened with several of Kamal ul-Molk's disciples occupying key positions and holding back, for another decade or so, the plunge into modernity beyond Impressionism. Meanwhile miniature painting in the Safavid style continued to be practised by a residual school of artists, best represented by Hosayn Behzad.

During World War II, contact with Western culture increased when the Allied Forces occupied Iran in 1941. After the war many Iranians travelled to Europe and the United States to pursue their education abroad, and some of them studied art. A number of group exhibitions were organized in Tehran, which included most of the so called 'practising modernists'. The most outstanding was an exhibition held at the Iran-Soviet Cultural Society (VOKS) in 1946, followed by a series of exhibitions held at the Mehragan Club, home of the National Teachers' Association during the early fifties. All these shows continued to bear the stamp of the Kamal ul-Molk school.

The Formative Years

Proper modernism was introduced into the Iranian art movement with the return of a number of artists who had finished their studies abroad, notably in Italy and France. They injected avantgarde norms and styles into all forms of the visual arts. Fired by examples of rapid modernization in many fields of Iranian life and culture, they tried to catch up in the arts. The most important figure responsible for introducing modern trends to the Iranian public and artists alike was the painter Jalil Zia'pur (b. 1928). A graduate of Tehran University's School of Fine Arts, he continued his studies in France under Cubist painter André Lhote. Upon his return he started, with the help of his friends, an art club and a monthly publication called *Korus-e-Jangi* which soon carried the banner for modernism and became the platform around which avantgarde painters, poets and dramatists rallied. Quasi-Cubist, Expressionist and even Abstract works started to invade Tehran's early art shows creating a public debate on the merits of modern art. This continued side by side, for almost three decades, with the 'new versus classical poetry' controversy. Besides Zia'pur, Kazemi and Javadi-pur may be credited as the first pioneers of modern art in Iran.

By the mid-fifties, Iranian artists advocating modernism started to receive official encouragement from the Department of Fine Arts (later to become the Ministry of Fine Arts). Officials realised that there was a need for a major exhibition, to give impetus to the modern art movement, while preparing Iranian artists to participate in international artistic events like the Venice Biennale. Marcos Gregorian (b. 1925) is a painter who upon finishing his art studies in Italy in 1954 became a source of new ideas inspired by Western art and an enterprising activist in setting up exhibitions. He opened the first art gallery in Tehran, the Gallerie Esthétique (1954–1959), and organized in 1958 the first of five biennale exhibitions. The Department of Fine Arts provided the budget for all the Tehran Biennales and the first four were held at the Abyaz Palace, within the Golestan Palace compound, and was open only to Iranian artists. The fifth and last biennale took place at the Ethnographical Museum in 1966, and artists from Turkey and Pakistan were invited to join. The reasons behind the demise of this important artistic event were never made public.

An important issue that bothered many young artists of the fifties and sixties was to find characteristics that would distinguish their works from those of artists elsewhere. They wanted to find a relationship between the art works they were producing, be it painting, sculpture or ceramics, and their country's cultural heritage. They were encouraged in their quest by officials of the cultural establishment who wanted to see the creation of a national school of art, linked with the glorious past of Persian art. To this end, some artists started taking on subjects that would immediately be recognized as 'Iranian', while others employed motifs borrowed from the bas-reliefs of Persepolis and ancient Islamic manuscripts. All were interpreted through modern Western styles, such as a Cubist rendition of a family gathered around a kerosene lamp or a local bazaar with turbaned figures and *chador* clad women painted in a semi-abstract, stylized manner. This assemblage of local subjects with modernistic techniques did not always succeed, and it certainly won no great acclaim from the Biennale juries, yet the efforts continued and they eventually bore fruit.

The Prime Years

Persian modern art was born in the early sixties under the name Saqqah-Khaneh, an art movement considered to be a manifestation of latent nationalism. Saqqah-Khaneh is a small public watering place found in the old sections of every town and village in Iran where passers-by may help themselves to a cool drink. Set up in a recessed niche with its cistern and brass bowl, Saqqah-Khaneh is set up as an act of benevolence in memory of Imam Hosayn, grandson of the Prophet Mohammad and the third Shi'ite Imam who was martyred with his followers at Karbala (in present day Iraq) in a battle with the Umayyad army (680 AD) after being tortured through two hot and waterless days. Therefore the Saqqah-Khaneh is considered a holy place where candles are often kept burning and green and black drapes are displayed, while the protective wrought-iron grillwork and sides of the cistern are engraved with decorative motifs and Koranic verses. Together these elements form a specimen of religious folk art. Searching and finding cultural and religious symbols and tools for artistic expressions, the artists of the Saqqah-Khaneh looked into cults, rituals and products of folk culture to inspire them. What made this movement revolutionary was the modernistic tradition and the sense of freedom from the bonds of past cultural clichés. This was the first attempt in the twentieth century for Iranian artists to pick from their own backyard sources of inspiration.

When Hossein Zenderoudi displayed, in the Third Tehran Biennale, canvases that, for the first time, brought together geometric patterns covered with talismanic writings on a background of green, yellow, orange, red and black that recalled Shi'ite religious ceremonies, Karim Emami, the leading art critic, used the word Saqqah-Khaneh to describe the mood invoked by Zandarudi's new style. The name caught on and became descriptive of works by artists who borrowed their subjects from Iran's storehouse of decorative motifs, including Persian calligraphy, to create modern compositions related to their cultural heritage.

The Saqqah-Khaneh artists, also called neo-traditionalists, came closest to creating a local national school of Iranian modern art by being flexible in their use of motifs and patterns and in their choice of colours. Saqqah-Khaneh paintings and sculpture bore direct links with Iran's cultural and religious heritage. Among the better-known names associated with this school are Zenderoudi, Tanavoli, Pilaram, Arabshahi, Tabrizi, Ovesi and Tabataba'i. Hossein Zenderoudi (b. 1937) was a graduate of Tehran's Secondary School of Fine Arts for boys and the School of Decorative Arts. He started by doing iconographic works before moving to calligraphic paintings and seal impressions that created lattice-like visual rhythms. Parviz Tanavoli (b. 1937) graduated from the College of Fine Arts at Tehran University and the Berrera Academy in Milan where he studied with Mario Marini. The leading Iranian sculptor, he works with different media and is inspired by traditional metalwork, calligraphy and old Persian legends.

Farman Pilaram (1937–1983) was a graduate of the School of Decorative Arts in Tehran, a modernist painter and an accomplished calligrapher. He borrowed his geometric forms from Shi'ite iconography and added to them seal impressions before turning to bold, large calligraphic paintings. Mas'ud Arabshahi (b. 1935) is also a graduate of the School of Decorative Arts who works with ancient motifs taken from Achaemenian, Assyrian and Babylonian rock carvings in decorative and colourful compositions. Although Arabshahi avoided borrowing from Shi'ite iconography, he is considered a Saqqah-Khaneh artist in spirit and outlook. During the seventies he was officially commissioned to decorate with bas-relief, walls and facades of public buildings, among them the Ministry of Industries and Mines. Sadeq Tabrizi (b. 1938) is a prolific artist and a graduate of the School of Decorative Arts who works with pottery, collage and painting, borrowing elements from calligraphy, folk art, and Persian miniatures and injecting them with humour. Mansur Qadriz (1935–1965) was another graduate of the School of Decorative Arts who was generous with his use of motifs but economical with his colours, using only two or three hues; a car accident caused his early death. Naser Ovesi (b. 1934), a diplomat and an artist, executes figurative paintings that are reminiscent of Saljuq, Safavid and sometimes Qajar art. He makes use of calligraphy and decorative patterns taken from wooden blocks used for printing on cotton. Women and horses figure in Ovesi's work which, by time, have become more complicated and elaborate, showing a profusion of gold and silver. Jazeh Tabataba'i is a painter and sculptor who borrowed from Iranian folk art a year or two before the Saqqah-Khaneh school was defined. In his works, Tabataba'i satirizes Qajar stereotypes while combining them with decorative elements taken from wooden blocks, book illustrations, calligraphy and metal engraving. His humorous and imaginative sculptures are made up of pieces picked up from scrap heaps. He established the Iran Modern Art Gallery, which was active during the sixties.

There is a parallel between Saqqah-Khaneh and Pop Art, if we simplify Pop Art as an art movement which looks at the symbols and tools of a mass comsumer society as a relevant and influencing cultural force. Saqqah-Khaneh artists looked at the inner beliefs and popular symbols that were part of the religion and culture of Iran, and perhaps, consumed in the same way as industrial products in the West (but for different reasons and under dissimilar circumstances). In short, if we could recoin the movement in reference to Western art, it should be called 'Spiritual Pop Art'.

Later other artists, outside the Saqqah-Khaneh movement inspired by the same idea, produced work that drew on Persian culture. Marco Grigorian's works are noteworthy among those of the Saqqah-Khaneh. Prolific and talented H. Zenderoudi branched out into calligraphy and still paints creatively without repeating himself. He influenced fellow artists as well as young disciples, among them Reza Mafi (b. 1943). Mohammad Ehsa'i (b. 1939) and Sadeq Barirani are two more calligraphic artists who took their inspiration from Saqqah-Khaneh before concentrating solely on script. Sculptor Tanavoli constructed pieces reminiscent of religious shrines and other symbolic religious invocations and objects.

Some artists' concern with finding an artistic identity led them to depict the Iranian landscape, instead of exploring Persian folk and artistic sources. Sohrab Sepehri (1928–1980) was a painter and a poet. A graduate of the School of Fine Arts at Tehran University, he studied lithography at the Beaux Arts in Paris and woodcut techniques in Tokyo. His subsequent work showed traces of Japanese design. His semi-abstract works are noted for their simplicity and have a watercolour effect that focuses on the landscape of the arid desert around his native Kashan, as a major source for his imagery. Parviz Kalantari (b.1931) and Sirak Melkonian were also drawn to the desert as well as local village architecture.

In the late sixties and early seventies, there was a proliferation of the arts scene with artists painting in different individual styles and covering the entire spectrum of Western art: Abstract, Pop, Minimal, etc. Among those artists are Abul Qasem Sa'idi (b. 1926) who has trained at the Beaux Arts in Paris and had a calligraphic quality to his line. Naser Assar (b. 1938) is a Paris based artist known for his large monochrome canvases in soft hues. Monir Farmanfarma'ian developed the decorative and formal qualities inherent in glass paintings of the nineteenth century to create modern works, in mixed-media, combining both painting and sculpture. Ghassem Hadjizadeh (b. 1949), a young artist of the seventies, put to innovative use old nineteenth century photographs as background to highly personal representational paintings. The works of Nikzad Nojumi, Bahman Nayfar (b. 1945), Hanibal Alkas, Nahid Haqiqat and cartoonist Ardashir Mohasses (b. 1938) are powerful expressionistic paintings. All of these artists, at some stage in their careers, drew upon Iran's past in their search for a contemporary statement. There were others, however, who followed international idioms and never concerned themselves with local and indigenous sources. Among these are Manuchehr Yata'i (b. 1922) with his abstract-expressionist still lifes and portraits, Bahman Mohasses (b. 1930) who developed a personal imagery of minotaurs and nightmare creatures, Behjat Sadr with his rhythmic geometrical abstracts and Mortaza Sazgar's geometric designs worked into fine textures.

An atmosphere of renaissance pervaded the sixties and all the arts in Iran flourished. Architecture, music, theatre, cinema and poetry went through a transformation. A private arts club and cultural centre 'Rasht 29' was founded by sculptor Parviz Tanavoli, Oxanna Saba and Kamran Diba an architect, painter and artistic catalyser. For a few years it became a locale frequented by the cultural milieu where painters, musicians, actors and writers would meet and exchange views and attend the club's programme of poetry reading, informal theatre, music and for the first time in Iran an art auction which was attended by two important patrons: Queen Farah Pahlavi and Prime Minister Abbas Hoveyda.

Art Criticism

Karim Emami was the pioneer art critic who reviewed exhibitions in the English edition of *Kayhan International* but, unfortunately, became less active in the seventies. Behrouz Souresrafil took the job of art critic with the intellectual daily, *Ayandegan*, and was quite active up to the time of the revolution while Ehsan Yarshater was the first Iranian to write books on contemporary art in Iran.

Art Institutions

In 1961 the establishment of the School of Decorative Arts forms a landmark in the history of Iranian modern art. It offered degrees in the applied arts such as interior decoration and graphics among others, for graduates of Iran's Secondary schools of Fine Arts for Boys and Girls who were not admitted to the School of Fine Arts at Tehran University. A number of successful, innovative and talented artists graduated from this School and some soon rated it above the College of Fine Arts as a breeding ground for artists. The first group of professors and instructors assembled at the College of Decorative Arts, as it was initially called, were instrumental in instilling in their students a less formal, more flexible approach to the choice of subject and the treatment of material, than those who taught at the College of Fine Arts. In the late seventies the College of Fine Arts under its Dean Mehdi Kowsar, expanded its programme and had a host of noted artists on its faculty.

The Ministry of Culture (formerly the Department of Fine Arts) under Mr Pahlebod, played a significant role in the development of Iranian modern art. In addition to organizing the five Tehran Biennales, it set up and operated two exhibition galleries: Oftab and Mehrshah. It also provided subsidies for other galleries. Artists were sent abroad on scholarships to study and were prepared to participate in international art exhibitions such as the Venice Biennale and the Salon d'Automne in Paris. Government ministries started commissioning artists to do work for public institutions and a number of museums of modern art were established. Foreign cultural societies, such as the Iran-America Society and the Goethe Institute encouraged young artists by holding exhibitions for them. A number of commercial galleries opened in the sixties and early seventies and these helped stimulate artistic activity. Among them were Qandriz, Saba, Negar, the Mess, Borghese, Seyhun Zand and the Saman; the last four were commercially on a par with Western galleries. Private collections of modern art were started by Ebrahim Golestan and Kamran Diba and, in later years, the Lajevardi family built a formidable collection of contemporary Iranian art. By the seventies, corporate collectors began to emerge, led by the Behshahr Group who eventually built up a collection of 400 works of contemporary Iranian paintings. Queen Farah had an extensive collection by contemporary Iranian artists which she later donated to various museums. The late Prime Minister, Abbas Hoveyda, also amassed an important collection for the Prime Minister's Office.

In the late seventies, the general characteristic of the Tehran art scene, just as in the West, was pluralism of artistic tendencies. The major event of the decade was the inauguration of the Tehran Museum of Contemporary Art in October 1977. The Museum, along with several other museums and cultural centres, was under the umbrella of the Farah Pahlavi Foundation and it initiated a new phase of artistic activity which was cut short, however, by the 1978 Revolution.

The Tehran Museum of Contemporary Art had a collection of works by major Western artists, ranging from the Impressionists to the latest movements of Minimal and Conceptual art of the seventies. The other aim of the Museum was to build a permanent, in-depth collection of Iranian art which was, both in quality and quantity, the most impressive of Iranian modern works. The Museum has departments in painting and sculpture, works on paper, graphic art, photography and architecture. During the post-revolutionary period the collections were kept intact, although the museum had to shift its attention from international art to revolutionary art and political propaganda. In recent years, the Museum has re-installed, in rotating exhibitions, part of its permanent collection, but in essence it has allotted most of its space to temporary exhibitions by contemporary Iranian artists while photography and graphic art, mainly posters, occupy an important place in the post-revolutionary scheme of events.

The Niavaran Cultural Centre, another project of the Farah Pahlavi Foundation, was innaugurated in 1978, the year of revolutionary turmoil. Afterwards this newly-built edifice became a centre of revolutionary art activism and survived the revolution. It has large exhibition galleries, an auditorium and a library.

During the seventies, there were some fifty to sixty full-time artists, holding at least one annual exhibition in the ten to twelve art galleries that existed in Tehran or some key provincial centre, such as Shiraz or Isfahan. Other artists made a living working in book illustrations (e.g. Farshid Metqali, Bahman Dadkah, Parviz Kanlantari), commercial art (e.g. Mortaza Momayyez and Qobad Shiva) and animated films (e.g. Nur al-din Zarrin-kelk).

Post-Revolutionary Period

At present, among the various active artists, one group of religious and fervent followers of the revolution stand out. They work for the art unit belonging to the Office of Islamic Propaganda and are figurative artists celebrating the revolution, martyrdom and so called Islamic precepts of morality.

Aside from these officially sponsored artists, a multitude of unknown artists exhibit their work at the Museum of Contemporary Art; a few architects, and other professionals-turned-painters, show at privately rented spaces and bookstores. Others like Parvaneh Etemadi, whose style of visionary realism has gained her recognition in the United States, shun public exposure and work at home. Among expatriate artists, not all reflect the experience of exile in their work, but one woman artist who does is Behjat Sadr. She uses large photo-collages, mostly of Persian scenery framed by bold abstract brush strokes which invoke the impression of a window view, perceived from a claustrophobic interior, opening onto past memories of a beloved land.

Soon after the Revolution most of the burgeoning galleries closed down, art patrons left or withdrew their patronage, museums stopped their work to revise their policies and future plans and a great number of established artists went to live abroad.

Since the 1978 Revolution official patronage of avantgarde art has disappeared, and no ultramodern works imitating the very latest Western styles are being created. The Tehran Museum of Contemporary Art has been sponsoring a number of group shows that include works which may be classified, for convenience, as revolutionary art; they are either wholly naturalistic, reminiscent of Kamal ul-Molk's technique, and propagandist, or surrealistic canvases illustrating the theme of martyrdom. This last genre combines pictorial elements from Shi'ite folk art and Persian/Arabic script, the same sort of source material that the Saqqah-Khaneh artists were tapping years earlier. As a matter of fact, calligraphic painting is the only form of art that continues to thrive in Iran without a setback.

See colour pp. 76–77 for plates of the following artists' work:

SIMIN MEYKADEH
HOSSEIN ZENDEROUDI

GHASSEM HADJIZADEH
Iran, b. 1947
Trained at the High School of Fine Arts in Tehran, Hadjizadeh has developed, or rather found, a unique style in which he marries the two adversaries, painting and photography. A member of the Saqqah-Khaneh [see Zenderoudi] school of painting in Iran, he has established a method by which he integrates old, yellowing photographs in his paintings in a symbolic manner that contains fictional nostalgia with pragmatic modernism. He utilizes modern technology to relate messages from the past that are significant to the present, depicting events and personalities and using them as symbols. Hadjizadeh is an original artist who has succeeded in manipulating the past and the present to serve his innovation.

Sophia
Mixed media on paper
110 x 95.5 cm
1987

ALI NASSIRI
Iran, b. 1950
Nassiri is one of the promising young Iranian artists. He attended the Cannock House School foundation course in arts and architecture, the RIBA, and St. Martin's School of Art. His inspiration is derived from Islamic calligraphy, from Mevlana and the Persian poet, Hafiz.

Untitled
Chalk and ink on wood
76 x 100 cm
1985

RAVI SAMIMI
Iran
Samimi belongs to the classical school which was popular up until the sixties. He painted many oriental scenes which varied in subject and composition reflecting his respect for nature and his deep feelings for his subjects. Samimi's style is traditional. He uses restrained colours with close attention to details. His figures are clearly depicted with facial features displaying his skill as a painter to the full. He has earned a distinguished reputation as a traditional painter.

Bikdashi Derwishes
Oil on canvas
40 x 70 cm
1952

PARVIZ TANAVOLI
Iran, b. 1937
Born in Tehran, Tanavoli studied sculpture at the Fine Art School of Tehran, and in Milan, Italy. He has taught sculpture in Iran and the USA. He retired from Tehran University in 1981. He has exhibited widely and his works have been commissioned worldwide. He was also an influential figure in the Saqqah-Khaneh movement. He is the author of numerous articles and books on art, especially on the art of Iran. Tanavoli has a deep feeling for the traditional arts of his country. *The Walls of Iran* are the synthesis of Tanavoli's work, the culmination of thirty years of uninterrupted effort to achieve an independent and personal style of sculpture.

Hich
Bronze
17.5 x 5.5 x 5 cm
Undated

Group of Modern Art'. They made a proclamation, the first to be made by any artistic group in Iraq. At that time Salim was full of enthusiasm, determined to create an Iraqi artistic identity. After studying the works of the Abbasid painter, al-Wasiti, he believed that it was possible to find a style which would combine the past and the present. As a consequence, he announced in the proclamation that: '. . . A new trend in painting will solve the [artistic] identity problem in our contemporary awakening by following the footsteps of the thirteenth century [Iraqi] painters. The new generation of artists finds the beginning of a guiding light in the early legacy of their forefathers.'

This was the real beginning of the search for a national artistic identity. It was to be an identity that did not find fulfilment in outdoor scenes alone but raised instead the question of incorporating a message and philosophy within the composition of the work of art. Modern Iraqi art began with the first exhibition of the Baghdad Group where they announced the birth of a new school which would '. . . serve local and international culture.'

Jawad Salim (1921–1961) is another important figure in the formation of the modern art movement. He guided it towards internationalism. He was the first artist to call for an equation between traditional heritage and modernism, by recalling the artistic legacy of ancient Mesopotamia and Islamic art and interpreting it in the context of contemporary international art movements. He intended to link the ancient and modern worlds and also change society's outlook on art. Salim came to know and appreciate the aesthetic values of ancient art while working at the Directorate of Antiquities in Baghdad. He was sent on government scholarships, first to Paris (1938–39), then to Rome (1939–40) and after World War II he continued his studies in England (1946–48). He was fond of music and poetry and had qualms about practising sculpture and painting together. Finally, after having painted his most mature works in the fifties he decided to relinquish painting and concentrate all his energy on sculpture. The culmination of his career was his *Monument for Freedom*, now a landmark of Baghdad.

The other person who pushed the Baghdad group forwards is Shaker Hassan al-Sa'id (b. 1925). He not only shared Jawad Salim's beliefs and ideals, but through his own intellectual research into Islamic heritage, was able to develop a style which incorporates indigenous and international trends. He studied social science at the Faculty of Education in Baghdad University, and studied art at night classes given by the Institute of Fine Arts, before he went on to the Academie Nationale des Beaux Arts in Paris. He became interested in folk art, legends, and stories from the Arabian Nights. After his return from Paris in 1956, he became an abstract painter with a mystical and contemplative aura. His symbols comprise wall cracks, graffiti, numerals and Arabic letters.

Khalid al-Rahhal (1926–87) had been a highly expressive artist since youth. He is possessed by a blazing spirit and is one of the important figures of the decade. He was impressed by antique sculpture. As a labourer on archaeological excavations, he gained first-hand knowledge of artefacts. By the time he graduated from the Institute of Fine Arts in 1947 he had already achieved a maturity in performance that gave his works a sense of the natural continuation of Mesopotamian statues. Although he sculpted according to Western schools, the Iraqi spirit overpowers his work and its presence seems inherent without any intrusion. When he went on a government scholarship to the Rome Academy in 1954, his past training helped him gain a firmer grasp of the fundamentals of European sculpture. In spite of the fact that he was also a painter, the sculptor in him was always dominant.

Other members of the Baghdad Group are: Qahtan A'wni (architect and artist), the late Faraj A'bou (painter), Mohammad al-Husni (sculptor), Khalil al-Ward (sculptor), Abdul Rahman al-Kaylani (sculptor), Rasul A'lwan (painter) and Fadil Abbas (painter) who after distinguishing himself in the fifties stopped painting. One of the people with Jawad Salim from the very beginning of the movement was Jabra Ibrahim Jabra, a Palestinian artist, writer and art critic. He wrote extensively on Iraqi art, particularly Jawad Salim. There were also Salim's family: his brother Nizar, his sister Naziha and English-born wife, Lorna, each of whom was an accomplished painter in his or her own right. Later members of the group are Mohamed Ghani (sculptor), Fuad Jihad, a painter with a Byzantine style, Ibrahim al-Abdali (painter), Mohammad A'rif, of Kurdish origin who was fond of painting mythological epics, and Khudair Shakarji (painter).

There are also artists who did not belong to either of these two groups. One of them is Jamil Hamoudi (b. 1924). A graduate of the Institute of Fine Arts, he injected the movement with intense cultural activity. In 1947 he went to Paris to study on a government scholarship. Along with Madiha Omar who had already had her art training in the United States, Hamoudi is one of the first Arab painters to use calligraphic forms in his search for a personal artistic identity that would set him apart from the West. Yet, it was through the work of Western artists, influenced by the East, that he discovered the value of the Arabic letter in all its different, abstract formations.

In 1953, a third group, 'The Impressionists', was formed around Hafid al-Drubi (b. 1914) who since the early thirties had been one of the founders of the Iraqi modern art movement. He is a founder of the Society of the Friends of Art and held his first exhibition in 1941, and in 1942 opened the first independent painting studio in Iraq. He trained at Goldsmith College in London and started his career by following traditional academic styles. He soon gave this up for Impressionism, and then turned to Cubism, which he followed for a long time. He used Cubism to portray city scenes with narrow, winding streets and open country landscapes. In 1951 Drubi was appointed to supervise the joint atelier belonging to the Faculty of Arts and Sciences. Discovering new talent and encouraging students to take up art were a challenge. His success at the Faculty's atelier made other colleges start their own studios.

Among the most outstanding students at the Faculty of Arts was Dia Azzawi, who later joined the Impressionist Group. Other members of the group were Sa'ad al-Ta'i (painter), Hayat Jamil Hafid (painter), Yassin Ka'abi (painter) and Dr A'la' Bashir (painter). The Impressionist Group obsessed artists of the fifties and thrust Iraqi art towards modernism. Dia Azzawi aptly described it when he said: 'The movement started as an attempt to create an Iraqi Impressionist School . . . but soon this conglomeration became saturated with personal research in abstraction, Cubism, and sensitive Impressionist colours.'

An Impressionist artist who played an important role in the fifties and who did not belong to any specific group was Khalid al-Jader (1934–1988). He graduated from both the Faculty of Law at Baghdad University and the Institute of Fine Arts at the same time. He was sent on a government scholarship to France and took his doctorate in the history of Islamic art as well as a certificate from the Beaux Arts. He was a member of the Salon de Paris. Upon his return, he was appointed Dean of the Institute of Fine Arts and later of the Academy of Fine Arts after its founding in 1962. Jader was a strict administrator who demanded his teachers and students keep high standards. In his paintings, he recorded Iraqi village life in greyish blue hues that became synonymous with his works. He was a conscientious artist who quietly forged his style without any distraction. He left Iraq to live in Morocco where he painted and did research on folk jewellery and art.

Najib Younis is an artist whose style wavers between Impressionism and Realism. He lives in Mosul, his birthplace, and taught for a long time at its Institute of Fine Arts. He studied art in Egypt and was influenced by the Egyptian School. He is highly expressive, and this is nowhere more apparent than in his paintings of crowds. His best works are those depicting members of the Yazidi sect, a notorious religious sect in the north of Iraq whose followers worship the devil.

One of the many activities of the fifties was the creation in 1956 of a 'Society of Artists'. Its members were well established artists and a few architects who promoted the arts. It had an exhibition hall, the first such space intended only for exhibitions. At this stage, the Institute of Fine Arts started to cultivate training in ceramics and employed two teachers, Ian Old, an Englishman, and Valentinos Karalambos, a Cypriot. Both contributed to creating highly qualified Iraqi ceramicists, among whom were two accomplished artists: Saad Shaker and Tariq Ibrahim. Old left Iraq in 1957, while Karalambos stayed on to train Iraq's best ceramicists and taught at the Academy of Fine Arts after it was founded in 1962.

In the fifties the government opened The National Museum of Modern Art and included in its collection the works of prominent Iraqi artists.

Two other important events also took place in the second part of the fifties. The first was the exhibition held at the Mansour Club in 1957. It included a vast number of works that displayed different trends and styles. Many works submitted for exhibition were refused for one reason or another. A second exhibition was held for their display. Both events showed bold renditions, indicating the high standard that Iraqi artists had been able to attain. They had achieved a degree of self confidence in their endeavours to form a distinctive artistic personality.

The years before the Revolution of June 1958, that ended modern Iraq's (1921–1958) constitutional monarchy, were characterized by a cultural period where all the arts, literature, music and visual expression went hand-in-hand. The social, political and economic development that had taken place made artists in all fields realize that they should not isolate themselves but instead should integrate into society while fulfilling their humanitarian and artistic role, within the general trend of their country's development.

The Revolution came like an earthquake to shake the very foundations of the art movement. Artists were torn between continuing to express themselves freely or putting their art at the service of government propaganda. Works done after 1958 and in the early sixties are highly emotional and artists had to comply with the demands of the Revolution. The best among them was a nationalistic mural by Faik Hassan, and Jawad Salim's *Monument for Freedom*.

The Sixties

The untimely death of Jawad Salim in 1961 struck a blow to the Iraqi art milieu and temporarily paralysed the art movement. In addition, Faik Hassan withdrew from the Pioneer Group in 1962. This threw the movement into a further period of stagnation that lasted until 1964, when new artists began to return from western Europe, the Soviet Union, Poland, China and the United States after having finished their studies. Their varied exposure and training, when combined with the more mature sense of local artistic heritage that had now evolved, injected the decade with new and audacious experiments. Jawad Salim's spirit along with Faik Hassan's talent and skill had imbued the Iraqi modern art with a continuous sense of discipline and devotion as well as with a sense that artists must extend their experiences beyond narrow, domestic boundaries, into the Arab world and towards internationalism. The unsettling political and social conditions that followed the 1958 Revolution, and especially the subsequent Arab defeat in the 1967 war with Israel, made artists more attached to their own cultural and artistic heritage. At the same time the era of modern communications was cutting through traditional styles, liberalising attitudes and opening everyone to the international exchange of cultural experience. The sixties generation, in particular, remained faithful to its three pioneer artists: Jawad Salim, Faik Hassan and Mahmoud Sabri. Each was noted for his method and had his own set of disciples.

In the sixties the government of Iraq established an Institute of Higher Education. Later it became The Academy of Fine Arts and now is called the Arts College. In addition to Iraqi teachers, there was a Polish couple, Roman Artomonsky and his wife Sophia, both abstract painters, and a Yugoslav called Lazeski who taught at the Institute and had a lot to do with guiding their students towards modernism.

In the first half of the sixties two private galleries opened. The Aya Gallery belonged to architect Rifa'at Chaderji and the Wasiti Gallery had behind it the architects Henry Zevobda, Mohammad Makkya and Sa'id Ali Madloum. Later on, Makkya left Iraq to settle in London and opened the Kufa Gallery, where today he exhibits works by Iraqi and other Arab artists. The private galleries offered additional exhibition space beyond that provided by the National Gallery of Modern Art which had opened prior to the Revolution. They also promoted the work of new artists, such as Isma'il Fattah, Mohammad Muhrilddin, Rafa Nasiri, Suad al-Attar, Rakan Dabdoub, Dia Azzawi, Saleh al-Jumaie and others. Each represented a new and different trend, ranging from abstraction to stylized realism.

Among the most outstanding exhibitions of the sixties were those of sculptor Mohamed Ghani Hikmat (b. 1929). He had returned from Rome, in 1961, after obtaining a diploma from the Rome Art Academy and spending time working with his teacher Jawad Salim on the latter's *Monument for Freedom*. Ghani's early works contained figures of ordinary men and women taken from everyday life and carved in wood. By the end of the sixties his figures became almost abstract and later on he was fascinated by Arabic calligraphy and ancient letter forms which he engraved on doors. These are considered among his best works. Recently Ghani has given his time to monumental sculptures for public places with subjects inspired by folk tales.

The first exhibition of Kadim Haidar (1932–1987), held in 1965, is looked upon as a landmark in Iraqi modern art. It was a one-theme exhibition of forty works based on the martyrdom epic of the grandson of the Prophet, al-Hussein. He was massacred along with all his family, women and children, by the Umayyad army at Kerbela in the seventh century AD. Haidar used this subject to depict the tragedy of man in a symbolic language and style, within a new artistic framework that was rebellious in form and content. Haidar was a highly educated man with an undaunted, experimental nature, who left his imprint on his country's art movement.

The phenomena of forming artistic groups, so prevalent in the fifties, continued into the sixties. In 1965 a group formed, calling itself the Innovationists. It lasted four years and consisted of a number of young artists like Salim Dabbagh, Saleh al-Jumaie, Subhi Charchafli, Ali Taleb, Faik Hussein, Talib Makki, Nida' Kadim (sculptor) and Taher Jamil (photographer). They held their first exhibition at the National Museum of Modern Art and their works showed signs of rebelling against traditional styles. Besides canvas, oils and watercolours, they utilized new materials such as printer's ink, posters, monotype, aluminium and collage. Most of the founders were among the first group of graduates of the Arts Academy. New members such as A'mer Obeidi, Ibrahim Zayer, Salman Abbas and Khalid Na'ib joined in while old members like Subhi Charchafli, Ali Taleb and Faik Hussein left the group.

In 1967 a new group formed 'Al-Zawya'. Headed by Faik Hassan, it included among its members Isma'il Fattah, Mohamed Ghani, Valentinos Karalambos, Kadim Haidar and Ghazy Sa'udi. They held only one exhibition before dispersing. Following the defeat of the 1967 Arab-Israeli War, the first nationalistic exhibition took place, based on the notion that art must support national events.

A new group calling themselves *Al-Ru'ya al-Jadida* (the New Vision) formed in 1969. It consisted of Dia Azzawi, Rafa Nasiri, Hashim Samarji, Saleh al-Jumaie, Isma'il Fattah and Mohammad Muhrilddin, though the last two never exhibited with the group. They made a challenging declaration, calling for freedom and revolution to uphold the future, and announced that '. . . revolution and art are linked to the development of humanity.' They defined their attitude towards heritage by stating that 'As long as we act freely towards it, [our artistic legacy] will not become a dictatorial force that pulls and imprisons us. We will take it as our duty to use it to conquer the world. We will speak a new language with its symbols, that belongs to a new life and a new man.' Soon Ali Taleb, Makki Hussein (sculptor), Tariq Ibrahim (ceramicist) and Nadim Ramzi joined the group. They held several exhibitions under numerical titles set by the number of participating artists.

One of the most outstanding members of the group is Dia Azzawi (b. 1939). He is a lively and dynamic artist, who studied archaeology at the Faculty of Arts, worked with Hafiz Drouby at the college's atelier and took evening courses at the Institute of Fine Arts. He was influenced by Jawad Salim and is considered his direct heir. For the past ten years he has lived in London where his forms have become more abstract, radiating an Oriental spirit. Through exhibitions he arranges for Arab and Iraqi artists, he has been able to introduce Arab art to the British public.

A poetic and sensitive artist, Rafa Nasiri (b. 1940) has been influenced by an ultra modern trend that combines, in his two dimensional paintings, pure colours, Eastern symbols and Western technique. He studied painting at the Institute of Fine Arts in Baghdad, then went to China and spent three years in Portugal specializing in graphics. He founded the graphic section at the Institute of Fine Arts where he currently teaches.

After graduating from the Institute of Fine Arts in Baghdad, Saleh al-Jumaie (b. 1939) went to the United States to continue his art training. There he came across new techniques. As one of the Innovationists, he had already shown an inclination towards using new and unusual materials in his collages, such as hammered aluminium sheets, treating the surface in a rough manner and employing graffiti, individual letters and poetry verses. Al-Jumaie moved to Beirut, then Guam and now lives in California.

Among other artists of the sixties who were also part of the 'New Vision' group is Hashim Samarji (b. 1938). A highly skilled artist, Samarji uses geometric formations composed of repetitive units, such as the square and the triangle, that together form moving combinations in order to express an eternal continuity. Muhammad Muhrilddin (b. 1938) is a graduate of the Institute of Fine Arts. He continued his training in Poland, where his works took on their modern properties. He is believed to have injected the Iraqi movement with modernism, through a style seen as a continuation of what Mahmoud Sabri had started in the fifties. At present he is a teacher at the Institute of Fine Arts.

Isma'il Fattah (b. 1934) is one of the six artists who signed the New Vision Declaration. He first studied sculpture with Jawad Salim at the Institute of Fine Arts and was influenced by him and by Khalid al-Rahhal's early works. He continued his training in Rome and was influenced by British sculpture, in particular the works of Henry Moore and Kenneth Armitage. Although he paints as well as sculpts, he is considered the best living Iraqi sculptor. He has executed colossal works, the most important is his *Monument to the Unknown Soldier*, that combines Islamic aesthetics with Western skill and technology.

Like all other modern art movements in the Arab world, the Iraqi movement has faced many difficulties, especially the drain of talent with unstable political conditions. The challenge of proving oneself internationally is always there. An Iraqi artist who was able to build a successful career in the West is Issam el-Said (1939–1988), the grandson of the late Prime Minister and political scion Nouri el-Said. A prolific artist of many talents, el-Said read architecture at Cambridge. He was a painter, sculptor, designer, art historian and expert on Islamic art and design. He worked with graphics, oils, enamel on aluminium, and paleocrystal (a material he developed) to execute his stylized drawings of Baghdadi scenes, calligraphic paintings and arabesque patterns for free standing art pieces, carpets and furniture and is known for his research in theories on Islamic architecture and design basing them on scientific equations. El-Said was also a member of Christies Contemporary Artists. His sudden and untimely death usurped the Arab art movement of one of its most cultured and intellectual artists before he was able to fulfil all his goals in his various fields of interest.

The Seventies and Eighties

The generation of artists who came on the art scene in the sixties carried Iraqi art outside its borders in the seventies, through exhibitions held in North Africa, Cairo, Damascus, and Beirut which for a time became a centre for Iraqi artists.

After the second Revolution of July 1968, the government adopted an open-door policy vis-à-vis art and started holding international as well as local art festivals and meetings. The first was Al-Wasiti Festival, held in 1972, followed by the meetings of the First Congress of Arab Artists in 1973. The latter induced the formation of the Union of Arab Artists.

The first half of the seventies witnessed outstanding activities by individual artists. In addition to one-person exhibitions, there was the exhibition called 'The Single Dimension' made up of a comprehensive collection of modern calligraphic paintings. It was held in 1971 at the initiative of Dia Azzawi, Rafa Nasiri, Shakir Hassan al-Sai'id, Mohamed Ghani, Abdul Rahman Kailani and Jamil Hamoudi. The Department of Arts took the exhibition under its wings and assisted its organizers. The exhibition documented the Iraqi experiment in calligraphy as a form of artistic expression; most of its artists had been influenced by the experience of European artists with Arabic calligraphy.

Several new groups formed in Baghdad and Basra, but most of them disappeared around the middle of the decade after holding one or two exhibitions. Among them was 'The Triangle Group' whose members were Mohammad Radi, A'jil Mizhir and Farouq Hassan. 'The Shadow Group' included Ali Taleb, Salman al-Basri, Shaker Hamad, Abdullah Shaker and Mou'ayad Abdulsamad. 'The Academician Group' was made up of young artists like Nu'man Hadi, Salah Jiad, Faisal Lu'aibi and Walid Sheet and 'The July 17 Group' had as its members Leila al-Attar, Salim Dabbagh, Siham Sa'udi, Amir Ubeidi and Khudair Shakarji. They had two exhibitions before dissolving. Some artists, like Suad al-Attar who came on the art scene in the sixties, reached artistic maturity in the seventies. She developed a style based on miniature painting with a highly skilled graphic technique. Today she lives in London and paints mythological figures on large canvases in a dreamy surrealistic style.

There are other artists of the seventies. Dr A'la' Bashir, a plastic surgeon and a member of the Impressionist Group, has a highly developed surrealistic style that is unique among Iraqi artists. Ali Taleb from Basra studied art at the College of Arts in Baghdad and then obtained his MA from Cairo; at present he teaches at the College of Fine Arts. Taleb was with the Shadow Group and believes art is but a reflection of reality. Sa'di Ka'bi, who taught for a while in Saudi Arabia, paints the desert ambience in earthy colours that reflect shadow figures. Amir Ubeidi also spent time in Saudi Arabia, and is inspired by the desert. Recently his stylized figures have turned into pseudo-geometrical, decorated shapes. Salman Abbas, after returning from Saudi Arabia, started painting shapes taken from local architecture, such as stylized domes and crescents. Mahmoud Ahmad studied art in the Soviet Union and uses social realism to paint rural subjects full of tragic despondency. Mehdi Moutasher lives in France and uses a visual, geometric, optic style that borrows its shapes from popular handicrafts. Salem Dabbagh's abstract works have a spatial and linear quality. Faik Hussein's plastic experience matured in the seventies despite his limited exhibitions before emigrating abroad.

Ceramics

So far, Iraq had had few noted ceramicists the like of Saad Shaker, who is an outstanding figure with a highly polished skill and sensitivity in the use of colour. Suddenly ceramics flourished and many artists embraced it, among them Abla Azzawi, Siham Su'udi and Nuha Radi. Radi is an innovative artist whose works are distinguished by their folkloric shapes, subjects and colours. Tariq Ibrahim uses free forms that reflect sensitive humanitarian feelings; he believes that ceramics have an expressive as well as an aesthetic role. Shinyar Abdullah studied ceramics in Baghdad and the United States and excels in his work. Muqbil Zahawi who is of Kurdish origin is a ceramic sculptor whose works range between miniature size and the gigantic, calling on Babylonian and Sumerian statues for inspiration. He is another expatriate artist whose works are better known abroad than in his own country. Recently the College of Fine Arts (formerly the Academy of Fine Arts) has graduated a number of ceramicists trained by Valentinos, Saad Shaker and Isma'il Fattah. There are training institutes that belong to the Ministry of Education where classes are held in pottery and ceramics, and not long ago, a Ceramics Society formed also to teach the subject.

Official State patronage increased in the first half of the seventies. The National Museum of Modern Art took over the patronage of plastic arts, increased its participation in international biennales and exhibitions, and raised the number of group exhibitions at the museum especially on national occasions or important political events. The tradition began of an annual exhibition on the occasion of the founding of the ruling Socialist Baath Party, which soon turned into an annual activity that broadly reflects the scope of activities of Iraqi artists. Among those who participated in organizing state exhibitions are Nizar Hindawi and Azzam Bazzaz, while Suhail Hindawi, a young and talented sculptor, gained prominence with Party exhibitions.

Iraqi Cultural Centres abroad witnessed increased activities, as a reflection on Iraq's artistic interests. The Iraqi Cultural Centre in London is one of the most active centres, arranging many important exhibitions, not only for its native artists but also for Arab and Third World artists. One of the main exhibits was The Graphic Exhibition of the Third World, both in London and Baghdad. There was also the Arab Graphic Exhibition and the Baghdad International Exhibition of Posters. There was an exhibition organized by the Iraqi National Art Committee to support Iraq, after the bombing of its nuclear reactor. In 1979, a traditional Baghdadi house was transformed into a Museum for Pioneer Artists, starting with works by Abdul Qadir al-Rassam until the early fifties. In 1984 the Orfali Gallery opened and later two other private galleries, the Naqqash and Abla Azzawi's galleries, also joined it as new exhibition spaces. The Saddam Arts Centre was inaugurated in 1986. It has vast halls that can hold colossal exhibitions, such as the Baghdad International Festival of 1986 and 1988 that literally had artists from all over the world. The Centre replaced the National Museum for Modern Art, whose permanent collection of Iraqi artists was moved to the new premises. An archives section was attached to it in order to document thoroughly the plastic art movement.

Over the last ten years the government has established many art institutes in major cities, such as Basra in the south and Mosul and Sulaimania in the north, as well as an Art College in the County of Babil. Art lessons are also available at the Institute of Applied Arts that belongs to the Ministry of Higher Education. At *Dar al-Turath Wa al-Funoun al-Sha'bia* (House of Heritage and Popular Arts), there is a special institute that offers a five-year course in painting, ceramics and handicrafts.

By the end of the seventies the experience of Iraqi artists matured, expanding into various methods and styles and proving that the large numbers of graduates from the different art schools had kept supplying the movement with energy and dynamism. The eighties that witnessed the tragedy of the Gulf War with Iran were supposed to hinder the progress of art, yet it appears that artists obsessed with death multiplied their work as if with creativity they wanted to make up for the loss of life. Besides the established names, a new generation of artists were born whose works show challenge and cynicism, reminiscent of the German Expressionists.

Modern art in Iraq began early and continued to develop under government and private patronage. Today this patronage has taken on more and more importance, making the country's contemporary art movement one of the most active in the Middle East.

See colour pp. 78–87 for plates of the following artists' work:

SUAD ATTAR
DIA AZZAWI
FAIK HASSAN
RAKAN DABDOUB
SALEH AL-JUMAIE
NOURI EL-RAWI
ISSAM EL-SAID
NIZAR SALIM
NAZIHA SELIM
ISMAIL SHEIKHLEY

ALA' BACHIR
Iraq, b. 1939

Ala' Bachir graduated from the College of Medicine in Baghdad in 1963 and is a specialist in plastic surgery. He studied Art at the Institute of Fine Arts in 1959. Bachir is a member of the Iraqi Impressionists Group and has been head of the Arts Association in Basra since 1975. Despite his membership of the Impressionists Group, he is a surrealistic painter with exceptional sensitivity. His works contain a great deal of intellectual symbolism, creating a dramatic effect on the viewer. His colours are essentially a spread of purple and his free use of form is more complex than is immediately apparent. Bachir is concerned with the human struggle and with all its anxieties. Sometimes his works contain disturbing and horrifying subjects and are meant to shock.

Tell Il Za'atar
Oil on canvas
100 x 130 cm
1976

WASMA KHALID CHORBACHI
Iraq, b. 1944

Chorbachi spent her childhood in Baghdad and went on to study in Beirut and Florence before taking advanced studies at Harvard University. Her artistic talent has been built on a search for her Muslim roots. The linear and geometric stamp all her work with an unmistakable Islamic identity. The blue–green hues of tiles rich with glaze carry the flow of calligraphy, and the holy words of the Koran take a central place in the pattern. She has distanced herself from her earlier Western training and now draws exclusively on Arab and Islamic traditions. By doing so she has found an inner peace: the imagined blues of a courtyard fountain and the soft greens of an oasis garden.

In the Name of God
Oil on silk
110 x 110 cm
Undated

HAFIZ DROUBY
Iraq, b. 1914
Hafiz Drouby was born in Baghdad. He was one of the original founders of the Friends of the Arts Association and a leader of the Impressionists Group, which was established in 1953. The French Impressionists had a great influence on Iraqi artists who nevertheless retained their use of rich, local colours. Drouby's works are cubist in style and his Baghdad scenes are executed in dominant blues and greys. Before his exposure to cubism his work was essentially post-impressionist, especially in his treatment of landscapes and figures. He trained first in Rome and later at the School of Art and Design, Goldsmith's College, London. Drouby has contributed a great deal to the development of art in Iraq.

The Market Place
Oil on canvas
79 x 95 cm
1980

ISMA'IL FATTAH
Iraq, b. 1934
Born in Basrah, Fattah graduated from the Institute of Fine Arts, Baghdad, in 1958 with diplomas in painting and sculpture. He also studied at the Academy of Fine Arts and at the San Jacomo Academy in Rome. Since his return to Baghdad, Fattah has closely examined the relationship between the human form and its environment. He expresses himself in a realistic style. His figures tend to be isolated yet solid. Although his sculptures and paintings may owe much more to modern trends than to ancient Assyrians and Sumerians, Fattah is still aware of his roots. He is now among the leading Iraqi artists, and his sculptural monuments and murals can be seen in many public buildings and squares in Baghdad.

Ashtar
Mixed media on paper
160 x 120 cm
1988

MOHAMED GHANI
Iraq, b. 1929
Ghani graduated from the Institute of Fine Arts in Baghdad in 1952 and in 1958 trained at the Academy of Fine Arts, Rome. He later mastered the techniques of bronze casting in Italy. Despite his European experience Ghani remains deeply rooted in his Iraqi heritage. He is much aware of the tragedy of contemporary events and is concerned with the human figure, which he handles in abstract terms. He is also noted for his scenes of Baghdad life which reflect simple charm. His monumental sculptures manage to maintain an intimacy between the work and the observer. Ghani is an instructor in sculpture and has completed some outstanding monuments and murals in Baghdad, including numerous sculpted doors in wood, copper and aluminium.

Figure
Bronze
73 x 133 cm
Undated

KHALID AL-JADER
Iraq, 1928–1988
Al-Jader graduated from the College of Law and the Fine Arts Institute. Later he studied for his doctorate in Islamic Art at L'Ecole des Beaux Arts, Paris. After returning to Baghdad, he helped establish the Institute and the Academy of Fine Arts and was appointed as dean of both institutions in 1961. Al-Jader's paintings are very close to nature. His themes are the scenes of daily life: people in the street or in the market, women and children. His colours are blues and greys and his consistency of treatment render his landscapes and villages very much alike. He never seemed to free himself from the French Impressionist influence of his early career, yet his work stems from Iraqi roots.

Baghdadi Souk
Oil on canvas
60 x 82 cm
Undated

JAFAR KAKI
Iraq, b. 1951
Kaki was born in Kurdistan, the son of a photographer. He studied at the Academy of Fine Arts in Baghdad, where he obtained his degree in 1976. He subsequently travelled to Spain to study at the San Fernando Academy, Madrid, and obtained his master's degree in 1984. He is currently preparing for his doctorate in Art. Jafar Kaki is a graphic artist, and he is highly specialized in miniprint, where there is a great emphasis on precision and attention to detail. In his works one can observe the strong lines and colours of abstract and semi-abstract paintings.

Rashy Sur 1
Print
72 x 58 cm
1986

FREISH KANIKIAN
Iraq, b. 1930
Kanikian is a sculptor as well as a ceramicist. He was born in the ancient city of Mosul and studied at the Fine Arts Institute in Baghdad from which he graduated 1957. He continued his studies at the Chelsea School of Fine Arts in London where he gained his National Diploma in design. His works are solid metal sculptures, inspired by his ancient Iraqi roots. Kanikian constructs his sculpture in a simple manner yet at the same time retains and reflects a solid and rich heritage.

Untitled
Copper and ceramic
22 x 19 x 55 cm
1978

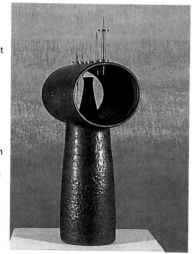

HASSAN MASSOUDY
Iraq, b. 1944
Massoudy was born and bred in Najaf. Between 1960 and 1969 he trained in Baghdad as a calligrapher in his own free time. He moved to Paris in 1969 and attended L'Ecole des Beaux Arts where he gained his diploma in 1975. He is a painter and a calligrapher. He has published detailed research on the aesthetic, social and technical aspects of Arabic calligraphy. He was influenced in his calligraphy by early masters such as Ibn Moqla, Ibn Bawwab and Ibn Saigh, but in spite of these influences he has set new trends within the discipline. He is regarded as one of the most distinguished contemporary calligraphers.

Poem
Etching
48 x 58 cm
1978

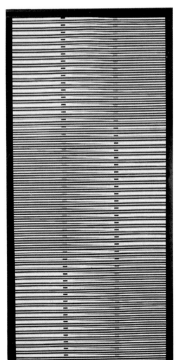

MEHDI MOUTASHER
Iraq, b. 1943
Moutasher has made France his home since the sixties but has continued to exhibit in Baghdad where he obtained his training at the Academy of Fine Arts. His work is well known in the Arab world and in Europe. His abstract canvases, where bars of colours move repetitively across the surface and the sensory pushes aside the message, have built a bridge between European arts and Arab understanding of abstraction. His work possesses a perhaps unconscious affinity with the traditional designs of kilims. Occasionally he reduces the background to the darkest black and allows the bars of colour to leap off the surface projecting themselves into a separate existence. Moutasher teaches at the Ecole Nationale Supérieure des Arts Decoratifs in Paris.

Untitled
Acrylic on canvas
95 x 194 cm
1982

RAFA AL-NASIRI
Iraq, b. 1940

Nasiri studied painting in Baghdad then went to Beijing and Lisbon to continue his training in graphics. He is a daring and innovating artist. He has made a concise study of the Arabic alphabet and deals with the problem of space by including Arabic letters, abstracting them from any meaning and adding to them a certain lasting spirituality. He has a strong grasp of different techniques and media and shows equal fluidity in painting and graphics. Rafa Nasiri is an artist who has succeeded in breaking free from his national boundaries but at the same time maintains a link with the cultural roots of ancient and modern Mesopotamia.

The Lover's Palace 'The Princess'
Acrylic on canvas
120 x 100 cm
1988

SAAD SHAKER
Iraq, b. 1935

Shaker's early training was at the Institute of Fine Arts in Baghdad from where he graduated in 1957. He completed his studies at the Central School of Fine Arts in London, where he obtained his diploma in 1960, specializing in Ceramics. He worked as technical assistant and lecturer for two years at the same school. He lives and works in Baghdad, where he teaches in the Ceramic Department of the Baghdad Academy of Fine Arts. Shaker is among the leading ceramicists in the Arab world. His works, fantastical shapes which allude to the natural forms of plants, shells or geology, are widely known. His ceramics combine a tremendous skill in execution with delicate, sensitive and sharp observation.

Completion
Ceramic on wood
36 x 28 x 15 cm
1979

Jordan
Wijdan Ali

Throughout history, the people of Jordan have experienced the rich panoply of cultures that spread across this cradle of civilization. In the middle of the fifteenth century Jordan came under Turkish rule and gradually became a backwater of the Ottoman Empire whose centre at Istanbul absorbed all cultural excellence. For five centuries the land slumbered, far from the seat of power and outside the glow of Ottoman art and culture.

Historical Background

Modern Jordan is a fairly new country. It was founded in 1924 by Prince Abdullah, the son of the Hashemite Sherif Hussein of Mecca, who led the Arab Revolt against the Ottoman Empire in 1917. From its founding until the early fifties, the country had to cope with the problems of building the infrastructure for a modern state – a reality common to all Third World countries. The country's major handicap was its lack of natural resources.

In 1948 the first Arab-Israeli war followed immediately upon the founding of the State of Israel in Palestine. Hundreds of thousands of Palestinian refugees poured into Jordan in the first two weeks alone. Wave upon wave followed afterwards, all needing homes, services, employment and schooling. The country had to continue its economic growth and at the same time supply its large new population with all the basic services including adequate education. To meet those new demands it had to depend on its meagre resources and foreign aid. Thus, in the first thirty years of its founding, Jordan faced practical problems of survival that hardly allowed the luxury of nurturing a modern art movement. This, of course, does not mean that other forms of indigenous artistic expression did not exist. Rug and textile weaving, embroidery, nielo work on silver, goldsmithing, pottery, painting on glass, woodcarving and calligraphy continued to provide the means for people to express their love for beauty.

The origins of modern art in Jordan can be traced to the twenties and thirties, when individuals from outside the country came to live in Amman. The first was Omar Onsi (1901–1969), one of the pioneer Lebanese painters. He came to Amman in 1922. During his short sojourn, he did watercolours of the desert and of Shouna in the Jordan Valley. It was unfortunate for local artists of the time that none of them was trained by this highly accomplished painter.

Ziyaeddin Suleiman (1880–1945) was a Turk who had studied in Paris. He moved to Amman in 1930 and died in Salt in 1945. Suleiman was a self-taught painter whose style contained impressionistic overtones, and a writer whose articles were published in the local papers and periodicals. He was the first artist in Jordan to live off his paintings. Among his friends were many intellectuals and politicians, including Prince Abdullah who was himself a man of letters and convinced Suleiman to make Amman his home. He held the first one-person exhibition in Amman at the Philadelphia Hotel in 1938.

The third early painter was George Aleef (1887–1970), a Russian. After the Bolshevik Revolution he moved to Palestine, where he stayed until the Arab-Israeli War of 1948. Aleef came to Amman with the Palestinian refugees and taught painting to a number of artists at his studio in Amman. Among his students were Muhanna Durra, Rafik Lahham and Naila Deeb. In 1967 he moved to Beirut where he spent his last years. He was the only one among his contemporaries who had students and was able to benefit local artists. His style was academic with strong colours. He worked in oils, watercolours and inks, painting scenes from Jordan and Palestine and Russian landscapes recalled from memory.

Jack Girdlestone (1894–1980) painted while he was with the Helen Keller Home in Beit Hanina in the 1960s and sold many of his naive works to tourists and friends in aid of the Home. In 1966 he moved to Amman as the unofficial representative of the Bible Land Society and held an exhibition at the British Council in 1974. A self-taught artist, he spent his free time painting scenes of the countryside, towns and cities, ignoring the rules of perspective and using basic colours, devoid of complicated shading. He was an artist who never sought fame and with the proceeds from his paintings, he helped his friends in refugee camps repair their houses and pay some of their children's university fees. His last exhibition took place at the British Council in Amman just before his death, in 1979.

The last artist among these early artists is Ihsan Idilbi (b. 1924). A self-taught painter of Syrian origin, his early works were Jordanian and Syrian landscapes and city scenes painted in a classical academic style. During one of his long stays in Damascus, in 1955, he met the Syrian artist Michel Kirsheh. After this encounter, his colours became softer and his style took on an impressionistic tone. In 1942, he organized the first group exhibition in Jordan, at the Ahli Club in Amman, and showed his work with Valeria Shaban and Rafik Lahham. He refuses to sell his paintings and gives them away to friends and acquaintances.

The major contribution of the early artists to the modern art movement in Jordan was their influence in developing art appreciation among their many acquaintances and introducing the public to easel painting. Through the works of Onsi and Suleiman, Impressionism found its way into Jordanian houses. Both artists were close to Prince Abdullah and enjoyed royal patronage; their works were acquired by the Palace and the Royal Family. When Aleef moved to Amman in 1948 his works were also acquired by the Palace. This type of Royal patronage was unusual for its time.

The annexation of the West Bank to Jordan sealed the fate of both the Palestinian and Jordanian people. Among the refugees who crossed the River Jordan, there were many artists; more were born in the country to parents of Palestinian origin, making the distinction between Jordanian and Palestinian art movements almost impossible. West Bank artists were considered Jordanian and many came to the capital to exhibit their works while Jordanian artists went to Jerusalem and other cities to paint and hold exhibitions. Palestinian artists, like Afaf Arafat and Samia Zaru, were employed by the Jordanian Ministry of Education to teach art at government secondary schools and teachers' training colleges, and to develop art courses within the government's curricula. Even now when the West Bank is under occupation and an independent Palestinian State has been declared in 1988, many artists of Palestinian origin opt to be called Jordanian because of their intrinsic ties with the country.

The Formative Decades 1950–1969

In the early fifties came the first encouraging signs of a modern art movement in Jordan. In 1951 the artistic committee of the 'Arab Club' (*Al-Muntada al-Arabi*), founded by the late Islamic scholar Sheikh Ibrahim Kattan, held the second group exhibition in the country. Eight painters – Ihsan Idilbi, Rafik Lahham, Muhanna Durra, Valeria Shaban, Kawthar Shafiq, Nihayat Hashim, Hashim Hajawi and Hisham Izzedin – took part. They were joined by three photographers: two professionals, John Darkajian and Mgrdich Salbashian, and an amateur Jawdat al-Khatib.

The first artistic group called Nadwat al-Fan al-Urduniya was formed in 1952. Its aim was to spread art awareness and appreciation among the public and encourage amateur artists. Some of the members who either painted or sculpted were Najah Khayat, Valeria Shaban, Rafik Lahham, Sami Nimeh, Khalil Amouri, Ihsan Idilbi, Muhanna Durra and Daad Tell.

One of the first women in Jordan and Palestine to study art was Fatima Muhib. Born in Jerusalem in 1920, she graduated as early as 1940 from the College of Fine Arts in Cairo and in 1942 obtained her master's degree in fine arts from Helwan University, Cairo.

In the late fifties the government, feeling the need for trained artists qualified to teach at its schools, sent the first students abroad on scholarships. Muhanna Durra, Rafik Lahham, Ahmad Nawash and Kamal Boullata went to Italy while Afaf Arafat (b. 1925) first went to Bath Academy (1954–57) in England, and later on was sent to the State University of Tennessee (1966) in the United States for her master's in art.

Art appreciation started to grow slowly with the wider intellectual awareness encouraged by new cultural clubs such as the Scientific Nahda Institute, the Cultural Co-operation Club (*Nadi al-Ta'awun al-Thaqafi*) in Amman and the U'ruba School in Irbid. These clubs invited artists to exhibit on their premises and awarded prizes. Meanwhile foreign cultural centres like the British Council, the Goethe Institute and the French Cultural Centre exhibited the works of local artists in Amman and Jerusalem and also brought exhibitions from abroad. This helped expose the public to different international trends in art and gave local artists the opportunity to meet the public.

In 1952 Dr John Kayaleh, an ophthalmologist, accomplished violinist and art lover, founded the Institute of Music and Painting in downtown Amman. He employed Armando Bruno (1930–1963), an Italian, to give painting and piano lessons. Bruno instructed a number of budding artists, among them Rafik Lahham, Muhanna Durra, Daad Tell, Wijdan, Suha Noursi and Naila Deeb. A demanding teacher, he injected the expressionist and impressionist still lifes and portraits of his students with spontaneity and animation. The Institute became a meeting place for young artists and intellectuals and was the first attempt at formal art training in Jordan.

An interesting artist of a different age group was Prince Nayef Bin Abdullah. Born in Mecca in 1914, he was the son of King Abdullah and the uncle of King Hussein of Jordan. Prince Nayef was a self-taught artist who had known both Onsi and Suleiman. He started painting as a hobby at a late stage in his life, but soon found himself immersed in his art. He was a naive artist who painted imaginative scenes recalled from childhood and youth. He enjoyed a primary sense of colour, a natural eye for a well balanced composition and a vivid imagination. He had many friends among artists like Rafik Lahham and Muhanna Durra, with whom he exhibited in the fifties. He never sought fame, refused to sell his works and had only two one-person exhibitions in Oslo and Madrid. He died in Amman in 1985.

In the early sixties students who had been sent by the government abroad on art scholarships began to return. Others also became interested in art and embraced painting as something more than a hobby. Rafik Lahham (b. 1932) came back to Amman in 1962 after graduating from ENALC (Ente Nationale Addestramento Lavoratori Commercio) and the San Jacomo Institute in Rome. In 1967 he went to the Rochester Institute of Technology in New York State, where he studied painting and etching and was the first artist in Jordan to work in printmaking. One of Jordan's pioneer artists of the modern period, he has experimented with different styles and subjects ranging from portraiture and rural landscapes to abstract compositions of Nabatean images, calligraphy and Islamic motifs. He alternates his media between oils, gouaches, watercolours, and graphics.

Ali Ghoul (b. 1938) obtained his doctorate in architecture from Newcastle, England. Although he wavers between abstract impressionism and full impressionism, Ghoul's favourite subjects remain haunting landscapes painted in warm, glowing earth colours, with palm trees and peaceful sunsets. He is a professor of architecture at the Jordan University. Muhanna Durra (b. 1938) studied at the Academy of Fine Arts in Rome and graduated in 1958. The first leading Jordanian painter, Durra established a distinctive style of his own with expressionistic overtones in bold monochromes. He is known for his striking portraits of bedouins and peasants and his later abstract cubism, depicting what looks like cityscapes and fractured structures piled one on the other. Durra's strength lies in his clever distribution of masses, his strong, confident lines and deft manipulation of sparse colour. His dexterous ink drawings burst with energy and grace. He is the first and only Jordanian artist to cultivate his own followers; even today traces of his style can still be detected in the works of other artists. In 1971 he was appointed Director of the Department of Arts and Culture and was the first Jordanian artist to receive the State Appreciation Award in 1977 for his contributions to the cultural development of Jordan. In 1983 he joined the staff of the Arab League in Tunis as Director General of Cultural Affairs before being transferred to Rome.

Ahmad Nawash (b. 1934) is one of the leading figures of Jordanian modern art. He graduated from the Academy of Fine Arts in Rome in 1964 and in 1970 obtained a diploma in lithography and etching from the College of Fine Arts in Bordeaux, France. He also spent two years in Paris at the Ecole des Beaux Arts (1977). Nawash's style is highly individualistic. He paints mutilated, infantile figures that sometimes float around his canvas brandishing their disfigurations as a mark of their tortured souls. At times they are securely planted on the ground, leaning on uneven crutches, mocking society's hypocrisy and man's cruelty to his brethren. Prone to bouts of depression, his works do not emanate joyful thoughts and have a disturbing effect on the viewer. Though they are not popular, Nawash never compromises to please the public. Wijdan (b. 1939), painter, writer and art historian, graduated with a BA in history from Beirut College for Women (later to become Beirut University College) in 1961 and was the first woman diplomat to enter the Jordanian Ministry of Foreign Affairs in 1962. She took art courses in Amman during college holidays, working with Armando Bruno and Muhanna Durra. She has used oils, watercolours, pastels, coloured china inks with hot wax and etching. She went through many stages before developing her own individual style of shimmering combed surfaces that reflect light through thin layers of colour. Among her best known works are those of her desert period. A highly self critical and demanding artist, she believes in the need to support the creative abilities of Third World artists who have had to battle against great odds to survive. She has been experimenting with Arabic calligraphy, in particular Kufic script, emphasising the aesthetic form of the letters more than their content.

Around the mid-sixties a new group of artists began to return to Amman after finishing their studies in Arab academies or art colleges. Mahmoud Taha (b. 1942) is a ceramicist and a calligrapher who graduated from the Baghdad Academy of Fine Arts in 1968, and studied calligraphy with the late Moustafa Hashim al-Baghdadi. He continued his training in ceramics at Cardiff College of Arts in Wales (1976). The leading Jordanian ceramicist, Taha's talent lies in his skilful experiments with coloured glazes and his ability to successfully join the traditions of his country's most ancient craft with contemporary techniques. His pieces incorporate Arabic calligraphy within innovative spherical forms. Aziz Ammoura (b. 1944) graduated from the Academy of Fine Arts in Baghdad in 1970 and obtained his master's in fine arts from the Pratt Institute, New York, in 1983. His early oil paintings of landscapes and figures have a warm impressionistic style, while his adept ink drawings follow a stylized monochrome pointillism. Lately he has developed an original style of abstract, calligraphic painting in layers of transparent oils and watercolours. Yasser Duwaik (b. 1940) is another graduate of the Academy of Fine Arts in Baghdad (1968) and Brighton College of Fine Arts (1972). He went through many changes before finding a style of his own that revolves around a sombre expressionism, laden with calligraphic symbolism. His latest works are inspired by the Intifada in the West Bank. Nasr Abdel Aziz (b. 1942) graduated from the College of Fine Arts in Cairo University and later did post-graduate work in film production. His obsession with bedouins, horses, and children is reflected in his stylized but animated desert scenes, executed in warm earth colours. Saleh Abu Shindi (b. 1938) graduated from the College of Fine Arts in Cairo and developed a distinctive style based on fluidity of line and form. With time, his colours have become sparse while his lines have gained richness and harmony. Among his best works are his black-and-white sketches of old Jordanian and Palestinian villages and intricate fantasy compositions. Kuram Nimri (b. 1944) obtained his bachelor's degree from the Fine Arts Department at Damascus University in 1966 and was sent in 1973 to the BBC in London for a course in the design of television film sets. A sculptor who uses olivewood, he works around the knots and grain, transforming it into abstracts of the human figure. Lately he has been mixing metal pieces from car scraps with wood, to come up with peculiar combinations of smooth and rough surfaces. Tawfic el-Sayed (b. 1939) went to Egypt in 1961, where he did research in art, and gained a scholarship to the San Fernando Academy of Fine Arts in Madrid, where he graduated in 1975. El-Sayed is a prolific painter and sculptor who is at ease with oils, gouaches, watercolours, china-ink, and etching. He also draws caricatures. He worked with Durra for some time and was influenced by his style, but then gradually developed his own, executing large abstract works in monochrome and polychrome and emphasizing line instead of form.

There are other artists of this same generation. Mahmoud Sadeq (b. 1945) trained at the College of Fine Arts at Baghdad University (1970), taking his master's in painting from the University of South Carolina and doctorate in art education from Florida State University (1983). Sadeq derives his motifs and colours from folk patterns and local rugs and puts them into linear compositions to form semi-abstract landscapes. Munira Nusseibeh (b. 1942) is a painter and sculptor who trained at the Ecole Nationale des Beaux Arts in Paris and then moved to Abu Dhabi. There she painted large canvases of tyrannical men and oppressed women, created out of tar, sand, gold leaf and oils. Gradually, her forms became abstract, turning into solid, featureless, geometric masses. Her statues range from naturalistic portraits to elegantly distorted, contemplative figures. In 1985 she moved to New York where she discarded her sombre colours for prismatic still life. Kayed Amr (b. 1942) graduated in 1970 from the College of Art Education in Cairo and continued his studies at Pennsylvania State University, USA, where he completed his doctorate in art education in 1982. Amr first created cityscapes depicting the rooftops and narrow alleys of his hometown, Hebron, always with a dove to symbolize peace and tranquillity. They were executed in a cubist-expressionist style using sombre earth colours. He then moved to pastoral landscapes of Jordanian and Palestinian villages in expressive, vivid colours. Moustafa Moustafa (b. 1944) graduated from the Febertal Fine Arts Institute in the Federal Republic of Germany in 1967. He later continued at the Hamburg Industrial University. His German-expressionist canvases depict, with sombre colours and tormented shapes, man's anguish, the despair of the Palestinians and their homeless wanderings. He works in oils, gouaches, watercolours, silk screen and is an accomplished photographer. In 1981 Moustafa moved to Germany. Zaki Shaqfa (b. 1945) is a graduate of the College of Fine Arts in Cairo (1969). He employs folk motifs, calligraphy and geometrical forms in his decorative paintings.

In the sixties, the Ministry of Tourism started to send the work of Jordanian artists abroad to international exhibitions. The first was the New York World Fair of 1965. Others followed in Baghdad, Damascus, Bari, Rome, Copenhagen and Berlin. In 1966 the government founded the Department of Culture and Arts as part of the Ministry of Youth. Its mandate was to support and promote cultural activities in the fine arts, theatre, music and literature. The Department opened an exhibition hall for local and foreign artists. Since 1977 it has changed from being a joint Ministry with the Ministry of Information to an independent one.

The activity of the 1960s came to a premature halt in 1967. In five brief, harrowing days Israel occupied Jordan's West Bank, dividing the land and the people. Palestinian artists living in the West Bank were cut off from Jordan and some, like Kamal Boullata, emigrated outside the Arab world. The military defeat and political setback spawned a new trend in art, not only among Jordanian and Palestinian artists but also among Arab artists in general. It bore a nationalistic message opposing occupation or expressing the nation's disappointment in its leadership.

The Growing Decades 1970–1989

The opening of the seventies witnessed a considerable increase in artistic activity. In 1972, on the initiative of Muhanna Durra, the Department of Arts and Culture founded the Institute of Fine Arts with a two-year basic course in painting, sculpture, graphics and ceramics; Durra became its director. Many artists had their initial training at the Institute. Among them were Youssef Husseiny, Nabil Shehadeh, Omar Hamdan, Ma'amoun Dibian, Youssef Badawi, Mazen Asfour and others. Some of the well established artists gave painting lessons in their private studios. These included Muhanna Durra, Rafik Lahham, Aziz Ammoura and Mahmoud Taha, who had a kiln and taught ceramics. By this time, the number of students opting to study art had rapidly multiplied. Scholarships were provided by the Ministry of Education to Turkey, the Soviet Union, Iraq, Syria, Italy, France, Germany, Spain and England. Some artists who went to study on their own chose other countries like the United States, Switzerland and Pakistan. In 1977 the Artists' Association was founded. It succeeded in establishing a headquarters for artists where they could meet and discuss their problems, and hold occasional exhibitions and lectures.

The Jordan National Gallery of Fine Arts

In 1979 the Royal Society of Fine Arts was created. It is a private non-profit organization whose goal is to promote the visual arts in Jordan, the Arab countries and the Third World. The Society's major achievement was the founding of the Jordan National Gallery of Fine Arts in 1980. The Gallery is the first art museum to open in Jordan and the first official forum to set high goals and standards for Jordanian artists. When it first opened, the Gallery's collection had only 75 works and 70 paintings on loan from Pakistan's Ministry of Culture. Since then it has amassed a permanent collection of nearly 1,000 paintings, sculptures, ceramics, and textile wall hangings by contemporary artists from the Islamic and Third World countries. It also has a small but highly prized collection of Orientalist paintings which includes among others works by Gerome, Le Compte de Nouy, Rudolph Ernst, David Roberts and Eugene Delacroix. The permanent collection of the Gallery is unique; it covers a geographic area that extends from Brunei in Southeast Asia to Pakistan, Iran, Turkey, the Middle East and North Africa.

The collection has expanded beyond expectation; it represents a well managed and safe repository, documenting, conserving and exhibiting art from the region. Samer Tabbaa was the first director, and since 1981 it has been under the efficient and dynamic direction of Suhail Bisharat. In its initial ten years, the Gallery has held 50 exhibitions in Amman, including group exhibitions from different countries such as Tunisia, Turkey, the United Kingdom, Spain, France, Yugoslavia, Germany, Egypt, Italy, Iraq and others. It has taken exhibitions of Jordanian artists abroad to Turkey, Poland, France, Egypt and England. This exchange in cultural activities has opened new horizons for local artists and been instrumental in introducing Jordanian and modern

Islamic art abroad. The Gallery has also taken exhibitions outside the capital, Amman, to remote places like Kerak, Mazar, Wadi Musa, Azraq and Tafila in the south and Anjara, Irbid and Ajloun in the north. It has directed exhibitions of contemporary Jordanian art and photography during four summer festivals held at the Roman city of Jerash. Villagers and bedouins have had their first opportunity to gaze at and comment on artistic works in two dimensions. The Gallery also holds one-person exhibitions for Arab, Islamic and Western artists. To celebrate its tenth anniversary in 1989 the Society established awards for artists from the Islamic and Arab world who have made outstanding contributions to the plastic arts. The Royal Society of Fine Arts also arranges for artists to go on training courses abroad and has given a scholarship to a gifted student at the Fine Arts Department of Yarmouk University. The ultimate goal of the Society is to have a museum which will include works by prominent artists from all Third World countries in Asia, Africa and South America.

The Fine Arts Department – Yarmouk University

In 1980, a Fine Arts Department was established at Yarmouk University in the north of Jordan. It is Jordan's first institute of higher education to offer art as a major. It opened with 50 students and now has over 500 students who can choose to specialize in:
1 Fine Arts (painting, photography, ceramics and sculpture)
2 Applied Arts (interior decoration, industrial design, commercial design)
3 Theatrical Arts (acting, stage design and directing)
4 Music (theory and practice in both Western and Arabic music)
Its faculty includes prominent artists like Aziz Ammoura, Mahmoud Sadeq, and Kayed Amr.

The opening of the Jordan National Gallery and the Department of Fine Arts mark the eighties as a milestone for the modern art movement in Jordan.

During the mid-seventies a number of new artists returned from training abroad. Ali Jabri (b. 1943) stands out among them. Jabri read English Literature at Bristol University and architecture and fine arts at Stanford University in California. He is one of the rare modern Arab artists who is equally versed in Islamic and Western culture. He is obsessed with preserving his heritage and has recorded with his sensitive and original neo-realist style, national events, like the Arab Revolt, and many sites that have disappeared, like the old port-city of Aqaba in the south of Jordan and the late King Abdullah's guest house in Ma'an. He has been instrumental in making the authorities aware of the importance of neglected historical sites and buildings. He trained in museology while on a study tour to France and the United States. When he came back he took over the design and installation of the Jordan Museum of Popular Traditions in Amman, which was founded by his aunt Mrs Sa'adia Jabri Tell. Jabri is a demanding perfectionist who roams Jordan's deserts and archaeological sites, its dilapidated urban neighbourhoods and its remote villages, recording them with his meticulous eye for detail and transforming their minutest mundane particulars into momentous features that pulsate with life and inner beauty. He is the only contemporary artist in Jordan who has always lived off his art.

Hafiz Kassis (b. 1945) is a graduate of the Fine Arts Academy in Istanbul (1972), where he studied painting and stained glass. He continued his training at the College of Fine Arts in Ravenna, Italy, where he learned the art of mosaics and is the only Jordanian artist who works in these two media. He is a skilled restorer and has done major work on the St. Salvatore Cathedral in Jerusalem, the Church of Santa Maria in Larnaca and the Latin Church in Salt, one of the oldest churches in Jordan. He has executed huge murals in mosaics as well as stained glass windows at the Catholic Church in Fuhais, the Rosary School and Casanova Hotel in Jerusalem, and the Terra

Sancta School in Amman. His oil paintings have the air of medieval stained glass with deep green, red and blue figures framed in thick black lines. Farouk Lambaz (b. 1942) graduated from Law School at the Syrian University in 1968 before he took up art as a career. He trained at the Institute of Fine Arts in Amman and specialised in graphics and poster design. He has developed a quaint, feathery impressionistic style in which he depicts, in pale earth colours, the desert and rural landscapes. Suhail Bisharat (b. 1942) obtained his BSc in Geology from London University and became a fellow of the Royal Geological Society in England. He worked as a geologist in Britain then joined Aramco and explored the Empty Quarter of Arabia. He first showed his paintings at the Aramco Annual Art Show in 1974. In 1976 he came back to Amman and worked on geological projects before deciding in 1980 to devote himself to a career in art. A self-taught artist, Bisharat chose an original medium; he paints with coffee and manipulates its shades of brown to depict landscapes and portraits that betray his formal scientific training and are reminiscent of the earth's contours and strata.

Samer Tabbaa (b. 1945) is a sculptor, painter and photographer, though he is best known for his statues. Tabbaa did his master's in fine arts, majoring in sculpture, at Kent State University, Ohio. He works largely in stone, creating a melodious harmony and three-way entente between himself, his piece and the viewer. He is equally versatile with wood and uses colour to accentuate his angular wooden shapes. Said Haddadin (b. 1945) is the first Jordanian artist to train in the Soviet Union where he obtained his BA in Fine Arts from Lvov College of Fine Arts in 1974. His well balanced canvases depict humanity's suffering through solid, stonelike, silent forms, in dismal colours of obscure blues, greens and browns. Fuad Mimi (b. 1949) studied television production and directing at the BBC and painting at St. Martin's College of Art in London. Upon his return, he worked with Jordan Television, and produced several series of documentaries on art and culture. A perfectionist who takes a long time to complete a painting he draws the Jordanian landscape in placid colours with small impressionistic brushstrokes. Abdel Raouf Shamoun (b. 1945) obtained his BA in Literature from the Jordan University in 1968. A self-taught artist and art critic, he took art courses at the Institute of Fine Arts in Amman. His style vacillates between surrealism and expressionism and is laden with symbols that try to transmit a social message. He is an artist who thoroughly researches a subject before depicting it.

One of the main events of the seventies was the arrival of Fahrelnissa Zeid. She moved in 1975 from Paris to Amman. A truly magnanimous artist of international standard and reputation, she was born in Istanbul in 1901, and studied painting at the Fine Arts Academy in Istanbul and the Academie Ranson in Paris. She had lived most of her life in the European capitals of Berlin, London and Paris, accompanying her diplomat husband, the Hashemite Prince Zeid Bin Hussein, youngest son of Sherif al-Hussein of Mecca. In Amman, society ladies flocked around her to learn painting. With them as her pupils, she established a private gathering called the 'Art Institute of Fahrelnissa Zeid'. Her pupils followed her abstract style and Byzantinesque portraits. Fahrelnissa Zeid is a versatile and prolific artist who has worked with watercolours, china inks, gouaches and oils, executing gargantuan abstract canvases in her highly textured individualistic style as well as miniature paintings bursting with energy and life. By filling up all available space on the canvas, she unconsciously adheres to a basic rule in Islamic art. Her portraits are on a giant scale and her imaginative vigour has led her to work in paleocrystals injected with chicken and turkey bones that form revolving pieces of sculpture, and free standing stained glass paintings. Her works have been acquired by major museums in the United States, Europe and the Middle East.

Of Fahrelnissa's students only Suha Shoman, Hind Nasser and Rula Shukairi have seriously pursued a career in art. Shoman (b. 1944) is a law graduate from the Sorbonne in Paris. When she first started painting, she followed her teacher's style, but after continuous experimentation, she succeeded in creating her own style of abstraction which depends mainly on a clever formation of masses and adroit use of colour.

In 1981, a number of artists broke away from the Artists' Association to form the Young Artists' Group. Heading this new formation was Ibrahim Najjar, born in Jerusalem in 1949. A graduate of the Fine Arts Academy in Cairo, Najjar continued his art education at Helwan University and obtained his doctorate in the History of Art in 1987. He follows a distinctive expressionistic surrealism based on mummified figures. His most distinguishing feature is the Dali blue he cleverly mixes with red, which overpowers all other shades and colours. Among the members of the Young Artists' Group who took part in its annual exhibitions were Mohammad Abu Zreiq (b. 1947), Ishaq Nahla (b. 1946), Hanan Agha (b. 1948), Arwa Tell (b. 1948), Hiyam Abaza (b. 1956), Adnan Yahya (b. 1960), Mohammad Isa, Dina Zubi and Youssef Badawi (b. 1959). Surrealism was the common artistic trait that united the group. The group dispersed after its last exhibition in 1988.

Mona Saudi (b. 1945) studied at the Ecole Nationale des Beaux Arts in Paris (1971) and then went to Italy to work in a marble factory where she perfected her technique. She moved to Beirut in 1969 and joined the Artistic Bureau of the Palestine Liberation Organization. In 1982 she came back to Amman and has been running Al-Wasiti art gallery. She works stone, rough granite and grainy marble into perfectly smooth, romantically intertwined, abstract figures. Nabil Shehadeh (b. 1950) started his art training at the Institute of Fine Arts in Amman after which he went to Chelsea College of Art in London. He has also lived and worked in Switzerland. One of the few leading abstract artists in Jordan, Shehadeh considers line and space before colour. His vivid imagination creates animated three-dimensional abstract compositions, full of pulsating movement.

There are a number of young Jordanians born in the 1950s who show great promise. Among them are Omar Hamdan (b. 1955), Daif Allah Obeidat (b. 1957), Ammar Khammash (b. 1960), Nawal Abdallah (b. 1951), Khalid Khreis (b. 1956), Youssef Husseiny (b. 1956), Omar Bsoul (b. 1951), Ma'amoun Dibian (b. 1952), Nasma Nimri (b. 1953), Hussein Daasa (b. 1962), al-Jaloos (b. 1960), Jamal Ashour (b. 1958) and Hazem Zubi (b. 1957).

Art Criticism

Jordanian artists have had little opportunity to learn from knowledgeable art critics who evaluate work without having to take into consideration personal sympathies and social niceties. The few who write in local papers tend to be either amateur art lovers like Rabah Sgayer, Dr George Lutfi Sayegh and Meg Abu Hamdan, or artists themselves like Abdel Raouf Shamoun, Nelli Lama, Ayad Nimr, Tawfic el-Sayed, Hussein Daasa and Mohammad al-Jaloos. Only those few Jordanians who have had the opportunity of exhibiting abroad have any experience of professional reviews. Mazen Asfour is a painter who graduated from the Institute of Fine Arts in Amman and went to Italy to study and specialize in art criticism. His return is impatiently awaited.

Exhibition Space

Apart from the halls of the Jordan National Gallery, the Artists' Association, the foreign cultural centres and major international hotels there is the Royal Cultural Centre. This complex includes a theatre and several halls where exhibitions are regularly held. Commercial art galleries have had limited success. The first to open was The Gallery (1972), owned by Nuha Batshon; it is the only one to survive and turn a profit. She shows Jordanian artists as well as a few Arab and foreign artists resident in Jordan. Other galleries have been short lived.

Art Patronage

In the West financial institutions, especially banks, began to take on the role of patrons of the arts after the Second World War. Turkey is the only country in the Middle East where bankers have played a prominent, supportive role to the arts from as early as the late 1920s. In the Arab World, the oil boom of the 1970s has yet to produce any noteworthy benefactors. Perhaps today we are on the verge of more sophisticated patronage.

Petra Bank was the first financial institution to collect art and patronize artists. In 1983, at the initiative of its chairman Dr Ahmad Chalabi, it opened an art gallery in its newly built headquarters and offered it to artists free of charge, as an exhibition space. Dr Chalabi, himself an art connoisseur and collector, is the first banker in Jordan to start a collection by Jordanian, Arab and Islamic artists and commission them to do works especially for the bank. It now owns an extensive collection of paintings and sculpture by prominent Islamic artists. Petra Bank has also funded a number of art scholarships for talented students. The Central Bank of Jordan has a small collection of art work started under its governor, Dr Mohammad Said Nabulsi. Its former governor, Hussein Kassim, opened a fine numismatic museum that specializes in Islamic coins. The Royal Jordanian Airlines also plays a vital role under the leadership of its chairman, Ali Ghandour. In 1980, he opened an art gallery for the airline where local artists as well as other Arab and foreign artists could exhibit their work. The airline offers free and reduced tickets to artists who travel on scholarships and for exhibitions and ships their work free of charge. It also contributes to the country's cultural activities by supporting exhibitions abroad, giving coverage to the arts during its in-flight films and devoting large sections of its in-flight magazines to painters and museums. The Arab Bank, the Arab world's oldest and most powerful banking institution, has recently taken a public role in the arts. At the initiative of Suha Shoman, the wife of its chairman, herself a painter, the Shoman Foundation opened an art gallery in 1988 where exhibitions as well as literary evenings, lectures, debates and seminars are held. A demanding patron, Shoman strains to build the gallery on high artistic standards. The Foundation, opened only a decade ago by the Arab Bank, has contributed to the support of culture and science not only in Jordan but throughout the Arab world.

Although big business may be replacing individuals as art patrons, patronage still depends entirely on the initiative of the individual running the institution. As yet all too few business leaders are interested in culture and the arts.

Conclusion

Rarely a week passes in Amman without at least one exhibition, either local or from abroad, opening in one of the city's many halls or galleries. There is intense artistic activity all year round and the number of students who choose to study art is on the increase. Artists, like any other group, can subscribe to the government's social security plan. The number of collectors has increased and many artists sell most of the work they exhibit. Nevertheless, art is not taken seriously, by either officials or the general public. Jordanian artists need to group under a more efficient and effective organization such as a union to safeguard their needs and rights as creative individuals.

Jordanian modern art has come a long way since the fifties. Having reached maturity in an age when art schools and styles are replaced by individual experiments and fads, a definite Jordanian school of art has not developed. Yet, in the works of artists from the sixties, like Muhanna Durra,

Ali Jabri, Aziz Ammoura, Mahmoud Taha and Wijdan and in more recent ones from a younger group like Jamal Ashour, Khalid Khreis and Adnan Yahya one can see the emergence of trends which could be characterized as distinctive of Jordanian modern art.

See colour pp. 88–100 for plates of the following artists' work:

NASR ABDEL AZIZ
JAMAL ASHOUR
SUHAIL BISHARAT
ALI JABRI
RAFIK LAHHAM
FUAD MIMI
IBRAHIM NAJJAR
AHMAD NAWASH
ABDEL RAOUF SHAMOUN
SUHA SHOMAN
WIJDAN
FAHRELNISSA ZEID

SALEH ABU SHINDI
Jordan, b. 1942
Born in Jaffa, Abu Shindi obtained his bachelor degree and a diploma in Art Education from the College of Fine Arts in Cairo. Abu Shindi's works are concerned with a compositional landscape blended with Islamic motifs and calligraphy. Using china ink and marker pen, he captures the decorative character of the Arabic script, and portrays the strong images of Jerusalem which feature in many of his works. His paintings reflect a sculptural effect, with the play of light and dark and emphasis on cultural details. Abu Shindi is also a teacher as well as a painter. He has held a number of leading posts in various Fine Arts departments.

Silent Conversation
China ink on paper
35 x 50 cm
1985

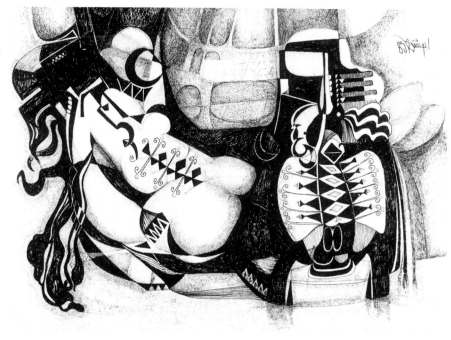

AZIZ AMMOURA
Jordan, b. 1944
Ammoura graduated from the Academy of Fine Arts in Baghdad in 1970 and obtained a scholarship to complete his master's degree at the Pratt Institute, USA, in 1983. He then took up the position he holds today as assistant professor at Yarmouk University's newly founded College of Fine Arts. A strong painter as well as a patient teacher, Ammoura takes his inspiration from the immediate environment, which he can compose with minute exactitude from retained visual images. His oils are executed with a masterful technique where precision of brushstroke and individuality in the selection of colours excel. His pen and ink drawings use a form of pointillism to create smooth, sensuous compositions where the round lines and poetic illusions exude a strange peace, purity and sadness.

Manuscript
Watercolour on paper
37 x 48 cm
1987

KAYED AMR
Jordan, b. 1941
Amr is a painter and teacher. Born
in Hebron, Amr first joined the
Higher Institute of Art Education
and later gained his bachelor
degree from Cairo University. He
then travelled to the United States,
where he gained his master's from
Central Connecticut State College
and his doctorate in art from
Pennsylvania State University.
Amr's work deals with his
immediate environment, drawing
on traditional themes. His paintings
rely heavily on geometrical lines
and blocks of massive colours, with
very little attention to details. Amr
has contributed to the development
of art education in Jordan both as a
Professor at the Fine Arts Institute
of Yarmouk University and as a
practising painter.

City of Peace
Oil on canvas
72 x 85 cm
1980

MUHANNA DURRA
Jordan, b. 1938
Muhanna Durra, whether in oils or
ink, displays an intense, observant
energy and a mastery of materials
and technique. Movement defines
his surfaces; his figures are
propelled with grace and his
landscapes with colliding light. His
oils deftly break down images into
polychromatic planes and shafts of
colour.
Born in Amman, he graduated from
the Academy of Fine arts in Rome in
1958. He helped establish the
Institute of Fine Arts in 1971 and
was appointed its director.
He is one of the pioneers in the
Jordanian art movement, with a
young, enthusiastic following, and
is known for his Bedouin portraits,
which stress the subjects' rough,
intense features. His cubist
cityscapes and landscapes that
stack colour one shade on another
are also very popular.

Composition 3
Oil on canvas
75 x 95 cm
1977

YASSER DUWAIK
Jordan, b. 1940

Duwaik has captured many traditional scenes in his impressionistic faceless figures that evaporate into smooth colours. His graphics are a combination of oriental design and calligraphy with bold geometrical forms. Dominated by a sun-like disc symbolizing reality, these secular abstractions have strong visual appeal; by changing the compositional position, and colour of the disc, its power changes and the visual elements are highlighted. Duwaik graduated from Baghdad Academy of Fine Arts in 1968. Subsequently he studied in England at Brighton College of Fine Arts. He then returned to Amman to teach and promote art in Jordan while maintaining his intense level of production.

Hebron
Oil on canvas
56 x 70 cm
1982

SAID HADDADIN
Jordan, b. 1945

Said Haddadin is a painter, teacher and caricaturist. Born in Ma'in Village, he is among the few Jordanians who have studied art in the Soviet Union, where he graduated from Lvov College of Art. After graduation he worked as a lecturer in drawing and anatomy at the Institute of Fine Arts of Amman in the Department of Culture and Arts. His paintings are a sensitive study of the human face and figure, which he expresses essentially as lines and colour. Although his works show the influence of early Picasso and Matisse, Said is searching for his own style. He tries to reconcile the subject he seeks to express with his means of abstracting it. His cartoons and caricatures are captivating and expressive.

The Youth
Oil on canvas
50 x 70 cm
1983

HAFIZ KASSIS
Jordan, b. 1932
Kassis has an immediately recognisable style as a figurative painter, where his strength of character is revealed in confident figures with a geometrical outline. Kassis was born in Beit Sahour, Palestine. He graduated from the Academy of Fine Arts in Istanbul in 1972. Later he continued his studies in Italy, completing training in art mosaics in 1981. Kassis has distinguished himself with a number of large mosaics in Jordan and has been involved also in some restoration works. His stained glass work reflects a great deal of his sensitivity and a sense of perfection.

A Face from my Country
Oil on wood
75 x 55 cm
1983

AMMAR KHAMMASH
Jordan, b. 1960
Khammash was born in Amman. He started drawing when he was ten and painting when he was fourteen. After finishing high school, Khammash went to the United States to study architecture at the University of Southwestern Louisiana. His deep interest in vernacular architecture has a strong link with the subjects he chooses to paint as well as the techniques he uses. An advocate of recording, protecting and refunctioning traditional structures, Khammash excels at depicting the countryside and village architecture in translucent watercolours that reflect the light.

Luzmilla Hospital
Watercolour on paper
30 x 45 cm
1985

KHALID KHREIS
Jordan, b. 1955
Khreis was born in Kerak and
studied at Helwan University,
Cairo, before going on to the
Academy of San Gorgo, Barcelona,
the Pietro Vanucci Institute, San
Cugat and the Institute of Fine Arts
of San Miquel de Allende in Mexico.
His abstract tendencies owe their
origin to his early years in Egypt.
His technique is unusual. His earlier
works used cardboard and he relied
on ancient motifs and symbols
which gradually shifted into circles
and rectangles. Whether in inks,
acrylics, watercolour, or mixed
media, Khreis has succeeded in
using a number of techniques to
express his sensitivity. His use of
natural earth colours, brown,
yellow and blue reveal delicacy and
maturity.

Contemplations
Acrylic on carton
100 x 70 cm
1987

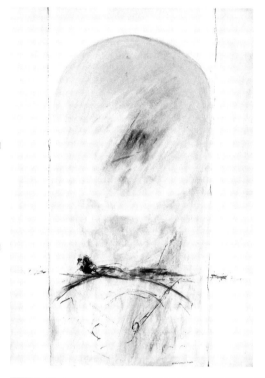

MOHAMMED MOUSTAFA
Jordan, b. 1944
Mohammed Moustafa graduated
from the Fine Arts Institute of the
German Federal Republic in 1968.
He subsequently studied industrial
design and drawing at Hamburg
University in 1969, and
photography at the Higher Popular
School in 1973. Moustafa has a
distinctive style which he has
arrived at after much
experimentation. He expresses his
personal philosophy and
impressions with deep sensitivity.
His highly developed technique and
the strength of his expressionistic
works cannot be measured by
conventional standards – they
impose their own standards on the
viewer, shocking and surprising at
once. Moustafa has great control
over his oil drawings, graphics and
photography, and despite their
different forms one can always
detect Moustafa's imprint. His
works are better known in Germany
than in the Arab world.

Untitled
Mixed media on canvas
100 x 110 cm
1979

KURAM NIMRI
Jordan, b. 1944
Born in Husn, Nimri graduated as a
sculptor from the Fine Arts College
in Damascus in 1970. He is among
the few Jordanian artists to have
studied under the tutorship of the
Egyptian-born artist, Ahmad Amin
Asem. After returning to Jordan,
Nimri taught sculpture at the
Institute of Fine Arts in Amman and
became immersed in his work as an
art consultant with Jordan
Television. Nimri has managed in
stone, metal and wood to carve his
medium into moving creative forms.
His olive wood sculptures are the
most striking and successful.

Human Figure
Wood sculpture
40 x 40 x 30 cm
1973

DAIF ALLAH OBEIDAT
Jordan, b. 1957
Daif Allah Obeidat was born in the
northern city of Irbid. He studied at
the Fine Arts Institute in Cairo,
where he graduated in 1982.
Obeidat's works deal with current
trends in a classical surrealist style.
His ideas rotate around human
injustice and the struggle of
mankind. Although his paintings
may show a close relationship to
European masters, his themes are
evidently much more Eastern in
spirit.

Untitled
Oil on canvas
90 x 120 cm
1982

MAHMOUD SADDIQ
Jordan, b. 1945
Mahmoud Saddiq graduated from the Baghdad Academy of Fine Arts in 1970. Later he continued his studies in the United States where he gained his master's degree from the University of South Carolina in 1980, and his doctorate from the Florida State University in 1983. Mahmoud Saddiq's earlier works were realistic expressionist in style reflecting his own emotions concerning his people and country. He gradually moved towards abstract expressionism where one sees less of the detail and where colour composition begins to dominate his large canvas. His work is derived from his cultural roots. He believes that one should express one's own intrinsic vision.

Rhythm
Oil on canvas
120 x 90 cm
1984

MONA SAUDI
Jordan, b. 1945
Mona Saudi is one of the few eminent Arab women artists who have devoted themselves to sculpture. She may take a rough marble block and smooth it into long, feminine, rounded curves which envelop a dynamic, perpendicular intrusion. Her less well-known graphic works are sculptural studies in two dimensions. Full of the ancient Middle Eastern symbolism of fecundity and procreation, they give an insight into the meaning of her large sculptural pieces where abstraction reduces the thought to its essence. She has pioneered the moving of sculpture from the interior courtyards of Jordanian houses to exterior, public spaces. While much of her work is intensely personal in its quiet, ethereal quality, her pieces for public display are more abstract and striking.

The Lover's Tree
Etching
73 x 36
1977

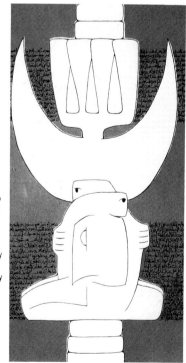

TAWFIC EL-SAYED
Jordan, b. 1939

Tawfic el-Sayed is one of the early pioneering artists in Jordan. He is a painter, sculptor, graphic artist, caricaturist and instructor. He was born in Safad, but grew up in Amman where he now lives. His artistic career began as a talented self-taught artist in 1950. In the sixties he left for Italy, Egypt and Greece. Subsequently he gained a scholarship from the Royal Academy of Fine Arts, San Fernando, Spain, and later studied at the Academy of Fine Arts in Rome. He spent a number of years researching anatomy and perspective. El-Sayed has shifted between realism, expressionism and abstraction. His brushstrokes are bold and thick. He continuously searches for a new means of expression while maintaining a basis of traditional technique.

Composition
Oil on canvas
90 x 135 cm
1980

NABIL SHEHADEH
Jordan, b. 1950

Nabil Shehadeh is a painter whose work explodes with the reflective energy of silent observation. Born in Jerusalem, Shehadeh moved to Amman at the age of eleven. His detachment from immediate surroundings and his early choice of the abstract may well represent an effort to transcend emotional ties to the human landscape. While highly skilled as a painter of pointillist watercolours, it is in his large abstract oils, some three by four meters, that Shehadeh achieves a distinctive collision of light and focus in layers of blue, brown and orange. Trained in England, Shehadeh has worked in Jordan and Switzerland.

Suggestion
Oil on paper
122 x 180 cm
1987

SAMER TABBAA
Jordan, b. 1945
Samer Tabbaa graduated in Fine Arts from the Youngstown State University, Ohio, and obtained his master's in sculpture from Kent State University. Tabbaa works mostly with stone and chooses his medium not only for its strength but also for the challenge it poses as an unworked piece. He has succeeded in creating a balance between form, mass and texture in his subject matter. He injects into his work a certain force, creating a harmony between artist and nature. Besides sculpturing Tabbaa also paints and engraves on zinc and copper, where the nature of the sculptor is clearly evident. Samer Tabbaa is one of the few artists who has had no trouble in breaking into the international arena.

Monolithic Gathering
Limestone
17 x 19 x 11 cm
7 x 40 x 12 cm
1977

MAHMOUD TAHA
Jordan, b. 1942
Taha moulds the clay of his native soil into full, smooth vessels that not only maintain an ancient tradition but also explore an innovative combination of textures, glazes and forms. Calligraphy, angular and stylized, functions as a counterpoint to the convex surfaces of his ceramics. In Taha's work the viewer may trace the natural hues of his ancient heritage. Taha is sensitive to the tension of tradition and change and does not hesitate to observe and explore new artistic interpretations of his rich, cultural roots. Taha graduated from the Academy of Fine Arts in Baghdad in 1968, and studied calligraphy under the famous calligrapher Hashim Moustafa al-Baghdadi. Later he continued his art training at Cardiff College of Arts in Wales.

Untitled
Ceramic
40 x 40 x 9 cm
1980

ADNAN YEHIA
Jordan, b. 1960
Adnan Yehia is a young and promising painter. His ink drawings are captivating, reflecting a deep concern for man's struggle, while his solitary figures reflect tragic anger, anxiety and turmoil. His works are characteristically the monumental rocks, symbolizing strength, and the bird, which is a symbol of hope and optimism in a widely destructive universe. One senses a combination of symbolism and realism in his works. Yehia studied art education at the Teacher Institute in Amman and following his graduation in 1980 continued his studies at the Fine Arts Institute in Amman.

If I did not survive
Mixed media
70 x 83 cm
1987

Lebanon
Wijdan Ali

The rays of the first dawn of modern art in Lebanon, according to Western concepts, go back to the reign of Mir Fakhruldine al-Shehabi, at the beginning of the seventeenth century. He was determined to push Lebanon into the mainstream of Western civilization by ruling according to Western inspired methods. In 1613 Mir Fakhruldine visited Italy and was impressed by Renaissance art and architecture. Upon his return to Lebanon, he built a palace in Beirut in the Venetian style he had seen during his Italian visit, and encouraged an open door policy towards European culture and art, marking his era as a new artistic age in Beirut and on the Lebanese coast.

In the mountains, the opening of missionary schools and convents by different European missions where Western art, in its various forms, was taught, marked the beginning of artistic rebirth, while the introduction of the printing press by these missions made religion the axis of political, economic, social and cultural life. Thus the emergence of modern schools, accompanied by the introduction of the modern printing press and an open door policy towards Europe, formed the base for a cultural, artistic and intellectual awakening in the country. The Gothic style in art was quite popular in eighteenth century Lebanon. It eventually gave birth to a local Gothic school of painting distinguished by its vivid colours and exacting lines. Works from this school filled the halls and corridors of numerous churches and convents in mountain towns and villages.

With the advance of the eighteenth century, relations between Lebanon and the West multiplied and European works of art started coming in from Italy and Austria. They left their imprint on local artists such as Canaan Deeb, who became impressed when he was studying with the monks by Michelangelo and Raphael. He later studied painting with an Italian artist called Giusti and became the court artist to the Shehab princes. He mostly painted religious subjects and specialized in portraits which were most popular in both the eighteenth and nineteenth centuries especially among the wealthy, the clergy and those occupying important positions.

In the meantime, a wave of Orientalism in all its forms, be it military, political, cultural or artistic, had swept through Europe and reached its peak by the mid-nineteenth century. Accordingly, Orientalist artists came in droves to Beirut and the Lebanese coast, recording on paper and canvas every rock and pillar, monument and crevice they set eyes on. Their fascination with the East and its quaint customs made them paint its people in their national costumes and during their local celebrations. As a result of this deluge of Orientalist artists a new school of art was born in Beirut, the 'Marine School'.

The Early Pioneers

Being part of the Ottoman Empire, a great number of young people from Arab countries, including Lebanon, went to Istanbul to pursue their studies in the Turkish academies. The artistic trend there was military painting, mostly done by army officers. This Turkish school of painting was yet another factor to influence the Lebanese Marine School. Its mark was apparent in the depiction of historical events and sea battles, with the inclusion of the largest number of people into the canvas in order to emphasise the historical importance of the depicted event. It concentrated on painting scenes of the Lebanese coast, with its fascinating scenery and luminous atmosphere, historical maritime events and ships. Among the important figures of this school was Ibrahim Sarabiyye known for his masterpiece commemorating the arrival of Emperor Wilhelm II of Germany at the port of Beirut; Ali Jamal al-Beiruti who had graduated as a naval officer from the War School in Istanbul where he later settled and taught painting; a young man from the Dimashqya family, Hassan Tanner; Mohammad Said Mir'i, who later emigrated to the United States; Najeeb Bekhazi, who emigrated to Russia; Najeeb Fayyad, Abdullah Misr, Mirlay Ibrahim al-Najjar, who was a medical doctor with the Ottoman army and the most outstanding figure among the group, and Salim Haddad, who later emigrated to Egypt where he gained fame.

Among the early pioneers in art there is also Ibrahim Alyaziji, who was well known for his improvements to the letters of the Arabic press; yet his importance regarding the arts lies in the exact drawings he made of his friends and relatives, both in colour and in charcoal. They radiate strength of expression, tactful use of colour and sensitivity of lines. Some of his works have been saved and are kept at the National Library in Beirut but, unfortunately, most of the works by artists of the second half of the nineteenth century were lost and those remaining tell us that this group of early pioneers were mostly amateurs, lacking the proper academic training and the right technical skill. What helped them in their pursuit of art was their raw talent and relentless dedication. An exception to the rule was Raiif Shdoudi, the only one to apply the normative principles of art during his rather short career.

First Generation of Pioneers

With the closing of the nineteenth century an important era for Lebanese culture started. Beirut had become the bridge between East and West, witnessing the birth of the theatre, the public library, commercial printing, the newspaper and the university which brought with them an increase of Western influences on the cultural and artistic life of the city.

The true pioneers of modern art in Lebanon appeared at the end of the nineteenth and the beginning of the twentieth century. Most of them had been to Brussels, Rome, Paris and London seeking the proper artistic training and gaining first-hand knowledge of classical and contemporary Western art. Among the first was Daoud Corm (1852–1930). One of the important artists of his generation, he went to Rome in 1870 to study with Roberto Pampiani who was the artist for the Italian court. After completing his training, he became a professional artist and was appointed to King Leopold and the Belgian royal family. He was invited by Pope Pius IX, whose portrait he did, as well as the portraits of Khedive Tawfik and his family in Egypt. Later when Khedive Abbas ascended the throne he invited him to visit Egypt and paint his portrait too. He also completed the portraits of several local governors in Lebanon.

With Daoud Corm there were Habib Srour (1860–1938) and Ni'amat Allah Maadi. They were mostly interested in religious subjects and their works decorated the walls of countless churches and convents.

Khaleel Saleeby (1870–1928) was the only one among this group to rebel against the popular genre of classical religious subjects. He followed the Impressionist school, emphasizing light, colour and movement. He was nicknamed 'the rebel' and was alienated from his peers, who felt secure in their classicism.

Others of the same generation were Philippe Mourani, who lived in Paris and painted in the classical tradition with an Eastern feeling, and Shukri Mousawer, who in spite of emigrating to the United States painted Oriental subjects after the European Orientalist School. This group of artists were the ones to introduce the principles of drawing coupled with the techniques of painting in oils and watercolours, showing the importance of light and shade according to Western classical norms.

Second Generation of Pioneers

Suddenly, and without a transitional period, a second generation of pioneers appeared. They were Youssef Hoyeck, Khalil Gibran and Youssef Ghassoub. In spite of the various contradictory influences exerted on them by Western art schools, which might have made them feel uprooted, they never suffered from a loss of identity. Without binding themselves to the local genre of traditional religious art, their aim was to take advantage of what the West and their predecessors had to offer, and produce original creations.

Youssef Hoyeck (1883–1962) studied in Rome and Paris and lived twenty years in the West where he was influenced by works of both the Renaissance artists and Rodin's tormented style, before coming back to settle in his own country and practise painting and sculpture. He was instrumental in the birth of modern Lebanese sculpture, and many of the fourth generation artists were his disciples.

Gibran Khalil Gibran (1883–1931) is best known for his contributions both to English and Arabic literature, yet he was an accomplished painter who had trained in Paris before emigrating to the United States, where both his writing and painting reached full maturity. There was a symbiotic relationship between the two forms of expression where his symbolism was manifested. His originality enabled his paintings to remain independent of any outside influences and in this lies his strength as an artist.

Youssef Ghassoub (1898–1967) differs from his contemporaries by having received his initial training in art with the father of Arab sculpture, the Egyptian Mahmoud Mukhtar, instead of a Western master. Later on he went to Paris and Rome in order to sharpen his technique. He left in Palestine, Syria and Lebanon more than one hundred works executed in his traditional academic style. A fourth artist, George Corm, should also be included with this group for his classical drawings and research in art.

Pioneers of Modern Art

The most important generation of artists appeared after World War I. They were the ones to lay the foundation for modern art in Lebanon, and their impact is still felt up to the present day. Their work exhibits a great spirit of freedom and originality, both in style and expression, that the two previous generations never knew. They were shown the right direction by Corm, Srour and Saleeby at the very beginning of their lives, helping them gain self-confidence, and establishing their artistic roots within the familiar atmosphere of their own national culture, while saving them the agitation and commotion that Western schools of art were going through in Europe, after the traumatic experience of the first global war.

The leaders of the third generation were Moustafa Farroukh (1902–1957), Cesar Gemayel (1898–1958), Omar Onsi (1901–1969), Saleeby Douaihy (b. 1912) and Rashid Wehbi (b. 1917). Like their predecessors, they also started their artistic lives by getting their training in the West and experiencing at firsthand the various new trends in art that were emerging on the European post-war scene, such as Dadaism, Fauvism and others, which soon spread to most parts of the world.

When this generation matured, they found that art in Lebanon was a luxury enjoyed within the confines of churches and palaces. Only the clergy and the rich could afford such a privilege. Having come from humble backgrounds and underprivileged families, the world of art was alien to them. Farroukh's father was an illiterate man, repairing copper utensils. Rashid Wehbi's father was a poor school teacher whose son's consuming passion for art made him sell his share of the family house in order to be able to paint. Cesar Gemayel worked on mountain roads breaking stones in order to save money and study pharmacy before the artist in him emerged. A life full of hardships and poverty was shared by the third generation of pioneers. Had it not been for their dedication and great talent, they would never have been able to be the founders of modern art in their country. The training they had in the ateliers of the previous generation of pioneers, before their departure to Roman and Parisian academies, was a major factor in assisting them in safeguarding their national identity and keeping their links with their heritage and culture. Farroukh, Douaihy and Wehbi started with Habib Srour, while Gemayel and Onsi trained with Khaleel Saleeby.

By the time this group went to Europe, religious subjects had been replaced there by the depiction of national events and heroes, which had an effect on their choice of subject matter. Upon their return to their homeland, they became instrumental in awakening a national feeling of pride in the recent history of Lebanon. They depicted Lebanon in all its aspects and from every angle. Today, their works consist of a wealth of documentation regarding the coastline and mountains, the people in their traditional costumes and local customs, recorded in the minutest detail. The only one among the five artists to abstract his subjects was Douaihy who was also known for his 'Douaihy style'. Still, he used indigenous forms like the Shalwar (local trousers worn by mountain people) turning them into abstract motifs. One of the main contributions of this group was to popularise art and make it accessible to the masses. By giving art lessons at schools, such as Sagesse and Makassed, they transmitted to their students the training they had at the studios of their predecessors coupled with whatever new Western techniques and skills they had gained during the years of their formal art education abroad. They laid the foundation for a modern renaissance in art, familiarising the public with an innovative style in oils and watercolours based on the Impressionist school. They were the ones to found a distinctive style that could be called a Lebanese school of art.

Exhibitions

Prior to the opening of the Academy of Fine Arts, there was a series of exhibitions encouraged and patronized by the French Mandate authorities in order to demonstrate the cultural aspect of their rule. Nevertheless, this made Beirut an important and active cultural centre. The major exhibitions were the ones held at the Arts and Crafts School in 1931 and 1932. Cesar Gemayel and Rashid Wehbi took part in the former, with Gemayel showing a nude drawing that aroused lots of interest among the conservative Beiruti society of the time. There was an exhibition by a French artist, Georges Cyr, who had settled in Lebanon and had a strong influence on artists of the younger generation. In 1934 an exhibition was held at the Saint-Georges Hotel by the newspaper *La Syrie* in which Habib Srour and Philippe Mourani took part as well as Moustafa Farroukh and Rashid Wehbi. Finally there was a big exhibition of Lebanese art held at the Parliament Building in 1936.

After independence, in the forties, three major exhibitions left their mark on the art scene: the Dhour Shoueir exhibition, organized on the occasion of the first cultural congress held in Beit Mery in 1947, an exhibition organized by UNESCO in 1949 at its headquarters, which was the starting point for periodical exhibitions held there every year since, and in 1953 an exhibition prepared by third generation artists for Lebanese art, entitled 'Bird Around the World'.

The Lebanese Academy of Fine Arts

In 1937, Alexis Boutros founded the Lebanese Academy of Fine Arts where foreign and local teachers gave lessons. Through it, the teaching of art and art education became accessible to those who sought it, regardless of their means or backgrounds.

The Fifties

When the Second World War ended, young people in Europe showed a desire to cut all ties with the past and to adopt new styles of art. In Lebanon a fourth generation of artists was emerging. It started emulating its Western counterparts. Although they never went through the harsh and cruel experiences of war, deprivation and demoralization which bred a rejection of old standards and values, yet, due to the inevitable communications between the two groups, Lebanese artists tried to live the experience of their Western counterparts by trying their hand at the different art movements that were then in vogue. Unfortunately, Lebanese artists could never be part of the world they were trying to penetrate. It was a world foreign to them, with different problems and complications that they could not relate to. For the first time they experienced the feeling of being lost between two worlds and belonging to none. The deluge of Western education and culture to which they were being exposed was another reason for the loss of identity that the fourth generation of artists was experiencing. Most of the artists of the fifties came from conservative societies in mountain towns and villages where for decades past mostly Arabic literature, history and culture were taught, alongside religion and a smattering of science. They descended to Beirut, attracted to the capital like moths to the light. There they were flooded by Western philosophy, literature, history, sociology, psychology, music, art, theatre and a new set of social codes and values, creating in them a psychological and cultural schizophrenia. In spite of the university degrees those young graduates had just obtained, there were not enough job opportunities to absorb them all, which caused disappointment and resentment among them, pushing some to focus their attention on the arts as an escape from their newly found frustrations. Thus, there were those who became Surrealists, Cubists or Abstractionists by just copying the forms without knowing anything about the components of those schools. Their works emerged full of superficiality and devoid of meaning, message or even the right principles of art. As a result of this abyss into which most artists in the fifties fell, some like Michel Murr (1930–1970) came to a tragic end while others succeeded in getting out of their dilemma and regained their national and cultural identity. There were a few who, due to the solid beginnings they had at the hands of the third generation of artists and in the classrooms of the Lebanese Academy of Fine Arts, were saved from committing the mistakes of the majority of their peers. Very few artists continued their blind imitation of Western styles. Those who were able to escape the dilemma emerged from the experience stronger than before, with a deeper understanding of their environment and culture, a stronger sense of belonging to both without bias or chauvinism and a drive towards individuality in style and expression. They constituted the fourth generation, characterised by their firm grip on technique and innovation in executing subjects relating to their way of life and environment. Among a group of painters are Fareed Awad (b. 1924), Shafiq Abboud (b. 1926), Jean Khalifeh (b. 1923), Mounir Eido (b. 1920), Said Akl (b. 1926), Yvette Ashkar (b. 1928), Rafic Sharaf (b. 1932), Paul Guiragossian (b. 1926), Adel Sagheer (b. 1930), Arif al-Rayess (b. 1928), Haleem Jourdak (b. 1927) and Helen Khal (b. 1923). All of them called for originality and innovation in style and rejection of the old familiar genres. As for the sculptors, there are Haleem Haj (b. 1915), the brothers Michael (b. 1921), Alfred (b. 1924) and Joseph (b. 1929) Basbous who were the main figures in developing contemporary sculpture in Lebanon, Salwa Rawda Shucair (b. 1916) experimenting with new materials such as plastic, aluminium and polyester, Mounir Eido (b. 1920) and the late comer Muazzaz Rawda (b. 1906). Each of the above mentioned artists has contributed in his own way to the advancement of plastic art in Lebanon. Some, like the sculptor Nazim Irani (b. 1930) and painter Wahib Batdini, preferred to stay within the boundaries of the pioneers' school and dealt with subjects directly connected to the Lebanese soil; others, like

Haleem Haj (b. 1915) and Sameeh Attar, remained within the framework of the classical academy.

In 1952, Nicholas Sursock bequeathed his house to the municipality of Beirut and it became the Nicholas Ibrahim Sursock Museum. In 1961 it started the first of 10 art salons. The museum also organized numerous local and international art and architectural exhibitions in Beirut and abroad. In 1954 the American University of Beirut opened its Department of Fine Arts. It had American artists on its faculty who gave art lessons, held art seminars and popularized the teaching of art. In 1957 the association of Lebanese Artists, Painters and Sculptors was founded in Beirut, further consolidating the position of artists.

The Sixties Onwards

When the time for the fifth generation of artists came, the post-war art turmoil in the West had settled down and artists came to realise the importance of having a solid base of academic training. The training that members of this generation received, whether in the West or in their own country, helped them find their own style and go through their personal artistic experiments, without loss of identity or alienation. In the meantime, Beirut had become the intellectual centre of the Middle East, with an influx of all kinds of local and international exhibitions from all parts of the world. The Fine Arts Institute had opened at the Lebanese University in 1965 and Beirut College for Women (Beirut University College) had already established its Fine Arts Department. Several Lebanese artists were enjoying international recognition, and the capital reached the peak in bridging the gap between Eastern and Western cultures.

Regardless of the various foreign factors affecting the Lebanese art scene, Beirut in the sixties had become a most interesting and exciting place for an Arab artist to live. It had enjoyed all the right elements of material prosperity coupled with the existence of seasoned art critics and countless platforms in daily newspapers, weekly and monthly periodicals, published in three main languages, Arabic, English and French, on whose pages they could air their views on local artists as well as international artistic events. In addition to exhibitions, almost every day, there were several workshops, seminars, lectures, symposiums and discussions on art held at the different galleries, universities, colleges, clubs, cultural centres and the UNESCO headquarters. Doubtless, all these elements played an important role in cultivating public taste and ingraining if not art education then art awareness among its educated members; and eventually developing among the rich and the intellectual middle class the habit of starting art collections and taking pride in owning a masterpiece done by a national artist. This accelerating desire to collect works of art led to a boom in the art market which in its turn led to the flourishing of art galleries, creating a demand for good works and encouraging the artists to increase their output while abiding by recognized standards. Thus we see the existence of a healthy circle of dynamic interaction between the artist, the public, the critic and the art dealer in an atmosphere of intellectual freedom, without any interference or pressure, either from the authorities or any other group. This created an art movement that interacted with other Arab as well as international art movements with openness, impartiality and audacious experimentations.

By calling for the freedom of the artist in expressing his individuality through his work, regardless of popular taste, which had deteriorated due to centuries of foreign occupation, cultural stagnation and aping of the West, the Lebanese art movement has contributed towards the enrichment of Arab plastic arts. This same art movement was able to establish for itself a new order that was more adventurous and freer than the old orders descending from the age of the Renaissance. It glorified individuality and originality as opposed to emulation and great proficiency. During the twenty-five years preceding the civil war, the Lebanese artist succeeded in introducing many modern artistic values pertaining to his subject as well as his style in the way of a new humanistic interpretation. He almost succeeded in introducing his art into everyday life and breaking the barriers between him and society's institutions and individuals by abandoning the marginal role it had been assigned so far. Among the independent innovators who have enriched and continue to enrich local and Arab plastic creative works are Amin Elbacha (b. 1932), Nadia Saikaly (b. 1936), Hassan Jouni, Farid Haddad, Assador Bazdekian, Odile Mazloum (b. 1942), Monir Najm (b. 1933), Amine Saghier (b. 1931), Wajieh Nahleh (b. 1932), Juliana Seraphime (b. 1934), Suha Tamim (1936–1986), Edward Lahoud, Paul Guiragossian, Hussein Madi and Moussa Tiebi.

The Lebanese civil war which started in the mid-seventies dealt a fatal blow to one of the most developed art movements in the Arab world. It not only put a stop to its growth but set it back decades by disrupting all the social and moral values as well as artistic values that had taken artists years to build, breeding in them a sense of banality, disappointment and despair. Difficult living conditions were brought about by the humiliation of the Israeli invasion, the breakdown of the economic order, the bloody internal sectarian and political feuds. The state of lawlessness that the country fell into gave rise to a segment of society whose creed was 'might is right' and who eventually succeeded in occupying a position of power, made a number of artists drop their emphasis on original expression and individuality in style in favour of decorative works that borrow from old indigenous motifs and were accessible to the general taste. Thus they chose the easy way out by lowering their standards to please the general public and produce what could be easily marketed. Still, judgement should be withheld, for the cruel living conditions under which artists have to live, coupled with their struggle for survival during the longest internal strife in this century, could easily lead to impotence in original creativity.

Most of the activities pertaining to art that were taking place before the civil war had to come to a halt. Many artists, in order to be able to continue their work, either chose or were forced to leave their country and live abroad. This drain of talent created a void in various fields of all forms of art. Even though artists continue to create and hold exhibitions and performances abroad, yet their efforts are scattered among several countries and continents, creating difficulty in communications between them and their public as well as among themselves.

The contemporary Lebanese art movement is a rare example of a natural and gradual evolution, based on solid academic training and the inspiration of its national heritage that culminated in an individual and authentic experiment of original creation and personalized style. Its creators practised in an environment of intellectual freedom, epitomizing the aim of most Islamic and Arab artists today. Suddenly, the rise of unforeseen elements of ignorance and brutal force trampled creativity and intellect, breaking the golden cycle and halting a truly advanced and liberated movement in art. Yet with the great wealth of talent that Lebanon has enjoyed for more than a hundred years, it could not negate its past achievements nor can it stop forever those of the future.

See colour pp. 101–106 for plates of the following artists' work:

CHAFIC ABBOUD
ETEL ADNAN
SALIBA DOUAIHY
AMIN ELBACHA
PAUL GUIRAGOSSIAN
SUHA TAMIM

EMMANUEL GUIRAGOSSIAN
Lebanon, b. 1954
Guiragossian worked with his father Paul until 1968. Later he entered the Academy of Fine Arts in Lebanon, then left for Paris and Florence. After completing his studies in anatomy in Düsseldorf in 1980, Emmanuel became associated with the German Neo-Expressionist Group. His work, on which his deep understanding of anatomy has had an important effect, has progressed through various phases, including realism, expressionism and abstract expressionism. Like the professional surgeon, he examines the human condition very closely, confronting the viewer at close range with a series of tortured ligaments or cracking bones. He is aware of the tragic events that surround him – war, peace, life and death. His paintings are full of pain and his brushstrokes bold with anger.

Untitled
Oil on canvas
80 x 60 cm
Undated

HELEN KHAL
Lebanon, b. 1923
Born in Allentown, USA, Khal graduated from the Fine Arts Academy in Beirut in 1948 then went to New York where she studied at the Art Students' League, graduating in 1950. Like most artists from this part of the world her style alternated between the impressionist and the abstract, yet through all her artistic experience, colour and light remain her main aim more than form or line. Her style is based on masses of colours depicting country landscapes, the sea, the desert, mountains and plateaux. Her use of colour is free and comfortable – mostly bright hues that define her spaces and forms by gradation.

Untitled
Oil on canvas
80 x 100 cm
1979

JULIANA SERAPHIME
Lebanon, b. 1934

Juliana trained in Lebanon, then at
the Florence Academy and the
Madrid Academy. She has
developed a futuristic art that
balances on the edge of surrealism
without indulging in its morbidity.
Her shapes reflect hope and
ethereal beauty, a world of happy
colours filled with nature, with the
'Flower Woman' at its centre.
Despite the delicate traits in her
portraits, she is an artist of iron
resolution who carefully studies
every image, elegant line and
fuchsia before putting it on canvas.
Whether in oil painting or graphic
drawing, she shows a firm grasp on
technique, a strength of expression
and a relentless desire for
perfection. Juliana is an established
artist who has penetrated the world
of art and beauty through
perseverance and talent.

Flying Horse
Oil on canvas
80 x 100 cm
Undated

Libya

Wijdan Ali

The modern art movement in Libya has depended mainly on individual artists, such as Taher al-Maghribi and Ali Moustafa Ramadan, who became prominent in the fifties. In the sixties most notable were Ali Omer Ermes and Farjani, a deaf artist whose output, however, is limited.

Students are exposed to art through lessons in secondary schools, of which some have good art sections, but that is as far as many artists progress in their art training. Both al-Fateh University in Tripoli and Garunis University in Benghazi have art classes which provide somewhat formal training. There is also the School of Arts and Crafts in Tripoli. In the past, a number of artists have gone to art colleges in Egypt and Europe, especially the Fine Arts Academy in Rome; among these were Taher al-Maghribi, Ali Gana, Bachir Hammouda and Ali al-Abani. Most of them returned to Libya feeling enthused by Western art schools and the Italian artistic spirit, others felt it a waste of time; the latter did their own thing and never referred back to their training, while some stayed for extended periods of time in Europe. Ali Omer Ermes stayed on in England and at present is possibly the only Libyan artist to be living and working abroad.

Formerly there were several artists' organizations; the most famous was the Libyan Painters' Association which later on was obliged by the government to merge with the writers, actors and others to form the Union of Libyan Artists. On the official side, the Fine Arts Section of the General Directorate of Culture, which is part of the Ministry of Information, is concerned with artistic affairs.

In the past, modern Libyan artists have had a rich artistic experience through exhibitions, travel and exposure. They were well trained in European and Arab academies, have been active teaching, writing and lecturing, and some of them, like Taher al-Maghribi, Ali Moustafa Ramadan and Ali Omer Ermes, have influenced other Arab artists.

Since 1980 when the Third Arab Biennale of the General Association of Arab Artists was held in Tripoli, cultural contacts between Libya and other countries have been precluded due to the government's policy and not much is known about the development of the modern art movement in Libya; at the same time there is virtually no information published outside Libya and access to information inside the country is also virtually impossible.

See colour p. 107 for plate of the following artist's work:

ALI OMER ERMES

Malaysia

Syed Ahmad Jamal

Malaysia comprises the mainland peninsula, Sarawak and Sabah in the big island of Borneo. Because of its position at the crossroads of maritime activity the Malay peninsular, known to Ptolemy as Khersonesos and later as the Golden Chersonese, has seen human activity since time immemorial. Cord-decorated pottery from cave dwellings show a good sense of form which was also evident in works done during the Hindu Sri Vijaya period from the seventh to the thirteenth century. Islam came to peninsular Malaysia in the fourteenth century and with it the beautiful Arabic calligraphy. The Malays who became Muslims infused Islamic principles into art works such as woodcarving, embroidery, weaving and metalwork. An interesting work of a high order of aesthetic plasticity is the group of stone menhirs about 90 kilometres south of Kuala Lumpur which include the 'Sword' stone which has a stylized human figure and the word 'Allah' carved in relief, and the 'Rudder' stone with a landscape showing mythical animals. Nearby is the grave of the 'Saint of Prawn River' with Arabic calligraphy in relief, dated 1467/8.

Malaysian art in the convention of easel-painting can be traced back to the topographic drawings and watercolour paintings by the British colonial officers from the eighteenth to twentieth centuries. The art of watercolour painting in the English tradition of romantic rendition of the landscape influenced a generation of artists.

Malaysian art as we know it goes back to the 1930s, introduced by British colonial educators and by a number of immigrant artists from south China.

After the Second World War art education was emphasised in schools and teacher training institutions. By the beginning of the fifties, Malaysia already had a few established and committed artists. In the early years of the fifties, a few personalities dominated the Malaysian art scene. Yong Mun Sen was one, with his uncomplicated landscapes, executed in fluid washes, of sun-filled spaces of ubiquitous village scenes and palm-fringed beaches. Mun Sen's highly accomplished oils were more resolved than his watercolours. Abdullah Ariff's works by comparison were more involved technically with a certain level of consciousness.

Cheong Soo-Pieng in Singapore and Chuah Thean Teng in Pulau Pinang, received formal art education in China. Their academic training was evident in the handling of form and in the sense of plasticity of the figure. The interaction of form and space relates their works to the Western pictorial tradition. The influence of post-Cubist schools is evident in their works. The immigrant artists founded the 'Nanyang' (South Seas) art academy in Singapore in 1937.

Art groups and organizations in the fifties were instrumental in the development of Malaysian art which was a response to the mounting excitement of Independence. The Arts Council, formed in 1951, played a big role in the development of art in Malaysia in the fifties and sixties. This independent body was responsible for supporting art activities such as music, drama, and the visual arts.

An important art group in the immediate pre- and post-Independence years (late fifties and early sixties) is the Wednesday Art Group, which met on Wednesdays under the leadership of Peter Harris, an expatriate art educationist who introduced modern concepts of art to a group of aspiring artists eager for knowledge and techniques in painting.

Another important art group is the Peninsular Artists' Movement founded in 1956 headed by Mohammad Hoessein Enas. The group was involved with realistic figurative presentation and identified itself with national identity.

By the time of Independence in 1957, the plastic arts had assumed a symbolically unifying form of expression for Malaysians transcending cultural barriers.

Art symbolized Malaysia's arrival in the contemporary age, from low-key provincialism to sophisticated internationalism. The artists' efforts were related to the forces that were forging the nation. By the time the momentum was reaching its ultimate goal of independence, contemporary aesthetics had become the universal norm.

The National Art Gallery was established in 1958. This official recognition boosted the confidence of Malaysian artists. Their works would be collected, properly housed and presented to the public in a national institution.

The first big effort to present Malaysian art overseas was the Malaysian Art Travelling Exhibition of more than 100 works. It was first shown in the Kelvingrove Art Gallery in Glasgow, as part of the Commonwealth Arts Festival in the autumn of 1965, and later in London and other European cities. The exhibition received favourable comments from European art critics.

The artists of the fifties and sixties subscribed mainly to the aesthetics of Abstract Expressionism. The immediacy and mystical quality of the mainstream art of the 1960s appealed to the Malaysian temperament, sensitivity and cultural heritage. With the tradition of calligraphy, they found in that idiom the ideal means of expression. Malaysian artists developed rapport with the bold gestures of Kline, Soulages, Hartung, Mathieu, Sugai and others. The gestural qualities of their works as expressive visual language have obvious affinity with the art of calligraphy, the cultural heritage of Malays and Chinese.

The sixties gave birth to a more critical approach to art. Malaysian artists questioned the validity of their work in the context of Malaysian culture and in relation to the international scene. The end of the sixties saw the artists' involvement with local materials and local environment as ingredients of visual imagery. They entered a new era of awareness, probing into their consciousness, environment, and cultural heritage.

The seventies saw the beginning of a change in direction in Malaysian art away from the strong influence of Abstract Expressionism. Malaysian artists not only worked in the realm of Hard-edge, Minimalism, Pop, Op, and other trends of the seventies but also postulated artistic situations involving perspicacity, mystical and metaphysical values, information, and knowledge traditionally outside the realm of painting. There also arose an awareness of the social role of the artist. The decade saw a growing awareness of a common cultural heritage with countries in the south-east Asian region.

The Malaysian Artists' Association was founded in 1980 to fulfil the need for a national body representing the artists.

The beginning of the eighties saw the flowering of art patronage. Art entrepreneurship also began to play a more positive role. The development of facilities for art presentation resulted in an increase in the number of exhibitions with emphasis on the younger artists.

The presentation of art works also became more sophisticated. Sales and attendance at exhibition openings were encouraging in spite of a general, world-wide economic recession.

Malaysian artists have turned away from complete reliance on the West for any move in avant-garde art; they are no longer intimidated by not being part of the latest trends in the international art scene.

The eighties saw a greater awareness of Islamic principles in art. In 1984 the Islamic Civilization Exhibition was an attempt to give shape to the notion of pictorial art created within the framework of Islamic ideological principles. In a seminar which followed the exhibition, it was posited that in a pluralistic society, Islamic aesthetic principles could be accepted by non-Muslims in the same way that Christian and Zen principles had influenced the works of Muslim artists.

In 1986 the National Art Gallery was accused by a group of Muslim fundamentalists of displaying pornographic paintings. A sensation-seeking tabloid capitalised on the question. The issue was debated in parliament, with the Gallery asserting differences between erotic, pornographic, sensual, sensuous and suggestive. The explanation was accepted and the matter closed.

The second half of the eighties finds Malaysia in a different emotional state from the first half of the decade. The euphoric mood injected by prosperity has turned to sobriety. Efforts at catapulting the country into the ranks of the industrialised nations by the twenty-first century have slowed down in the process of recession. The fall in the value of material commodities and political trends raises questions on traditionally accepted notions of the economic system, political and social structure.

Towards the end of the eighties art has become popular, especially with the younger generation. Busloads of school children descend on the National Art Gallery at weekends, from Kuala Lumpur and beyond. They respond to the works of art, especially painting, as something meaningful and related in some ways to their lives. It is interesting to observe the young visitors trying to fathom the meaning and mystery of the art works.

Malaysian artists are using media other than acrylic, oil or watercolour and venturing into paper-pulp, fibre, fibre-glass, photo-collage, clay, metal and various kinds of materials.

Among a number of Malay (Muslim) artists, Islamic principles have become central to their artistic commitment. The students and graduates of the Fine Arts Department of the MARA Institute of Technology have been involved in the realisation of art works within the framework of Islamic aesthetics.

Malaysian artists reflect awareness of the social role of artists. They have held exhibitions supporting the cause of the Palestine question, the Vietnam refugees, anti-nuclear devastation, natural heritage (ecology), shelter for the homeless and other socio-political issues.

The art scene has become active again in the late eighties. There has been renewed interest in art. Private corporations commission or purchase works of art for publicity projects. Hotels and offices have begun to enhance their premises with works by Malaysian artists, instead of imported reproductions, or allocate spaces in their premises for art displays. The private sector has shown interest in Malaysian art as a form of investment. Art activities have become popular items in official and cultural events.

The developing state of art has encouraged greater activity by artists, especially the younger ones who are mostly products of local art schools. But it is not all exhibitions. In 1988 the National Art Gallery held a seminar on 'Art and Society' followed by 'Art and Business' by University Sains, Penang, in 1989. Workshops by local and foreign artists in various areas of visual art have helped the late 80s become a lively period of Malaysian art. There is greater interest and interaction between art and the public, especially in the private sector. Malaysian art is in a dynamic state moving confidently towards an optimistic future.

See colour pp. 108–111 for plates of the following artists' work:

NG BUAN CHERS
ISMAIL HASHIM
SYED AHMAD JAMAL
SHARIFA FATIMAH ZUBIR

KHALIL IBRAHIM
Malaysia, b. 1934
Khalil Ibrahim's formal training was at St. Martin's School of Art in London. Ibrahim is one of Malaysia's leading exponents of the art of Batik painting. In his works the human form is a dominant theme. He places emphasis on the linearity of form and the movement of figures. His choice of vibrant colours and the overall simplicity of his works reflect sensitivity and are both fresh and appealing.

Eastcoast Series
Acrylic on canvas
107 x 132 cm
1988

NIRMALA SHANMUGHALINGAM
Malaysia, b. 1941
Her formal art training was at the Corcoran School of Art, the Fogg Museum of Art at Harvard University, and Oxford Polytechnic, England. Shanmughalingam's concerns are the human condition and its predicaments. She has devoted herself full-time to expressing her bitter feelings about the social and political status prevailing in the world today, particularly in Vietnam, Lebanon and Afghanistan. Reality is her source and the biting messages are stated in direct, unglamorous photo-journalistic imagery.

Beirut 4
Acrylic on canvas
121.9 x 205.7 cm
1983

LONG THIEN SHIH
Malaysia, b. 1946
Thien Shih is one of Malaysia's distinguished printmakers. Printmaking gained a special importance in Malaysia's art world during the seventies. Shih's formal art training was at the Ecole Nationale des Beaux Arts in Paris and subsequently at the Royal College of Art in London. Shih has immersed himself full-time in printmaking; whether in silkscreen, lithography or etching he has an ability, through humorous and bitter allusion, to focus our attention with sharp realism on the world we live in. Shih has played an active role in socio-political causes within the Malaysian art movement.

Artist and his Model
Oil on canvas
130 x 97 cm
1985

AHMAD KHALID YUSOF
Malaysia, b. 1934
Yusof's formal art education was in Liverpool, England, and at the Teachers' Training Institute, Cheras. He later studied at Winchester School of Art in England and at Ohio University in the United States. Yusof has explored the use of calligraphy and Jawi script forms as pictorial elements containing symbolic cultural connotations. In both acrylics and silkscreen work, he has succeeded in creating balanced calligraphical compositions with delicate lines and subtle colours.

Oh Stars! where is the Moon?
Acrylic on canvas
91.5 x 91.5 cm
1989

Morocco

Toni Maraini

The significance of modern painting in Morocco extends beyond the mere national importance of its existence and history. It has a relevance for contemporary art, whose strictly Western destiny is called into question each time it is confronted by works of art and movements from elsewhere.

Situated for centuries at the junction of several cultures (Saharan, Black African, Iberian, Phoenician, Berber, Carthaginian, Mediterranean, Middle Eastern and finally, Arab and Islamic), Morocco is infused by numerous, often unrecognised, aesthetic and intellectual traditions. Its contemporary art represents the essence of its affinities. Its painters do not well up from a cultural void; their painting is not the simple historical by-product of an art imported from the West.

For a long time, following this 'collection of roots' which caused them to discover what was modern before they realised their own inheritance, numerous painters undertook a search which revealed new horizons. Moreover, in their creativity, past, present and future did not follow a rigid chronology, but instead a system involving aesthetic pleasure, conceptual sense, the means of imaginative language and poetic intuition. This search affected a visionary and intellectual movement that belonged fully to the mainstream of the twentieth century, because they relied upon a primeval recollection and the desire to renew. The West should turn to Morocco for more than a search for sun, but try and participate in its complex and varied culture.

In releasing traditional, collective aesthetic norms from a multitude of individual visions, painting has assumed in Morocco the role of artistic conscience in the creativity and cultural education of a nation. This role has been very important in the evolution of a movement which has catalysed diffuse aspirations and understood how to profit from the support of vital, intellectual forces. Because it corresponds to something ever present and alive, and because it is able to communicate a language without a tongue (and thus without linguistic problems), painting has attracted to its mental hinterland a steadily growing number of works. Moroccan painting bears witness today to an exceptional journey within the panorama of the arts of Africa and the Middle East.

How should it be placed in the context of the modern movement and what is its history?

Modern Art and the International Movement

Modern art was born in the West, but apart from that it is not especially Western. We know that actually it was nurtured by factors from other civilisations and that certain eras and cultures created art forms that anticipated those of the twentieth century. It is also true that, from futurists to surrealists, numerous artists and theories of art spoke from the beginning of the worldwide importance of a universal art like the language of poetry. From its birth the modern movement saw itself as international. However, with the exception of certain isolated individuals, modern Western art has not been keen to admit into its artistic system (galleries, revues, museums, collections, etc.) contemporary groups and movements from other cultures.

As is well known, those artists who fought at the end of the nineteenth and beginning of the twentieth centuries to shake the foundations of the classical edifice of academic learning were all directly or indirectly influenced by the discovery of other artistic traditions. Without these influences modern art would not be the same. Such discoveries, whose historical import is often forgotten, fed the huge 'museum of the imagination', which today enriches our culture.

In 1912, the little almanac, *Der Blaue Reiter*, published, apart from works by Matisse, Klee, Delaunay, Kupka, Kandinsky and van Gogh, work from Japan, India, Egypt, Africa, the Pacific, works of popular art, works from the Middle Ages and work for children. A. Macke wrote, 'as if to mock European aesthetics, the forms everywhere speak an absolute language.'

It has been correctly observed that the interest shown by Western artists in African and Oriental art, as well as other arts in general, was prompted by their own uneasiness. In these art forms they rediscovered the academic tradition of the eighteenth and nineteenth centuries which had been censured and inhibited, and they tried to readmit it into the aesthetic awareness of their own period. We can be sure that today a similar phenomenon has forced many artists and non-Western groups into a polemic break with certain traditional norms in order to recover the original ethos and to inspire themselves with alternatives of modern art. The public has accepted, and with time even forgotten, that from Monet, Degas, van Gogh and Gauguin, to Picasso and Matisse, European painters have, on numerous occasions, discovered and sometimes adopted techniques, forms and symbols from other worlds of conception without losing their Western being. It has also heard about African form, Chinese calligraphy, Oriental arabesques, Japanese prints, of iconographies, images and universal matters otherwise ignored, and has learnt therefore to appreciate another aesthetic.

But what happens when it is told another story, the view from the other side, from the side of those who were 'discovered', for whom these art forms were seductive just because they were different? What happens when a culture classed as traditional meets modern works and welcomes the modern international movement? Usually the first reaction is one of surprise and rebuttal. One forgets whilst strolling in the streets of Kairawan, Tangiers, or Cairo, whilst visiting Java, Kyoto or Polynesia, that Klee, Matisse, Gauguin, Michaud or Tobey, to mention but a few, crossed paths with individuals whose histories were also in motion. From this forgetfulness and the idea of the 'unchanging tradition' and 'primitive purity' originated the shock felt by a public used to consider art as 'our business', without considering those who saw modernity as a curse from which other cultures should escape.

What modernity means must be investigated. Besides, has a modern international movement never existed except for the West?

Is it concerned only with a utopia, inherited and peddled by the project of modernity spoken of by J. Habermas?

Conversely, is it not true that the modern international movement really exists because different cultures took the project of the ideal at face value?

These questions are important because one should consider how each culture reacts in an international context to the blossoming of modern artistic thought.

It is more than just saying that everywhere and simultaneously the twentieth century has produced a new art – that is far from the case. Nor is it just saying that everywhere the West has reached will automatically produce modern painting. Neither colonialism nor neo-colonialism has exported or encouraged any form apart from in the most institutionalised aspect.

Some societies and cultures apart from the West have given birth to artists and movements of real import. In order for such art to exist it must benefit from the convergence of phenomena, convergence between potentialities, means, desires and needs, between certain turns of idea and visions of the world. The fact that certain forms, subjects and techniques, or certain styles, might on every occasion and for each culture be seen as proof of the other depends on the way in which each system itself responds to being expressed. In Morocco, for example, painting has dominated other techniques in art so far; a painting of surfaces, signs and symbols, a painting of spaces and images drawn from an iconoclastic cosmography and the organic matter of an ideal, geometrically pure world.

Historical Survey

Painting as a group of aesthetic rules and processes (pigments, colours, dyes, brushes, methods of application, etc.) apparently existed in Morocco before the arrival of the Europeans. This painting might either be integrated into an architectural space (ceilings, walls, panels, etc.), portable objects, and other surfaces and structures, or as part of the great Turco-Persian and Hispano-Arab traditions of illumination and miniature painting, that is to say a painting embellished by figurative imagery, an abstract structure and the line of calligraphy.

Within its own cosmography, the Islamic tradition used architectural space, the mandalic surfaces of the carpet and the spaces on the page and the manuscript wonderfully. It had no need to bring into focus, nor to borrow, this mobile space, this optical illusion of a square space which we call a 'picture', and which the miniature on the page doubtless anticipates whilst otherwise employing the illusory 'miniature setting' of the actual world.

Painting on an easel and its object-picture, however, came from the West. It cannot be said that they came with colonialism. Besides, under the French protectorate (in the north of Morocco, at the Escuela Preparatoria de Bellas Artes of Tetuan, the situation was somewhat different) 'the first introductory courses in drawing and painting . . . for young Muslims of both sexes' date from 1954,[1] whilst many Moroccans had chosen to paint pictures for a long time. We also know that exchanges, restricted to a few centres, had always existed between Morocco and Europe.

The excellent painter Juan de Pareja (c.1610–70), a Moorish slave of Seville, whose self-portrait hangs in the Metropolitan Museum in New York, was one of the best pupils of Velásquez. He was originally from Morocco and was also known as Juan de la Mora.

If we go back to the beginning of the century in search of documents to help us understand the historical genesis of modern art in Morocco, we discover that there were many individuals who were discreetly taking up painting at an easel, even though we cannot discover through whom or by what historical contacts (travel, acquaintances, etc.) and when the technique was brought from Europe.

The aristocrat el-Menebhi in Tangiers,[2] Abdesselam el-Fassi ben Larbi in Fez,[3] and Jilali ben Chelan[4] in Rabat, are recorded in archives. Their painting, which could be classified as neo-Impressionist, differs from the miniature paintings of their contemporaries (for example, the famous members of the Rabati family) as well as the work of popular painters.

The main merit of these painters, who considered themselves autodidacts, was to have escaped from the academic. Besides, the protectorate's administration did not set up a fine arts academy in Morocco. The time was not ripe for the acceptance of painters practising an intrinsically individualist art, which challenged traditional aesthetic knowledge and a certain conception of the real and its opposite.

However, in increasing numbers, painters were following, overtaking and transforming the example of their predecessors. Between the end of the 1940s and the beginning of the 50s, Aomar Mechmacha, Moulay Ahmed Drissi, Mohamed ben Allal, el-Hamri, Mekki Murcia, and Ahmed ben Driss el-Yaqoubi were exhibited, as well as the younger Farid Belkahia, Meriam Mezian, then Tayeb Lahlou, Hazdo el-Moznino, and many more. Certainly from the beginning, styles and tendencies were fairly varied. Some exhibited in the Salons. At the 5th Marrakesh Winter Salon, B. Saint-Aignan wrote enthusiastically of a renaissance of Muslim art in Morocco.

Because of the peculiar situation at the beginning of the period, these painters were for the most part self-taught. Those who had studied followed correspondence courses in art or followed an artistic fashion abroad. Others who had travelled a lot (such as Drissi and el-Yaqoubi) have been, perhaps too hastily, called 'naive painters' without trying to see how their works relate to popular pictorial and fantastic traditions.

When B. Saint-Aignan was writing, Morocco was engaged in its struggle for national independence. The intellectual ferment was enormous. Whilst in Morocco as before there were self-taught men and women artists, a new generation of painters (those born between 1930 and 1940) were to benefit at the time of independence (1956) from numerous study grants. Thus intent on pursuing their artistic development, F. Belkahia, J. Gharbaoui, M. Melehi, M. Meghra, A. Cherkaoui, S. Cheffaj, M. Chebaa and others left for Madrid, Rome, Paris, Warsaw, Prague, the Middle East and the United States. Imbued with different experiences, in contact with a Western world still optimistic about the historical import of modern art, their studies and development varied. However, it is this international range of experience, influenced by more than one culture, which identifies the art scene in Morocco. It is a situation which had to be created through a thorough renewal of structures, ideas and aims.

Upon their return to Morocco, some of these painters rebelled against the structural anachronisms and provincial culture.

Since other painters, often self-taught (such as Louardighi), had in the meantime been 'discovered', some maintained that 'naive' painting rather than the sophisticated complexities of modern art represented the true 'soul' of Morocco. There was speculation over the Moroccan claim to naive painting, a form of painting which, as we know, is a universal historical phenomenon. Meanwhile, many other artists, abstract and figurative, were exhibiting in foreign missions or in the other rare exhibition spaces. The idea was also advanced that a young Moroccan 'painting' had been born under the aegis of the Paris School. Without knowing which course to follow, exhibitions were organized in an unequal and heterogeneous way. With some rare exceptions (for example the Paris Biennale des Jeunes in 1959, which chose six Moroccan painters, of whom the famous critic, Lionello Venturi, wrote, 'a great surprise comes to us from Morocco, . . . where a modern, Western, truly seductive school of painting has been born', these mixed collections for a long time represented Morocco abroad.

We have all seen Third World exhibitions put together by circumstances and administrative ideologies. So it is surprising and unusual that artists in Morocco have succeeded after long battles in modifying this state of affairs and created a situation defined by its own peculiarities, its interests, and the quality of its output. Between 1964 and about 1970, a handful of artists, returning from their stays abroad and as a reaction to the local situation, have become the promoters of a new move beginning with the Ecole des Beaux Arts in Casablanca under the direction of Farid Belkahia who returned from Prague in 1962.

Their aims and art experienced difficulties. Belkahia, Melehi, Chebaa and other painters supported the action of Gharbaoui, Cherkaoui, Ataallah, Hafid, Hamidi, Cheffaj, and others. They saw themselves as the artistic conscience of the culture and the age. By criticising the politics of cultural missions at the time, poor artistic management, the lack of adequate facilities, discovering the basic modernity of some forms of popular, traditional art and pursuing very real research, organising independent exhibitions and initiating a debate on the practice and teaching of the arts in Morocco, they were responding to an historic need.

Painters from other Moroccan towns (Tetouan, Rabat and Marrakesh), as well as other creative people (writers, poets, architects, etc.) were interested in everything painting could convey in thought and culture. The history of the years 1960–80 began at this point because this action corresponded to a given intellectual and cultural situation. It was marked by the opening of private art galleries, the creation of cultural magazines, the realisation of many spontaneous projects of great breadth, diverse research into the realm of the plastic arts, the regrouping of artists, and the contact during the 70s with the artists of the Maghrib and the Arab world. We have already mentioned many artists who had meanwhile been shown; autodidacts (Chabia, Fatima Hassan, Aherdan) who were not inevitably 'naive', and others from the schools and art courses in Casablanca, Tetouan, Rabat, Marrakesh: A. Hariri, H. Miloudi, L. Miloud, M. Kacimi, H. Slaoui, F. Bellamine, and A. Rabi, M. Meliani, A. Sayed, then Saladi, A. Boujemaoui, the Sadouk brothers and many others. Hamid Berrada called them 'Young Wolves' in 1976.

Attitudes, debates, regroupings and quarrels are characteristic of an artistic milieu rich in individuals with varied attitudes. Sceptics who seek norms, national styles and hierarchies asked whether Moroccan painting really exists. By its own vital essence, painting proves its existence. But what is it that drives an ever increasing number of individuals to become artists? What is it that brings a very young generation to choose, everywhere in Morocco and with the same determination as their elders, the plastic arts as a means of expression, even though one cannot speak of a true art market or a sufficient infrastructure for so many vocations?

We spoke of a language without a tongue, an aesthetic tradition wrought in the depths by complex thought, an anthropocentric mythology with no legend and a theology of the absolute from which a new imaginative order (or disorder) draws its signs and images; only the creative process can assuage the ill-ease implied for us. The moveable object which is the 'painting' with its network of changes which it forms between individuals and groups shelters the tongue of each, setting it free from rigid structures.

What if painting and plastic art in general were one of the privileged places of a silent revolution of the imagination?

Tendencies, Painting and Painters

Moroccan painting evolved at the frontiers of the Western artistic system and then followed the rhythms of its own situation and the plurality of its courses. It has made choices of style and thought which perhaps are answering the needs of each area of pursuit and the worries of its own culture as well as the needs and requirements of the classic institutions of the modern world. Because it is not slave to the constant search for novelty in the pure linear evolution of modern art, Moroccan painting has escaped from the crisis and constraint in modern art today. It has already responded with a kind of post-modern situation to this fact without bitterness and with vitality.

It would be pointless attempting to analyse styles and tendencies whilst trying to determine groupings, influences, and precise stylistic labels. Rather it is those tendencies and principal streams or modes of expression of this century (Expressionism, abstract, lyrical, conceptual art, geometric, sign painting, figurative expressionism, etc.) which characterises the worldwide field of research by individual means and groups. This does not mean for Morocco the evolution or mutation of modern Western art; numerous Moroccan artists live abroad and create for themselves a professional problem. It is certainly true that a cultural retreat, necessary as a place of contemplation with theoretical distance, has allowed Moroccan painting to be creative away from the foreign constraint of a system and therefore to make its own choices.

It is within the context of autonomy and a basically psychological and aesthetic mobility that its best work and the result of its true history should be analysed. Because they are – as Pierre Restany said at Grenoble in 1984 – transhumant migrants between culture and metaphysics, we can call them trans-occidental painters.

Guided by the Islamic idea and vision of the world which embraces everything like Western culture, aristotelianism and neo-platonism, Moroccan painters have never lost sight of what their varied language can do and how their pictorial sensitivity can enchant: signs, marks, symbolic shapes, pen strokes, deep and poetic spaces of colour and surfaces; the interplay and quest for balance between opposing principles, where the pure concepts of a shattered ideal order are returned to the matter of the world and its images/model. A brief review of two generations of painters who worked at different times would shed some light on modern Moroccan painting.

Jilali Gharbaoui (died 1971) painted in the 50s and 60s. He was one of the first radically abstract painters. In creating a mannered tabula rasa of figural forms as well as the traditional geometrical order, his media and main gestures marked a salutary break. More lyrical and structured, the painting of Ahmed Cherkaoui (died 1967) marks a further step in this direction: the 'scrawling' of childish, symbolic features by Gharbaoui are revealed in Cherkaoui's work as signs of a maternal language (tattoos, etc.) to recreate thereby the elements of a strong, delicate script, pictographs of signs drawn to space and matter. Cherkaoui worked in the 60s.

Farid Belkahia, Mohamed Melehi, Labiad Miloud, Mohamed Kacimi and Abdelkebir Rabi each chose a different route, which began for Belkahia at the beginning of the 50s and for Melehi in 1957. They pursued different avenues and explored the primeval memory which Moroccan painting constantly brings to the imaginative consciousness of a new aesthetic order.

At various stages in their work these painters created rich and intense work, fundamental to the problem of Moroccan painting. It was painting where the metaphor of sign and the power of form are in a constant state of flux between the plane of the surface and fleeting depth. Few words do them adequate service.

Younger artists, Fouad Bellamine, Abderrahmane Meliani and Moustapha Boujamaoui have not had, like Gharbaoui, the need to make a first sacrilegious break. More sophisticated, their work is driven by clearly established aims: Boujamaoui, delicate and methodical in his signs, structure rhythms,and the texture of his spaces; the painting of Meliani is characterized by a strong sense of the paradox between the image and its poetry; he was thus one of the first Moroccan painters to be interested in conceptual art and structures. Drawn towards the dialectic interaction of surface/sign/texture/stroke, the painting of Bellamine marks a path in the quest for pure concepts expressed in gesture and form.

Chabia is exceptional, certainly as an individual. Discovered by Gaudibert, admitted to the Cobra group for painting as well as mere art, the painting of Chabia has stirred up in Morocco a confused reverie of the woman/matter, mater imaginis, with whom it and the public play gleefully.

Notes

1   *La Vigie*, March 1954, cf. Bernard Saint Aignan, 'La renaissance de la peinture musulmane au Maroc', B. Saint-Aignan and Edit PEFA, Morocco, n.d.
2   Beginning of the century 1972; his work is still unpublished.
3   Cf. B. Saint-Aignan, op. cit., pp. 19–20.
4   Quoted by R. Vaillant in 1931.

See colour pp. 112–115 for plates of the following artists' work:

ABOU ALI ABDEL AZIZ
AL HACHIMI AZZA
ABDULLA HARIRI
MOHAMED MELEHI

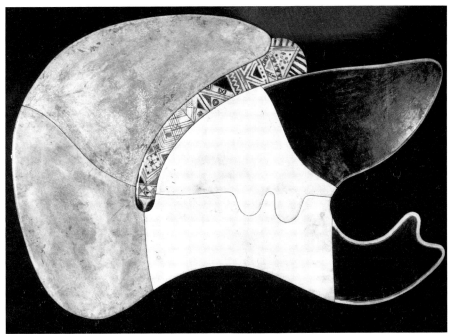

FARID BELKAHIA
Morocco, b. 1934
Belkahia transforms traditional Moroccan materials like leather by impregnating them with natural minerals, local dyes and herbs like henna and saffron and then stretching them into large abstract forms. Born in Marrakesh, Belkahia draws on magical symbols and rituals to make gigantic, abstract signs. Trained at L'Ecole des Beaux Arts in Paris, Belkahia then became the director of the School of Fine Arts in Casablanca where he still lives and works. His tattooed surfaces are often interacted by smooth fissures that suggest some primordial, almost organic unity between the separated sections. There are those who claim he is an artisan, not an artist but the debate is meaningless. His work has undoubtedly reaffirmed Morocco's artistic traditions and modern energy.

Untitled
Henna on wood and leather
117 x 175 cm
1981

MAHDI QOTBI
Morocco, b. 1951
Mahdi Qotbi was born in Rabat where he studied at the School of Fine Arts. He continued at the School of Fine Arts in Toulouse and subsequently at the School of Fine Arts in Paris. Qotbi is preoccupied with the Arabic script which is essential to all his works. He derives his inspiration from his native traditional Islamic culture. He covers his surfaces with fine calligraphy producing images that undulate and change. Qotbi is a very capable artist who has managed to produce fragile and intricate works. Qotbi has succeeded in controlling the direction and pressure of his ink, hues and situation of colour which have resulted in subtle and delicate works of art.

Arabic Calligraphy
Mixed media
50 x 80 cm
Undated

OMAR YOUSSUFI
Morocco, b. 1950
Youssufi's works are meant to be
touched and turned. He takes sand
and encloses it in compositions of
wood and carved amulets that
suggest some primeval force. Holes
hidden in the composition release
sand as the work is turned, creating
a multitude of compositions as the
sand flows. Youssufi studied at the
School of Applied Arts in
Casablanca and then at the School
of Art in Luminy, Marseilles, before
going on to the School of Fine Arts in
Aix-en-Provence. He has drawn on
his training in ceramics to produce
the delicate little carved tablets
and amulets that live inside his
compositions in sand.

Sand Sculpture
Sand, ceramic, wood and glass
35 x 70 cm
Undated

Pakistan

Wijdan Ali

The geopolitical factors that influenced the destiny of Pakistan have played a vital role in the formation of its modern art movement. Throughout history Pakistan had been part of the Indian subcontinent, until 1947 when the British withdrew from India and civil war broke out, dividing villages and towns against each other. Partition ensued and a new state was formed comprised of forty million Muslims.

Before Independence

During the period prior to partition, the most powerful art movement of the twentieth century in India was the New Bengal School. The Mayo School of Art in Lahore, founded in 1875, was another important institution.

In Lahore, the capital of the Punjab, a number of artists painted in watercolours, in a softly colourful and dreamily poetic style. One of the most prominent artists of this school was Abdul Rahman Chughtai (1897–1975). Although he was attracted by European artistic experimentation, he refused to follow any of them for his aim was to resuscitate the traditional Mughal style. Because of him the new Mayo School adopted both Western tonal harmony and the drawing base of the Mughals.

A young artist, Amrita Sher Gill, is considered the most gifted painter of her generation. She studied painting in Paris and produced works of great originality. She moved to Lahore in 1935, where she worked until her untimely death in 1939. She led the revolt against traditional Indian art and was the major force in introducing the influences of Cezanne and Gauguin to the subcontinent.

One of the early artists to study abroad was Fayzee Rahamin (1880–1964). A European by birth, he settled down in the subcontinent and became totally Indianised. He trained at the Royal Academy in London, worked with the noted British portraitist, Sir John Singer Sargent, and was first known as a portrait painter. Steeped in Western art traditions, he gradually shed them to become totally immersed in the cultural and artistic traditions of his adopted country. He recognized the difficulty the Indian artist faced in keeping his identity by following European schools and wanted to create a movement in art based on native traditions.

Post-Independence

After independence, artists in Pakistan found themselves in a shockingly difficult predicament. They had gone through the traumatic experience of exodus and war and had endured the birth of a new nation. Foremost among their problems was emerging with a fresh identity to suit their new situation. Lahore was the only city in Pakistan with any kind of art activity. It enjoyed historical continuity with the seventy-year-old Mayo School of Art, which became the Lahore National College of Art in 1958, and the Fine Arts Department of the Punjab University, and produced the bulk of art teachers who later manned art departments in scores of schools throughout Pakistan.

Sheikh Ahmad was one of the early artists who came to Lahore. He first studied art in the United States and later went to England where he taught at the Central School of Art before returning to his native country and joining the staff of the Mayo School of Art. During his early career he did lithography, which he had learned in the United States. It demonstrated his strict training in draughtsmanship and his acute sense of design. A pioneer art teacher who taught scores of young artists, he helped organize the Institute of Art and Design in Karachi and is known for his volatile genre paintings and naturalistic portraits. Two of Sheikh Ahmad's contemporaries were Ustad Latif, a watercolourist who like A. R. Chughtai experimented with wash-painting, and Ustad Atta Mohammed, a gifted decorative designer unmatched in his skill.

S. H. Askari, like Fayzee Rahamin, came from Lucknow and settled in Karachi. In spite of the wide range of subjects that he had tackled, Askari is best known as a portrait painter of important personalities. He illustrated poetry books, designed stained glass windows for a chapel, was commissioned to do huge murals, like the one depicting the battle of Kerbela for the Nuwab of Rampur, composed panels in relief and made statues. He painted imaginary Mughal princesses in a style that conformed to his aesthetic ideal of a delectable kind of beauty. He worked with smooth and tight brushwork; his figures are accentuated by dark shadows around the lit faces with emphasis on the highly ornate and rich dress and ornament, against a background of fabulously adorned palaces. Although he conformed to all the guidelines of a highly polished academic style, his canvases remain devoid of characterization, animation and warmth.

Anna Molka Ahmad is the most outstanding artist in the field of art education. Of English origin, she came in 1939 from Patrala with her painter husband, Sheikh Ahmad, to settle in Lahore. While her husband taught at the Mayo School of Art, she devoted her energies to setting up the Fine Arts Department at the Punjab University. When the department first opened in 1940, it only accepted women students; in 1956 it became co-educational. Post-graduate classes were soon established and four of the early graduates were employed to teach in the department; they were Anwar Afzal, Zakia Mallik, who only recently retired, Nazim Qazi and Sheikh Razia Feroz. Anna Molka consistently advocated the teaching of art at primary and secondary schools, while at college she demanded a high standard of proficiency in draughtsmanship, regardless of the idiom the artists might later adopt. Herself a prolific artist, she paints portraits, huge canvases of Punjab landscapes and philosophical subjects in bright oil colours.

Ustad (Master) Allah Bukhsh (1895–1978) was already famous when Pakistan was created. A self-taught artist, he started his career early, learning to draw in the traditional manner and depicting mythological and legendary figures. He learned his craft by doing cinema posters, studio sets and theatre backdrops, and trained for a while with Ustad Abdullah in Lahore. After independence, he glorified the rural life of the Punjab in genre paintings through its fairs, festivals, weddings, ceremonies and rural landscapes. He relied on chiaroscuro and perspective to create an illusion of reality. His followers created the Ustad Allah Bukhsh Academy and work today to keep the torch of their master burning.

Miniature Painting

The only form of painting that can be called authentically indigenous is miniature painting whose origins go back to the Mughal Empire. The emphasis was on stylisation of nature, decorative detail and a highly graphic and flattering technique of portraiture. Only after the impact of Western political and cultural contact, at the beginning of the nineteenth century, did this local tradition in art suffer a major setback. Yet because of the long and rich history of miniature painting, there continued to be miniaturists after independence, depicting palace themes and historical events. The doyen in Pakistan was Haji Mohammad Sharif (1889–1978) who traced his ancestry two hundred years back to Allah Ditta, the court painter of Patiala Raj. After independence he taught miniature painting at the Fine Arts Department of Punjab University and later joined the staff of the National College of Arts. He used to prepare his colours from vegetable and mineral ingredients, according to his own formula. He also prepared his own paper, feather quills and brushes and beat raw gold into gold leaf for his illuminations. After his death, no one except Ustad Shujaullah ventured into this field of classical painting.

Immigrant Painters

After partition, a number of established artists emigrated from India to Pakistan. Fayzee Rahamin came from Bombay and S. H. Askari from Lucknow; they both settled in Karachi. A. Sayeed Nagi came from Amritsar and was a prosperous artist, which is a rarity. He was in great demand for his bright, slick renditions of indigenous subjects, such as snake charmers and flamboyantly dressed fishermen, as well as his fair fleshy nudes with doll-like faces. Another artist who came from Amritsar to settle in Karachi was Mubarak Hussain. His paintings, which depict different parts of the countryside, range from his early soft-graded tones and gentle contours to his more recent works, treated in a vigorous style, with daring oblong patches of colour. None of these artists had any direct influence on the young promising artists of Karachi. It was another immigrant artist, Shakir Ali, who left the deepest imprint on the new generation.

The Fifties

The distance between the traditional style in art and the modernistic, that took Western artists centuries to cover, was bridged by only one generation of Pakistani artists within a mere decade, leaving their public bewildered and far behind. The impact of the Post-Impressionists and the art movements that followed in the West after the First World War is almost non-existent in the works of the traditionalist artists of Pakistan. Dadaism, Cubism and Expressionism never touched Chughtai and his contemporaries. This isolation was the reason why the next generations of artists did not look to their elders for guidance: they had absorbed the new ideas of art that had spread like wild fire throughout most of the world after the Second World War. Thus the traditionalists left no pupils to continue their quest for the preservation and the evolution of the traditional schools of art in their country.

The fifties constitutes an important decade in the modern art movement of Pakistan. Scores of new artists came into the field and adopted new styles and experimented by taking new directions in their creative work. An exhibition in Lahore in 1953 by Zainul Abedin was the starting point for a series of exhibitions of modern works in which the public discovered a contemporary style different from the conventional one they had known since childhood.

One of the first modernistic artists was Zubeida Agha (b. 1922). She held her first abstract exhibition in 1949 and her revolt against traditional painting, which she rejected for its stiff imagery and lack of vitality, was met with opposition and ridicule. She obtained her initial training at the studio of B. C. Sanyal alongside Amrita Sher Gill. She also worked with an Italian artist, Mario Perlingieri, who was a prisoner-of-war stationed at Walton Camp in Lahore and a one-time pupil of Picasso. For her formal art training she went to St. Martin's School in London and the Ecoles des Beaux Arts in Paris. She returned to Pakistan in 1953 to settle in Karachi. In 1955 she had her second show. The artistic climate and public taste had already changed so much that it was received with great enthusiasm and she was given credit for her talent and originality. Her fascination with the magic of light made her use pure colours, blending them in effective harmony. Today she is considered the best colourist of her country.

One of the most imaginative and innovative painters of Pakistan is Ismail Gulgee (b. 1926). An engineer, he realized his artistic talent and inclination late in life. He started with strong realistic portraits and compositions, then moved to abstract oils. When working in Kabul, Afghanistan, he developed a unique genre of portraiture executed in marble mosaics and semi-precious stones (lapis lazuli). Accordingly, he was commissioned to do the portraits of several Eastern and Western heads of state. In his abstracts he incorporates tiny cut pieces of mirror and also manipulates ornamental calligraphy, coloured beads, as well as gold and silver leaf in the tradition of Mughal Kunkandari, in order to enhance the rich colours of his canvas with different textures and effects.

The most prolific artist in Pakistan was Sadequain (1930–1987). Calligrapher, poet and painter, he graduated from Agra University and came on the art scene in the mid-fifties with an exhibition in Karachi. He was a figurative painter with allegorical significance. Although he betrayed no influence of any other painter, his works, with their thick lines and dark sombre colours, recall distant Cubist trends. He was the first to do large murals in public buildings such as the Jinah Hospital (1955) and Karachi Airport (1957) and used symbols in great profusion to register his social comment on humanitarian themes. He was the first to adopt free form calligraphy in his compositions. He illustrated the Koran and the Hadith (traditions of the Prophet) in vivid colours and bold compositions. More than any other painter he popularized painting for the average citizen by appealing to his combined religious and aesthetic senses. The National Council of the Arts devoted a museum to him in Islamabad and another one in Karachi and he was decorated by the State. Sadequain is an artist who represented the evolution of Pakistani modern painting through most of its forms and stages.

Undoubtedly it was Shakir Ali (1914–1975) who had the most influence on the art movement of the fifties. He was born in Rampur (India) and trained at the J. J. School of Art in Bombay and the Slade School of Art in London. He later went to France and worked with Aure L'Hote, a proponent of Cubism. In 1951, he went to Karachi and became the principal of the National College of Art where he remained until his death. He employed motifs of birds, flowers and the sun, through which he expressed his protest against injustice and cruelty, and affirmed his belief in the freedom and dignity of the individual. The first exhibition he gave of his abstract works baffled the public as well as other artists. His imaginative distortions, patternization of space, the calculated juxtaposition of colours and audacious employment of textures, were a departure from the familiar and recognizable approach. In the mid-sixties, he executed murals with calligraphic motifs for the Punjab Public Library, where he employed calligraphy alongside his familiar symbols. Many young artists from the National School of Art, as well as others, came under his influence; among them were Moyene Najmi, Anwar Jalal Shemza, Ahmad Parvez, Iqbal Geoffry and Kamil Khan. Besides his leadership in painting, he also influenced commercial art by injecting it with fresh energy.

The new modern vision proved to be exciting to six new artists of the fifties who broke away from the academic style and worked with the modern idiom. They were Moyen Najmi, Ali Imam, S. Safdar, Ahmad Parvez, A. J. Shemza and Kutub Sheikh. They condemned the works of Chughtai and Ustad Allah Bukhsh as being 'old-fashioned' and 'lagging behind the spirit of the times'. Instead, they adopted contemporary styles that varied between Impressionism, Expressionism, Cubism and Abstraction.

Moyen Najmi (b. 1928) is a self-taught artist who studied with the Russian painter S. Roerich in Simla. He painted landscapes and street scenes in an impressionistic style before turning his attention to abstract art. Ali Imam (b. 1924) studied initially at the Nagpur School of Art and Sir J. J. School of Art in Bombay. Imam's sensitive canvases betray a dreamy impressionism which portrays his country's women in their everyday life, shrouded by a veil of harmonious colours and solid structural forms. He was the first artist to open an art gallery in Karachi in an attempt to bridge the gap between the artist and his public. Sheikh Safdar (b. 1924) is another self-taught artist. When he first came to Lahore he was painting voluptuous women wearing tight saris. After the modern trends swept through the city, he started superimposing a geometrical space division on the whole canvas over the central figure, in an attempt to combine the traditional and the modern. Later he exchanged his female figures for houses, lit windows in apartment blocks and fields. Ahmad Parvez (1926–1979) was one of the most dynamic colourists who traced his artistic heritage back to the Mughal masters. He began painting still life and powerfully distorted figures in order to accentuate the peculiar characteristics of the image, using thick black lines, deep dark colours and strong contrasts. Shemza (1928–1985) attended a two-year course at the Slade School of Art and taught basic design in an art school in London. He rejected the traditional three-dimensional plasticity of Western art and developed a purely linear style and later on worked with different forms of Arabic and Persian calligraphy. Finally, Kutub Sheikh started evening classes at the Arts Council in Lahore. He left for Germany in the seventies, where he still lives and works.

Khalid Iqbal (b. 1929) greatly influenced painters of the sixties and seventies. A pupil of Anna Molka Ahmad and a graduate of the Slade School of Art in London, he combines in his landscapes an acute sense of tonality and precision in defining space and constructing forms, which is far from emotionalism. Among his group is Zulqarnain Haidar, Ghulam Mustafa, Iqbal Hussein, Ijaz Anwar Kaleem and Rashid Khan.

Sculpture

In contrast to painting, which has evolved rapidly over the last two decades, sculpture took a much slower route, with considerably fewer adherents and advocates. Ozzir Zuby and Nasir Shamsie are both contemporaries of Zubeida Agha and Shakir Ali, and like them they were influenced by the modern trends. Zuby paints as well as sculpts, and in his paintings strong lines form masses peculiar to sculpture. A graduate of the Mayo School of Art, he was influenced during his formative years by his teacher Ustad Allah Bukhsh. In the late forties and early fifties he was doing linear paintings of hills with human features and humans who looked like rocks and hills, showing a distinct influence of Ustad Allah Bukhsh and a mannerism that goes back to the days of Persian miniature painting under the Safavids. In 1950 he went to Italy for further training at the Academy of Fine Arts in Rome, after which he was considered more of a sculptor than a painter. He did a series of busts of Pakistani intellectuals, poets and writers. Nasir Shamsie is another sculptor and one of the few artists to have a one-man show sponsored by the Karachi Fine Arts Society in the early days after Independence in 1949. After an extended stay in London where he studied commercial design, he came back to work as a commercial artist before concentrating on sculpture. He did big pieces as well as reliefs and mobiles, with emphasis on line more than on mass. Novera Ahmad (b. 1935) was born in Chittagong, in what was then East Pakistan (Bangladesh today). Despite her family's efforts to discourage her from studying sculpture, Novera Ahmad managed to study at the Byam Shaw School of Art in London. She later went to Cumberwell School of Art where she studied sculpture. She also worked for a short while in the studio of Jacob Epstein. After her return to Pakistan in 1957, she went to Rangoon to study Burmese traditional wood carving. She does free form sculpture and murals in relief and works with clay, plaster, marble powder, wood and cement. The three sculptors have been strongly influenced by contemporary British sculptors like Henry Moore.

Art Societies and Art Councils

Immediately after the creation of Pakistan, a number of small art societies were established in the main cities of Lahore, Dacca and Karachi. They organized all kinds of art shows, ranging from one-person to group exhibitions, with subjects varying from Chinese rubbings, American silk-screens and European modern paintings to Bengali watercolours, etchings, woodcuts and lithographs. With the accelerated growth of art programmes and activities all over the country, Art Councils gradually took the place of small art societies. The first to be formed was the Pakistan Art Council in Lahore in 1953, followed by one in Dacca in 1954 and another one in Karachi in 1955. The Art Councils are public bodies administered by the private sector through boards comprised of eminent personalities from the world of art and culture. They raise their own funds and, during difficult times, receive sporadic grants from the government. A co-ordinating committee, with representatives of the individual Art Councils, meet periodically to review and co-ordinate art programmes on a national level. Apart from organizing exhibitions, the Art Councils have established galleries where their permanent collections of Pakistani art are on show to the public. In large cities like Lahore and Karachi, the Councils also offer evening classes in art which attract large numbers of amateurs and semi-professional artists. Besides taking a great load off the government's shoulders in the field of art patronage, the formation of Art Councils has helped spread a certain amount of interest as well as an artistic awakening among people throughout the country.

The Sixties

The sixties witnessed an accelerated momentum in the art movement. The 1965 war with India changed the trend in art and directed it towards realism. The first artistic event to involve artists in their country's national crisis was an exhibition of war paintings staged by Air Marshal Noor Khan. The political involvement, particularly of student and working class movements, provided great impetus to artists who maintained that art should not serve a social elite but apply itself to social and national issues by portraying everyday life and people, as well as important ideas of the time.

A new generation of artists appeared in both Lahore and Karachi. In Lahore, a group of highly gifted graduates (1961–62) of its art institutions made their impact on the art scene; one of them was Zahoorul Akhlaq (b. 1941). Painter and sculptor and a graduate of the National College of Art, he aesthetically enriched his paintings by employing traditional design elements. His disdain for undisguised ornamental effects pushed him towards total abstraction, while adopting ancient inscriptions and calligraphy. In his later canvases he expresses his concern about the dangers of the spread of nuclear weapons and the effects of nuclear fallout on humanity. He has gained recognition in Sweden and New York, where he worked in the Print Making Workshop. Ghulam Rasul (b. 1942) is a student of Anna Molka Ahmad who had further training in the United States and France, and returned to Lahore in 1972, determined to develop an indigenous style. Rasul is called the landscape artist of the Punjab. His early works have features of Mughal miniatures, but after his sojourn in France his landscapes became more stylized, with larger areas of harmonious colours. Saeed Akhtar (b. 1938) a graduate of Punjab University, teaches landscape painting at the National College of Art in the style of Ustad Allah Bukhsh and Anna Molka. He continued his training at the Slade School of Art in London and returned with a style of his own. His landscapes have fewer details than those of his teacher Anna Molka. His followers in the Punjab are, among others, Misbahudin Qazi, Nazir Ahmad and Shahid Jalal.

One of the finest and most sensitive artists of his generation is Colin David (b. 1937). Another graduate of the Fine Arts Department at Punjab University and a brilliant student of Khalid Iqbal, David later on succeeded in developing his own personal style based on a form of neo-realism. He teaches at the National College of Art. His figures are depicted in a direct representational manner against a simple background, using neutral colours and sometimes highlighting the canvas with a splash of red, yellow or orange. Instead of sensuality, his female figures radiate grace and femininity. Jamil Naqsh (b. 1937) inherited his love of painting from his father, Abdul Basit, who was an accomplished artist of the Mughal School. His initial training was at the National College of Arts. He persistently paints women and pigeons in inexhaustible forms and postures. With time, both subject and artist matured, adding to the canvas a soft feeling of texture and a touching unity between the pigeon and the nude. Bashir Mirza (b. 1941) is also a graduate of the National College of Arts. An articulate painter, he depicts nudes in aggressive erotic postures, although his later works betray more poetic sentiments. Ijazul Hassan (b. 1940) is another neo-realist painter who trained in Lahore and at Cambridge. After an attempt at Op Art, he started painting common scenes and mundane objects to express social criticism. Mansour Rahi (b. 1939) graduated from the Art School of Dacca and came to Karachi in 1963. In the seventies he turned to pure abstraction and became principal of the Karachi School of Art where he trained a number of young artists, among them Mashkoor Raza, Lubna Agha, Sumbul Nazir, Ghalib Baqar, Abdul Hai and Tareq Javed. Other painters of the sixties and seventies are Mansoor Aye, who has worked on the theme of girls and the moon for the past twenty years and recently has introduced peacocks, birds and butterflies to his canvases; Laila Shahzada paints elaborate scenes based on archaeological finds from Gandhara and Mohenjodaro, and has influenced a young artist, Ayuc Azam, who follows in her footsteps in a less elaborate manner; Jamil Amad was discovered in the slums of Karachi by an American visiting artist, but his career was interrupted by ill health and tragedy. Maqsood Ali paints Sind deserts with bright, bold colours: his squares and cubes are reminiscent of rilli quilts from Sind province; Lubna, Naheed Ali, Qudsia Nisar, Mehr Afroz, Zubeida Javed, Khalid Latif, Manan Azumi, Zahir Janjua, Ejaz Anwar, Ghazanfar, Zarina Hashimi and Mansoora Hassan all follow international styles, but each has developed individual idiosyncrasies of expression that reflect his or her personality.

The Seventies

The decade of the seventies was, in many ways, a period of stagnation for the arts. The political and social climate of the country left its mark on artistic creativity. Political unrest, repression and internal strife stifled the output of both artists and intellectuals. The ranks of the formalist school expanded and great artists like Sadequain devoted their energies to developing free form calligraphy and executing gigantic calligraphic murals. While all forms of experimentation with painting and sculpture suffered from the prevailing conservative climate, calligraphy gained new impetus. Among others who adopted the written script as a means of expression were Ozzir Zuby, Sarder Muhammad, Aslam Kamal, Shafiq Farooqi and Moojid. The most positive aspect of this decade was the interest in art that spread to other parts of the country. Baluchistan and the North West Frontier started to teach art in their universities. In Peshawar, a number of local artists appeared: Jahanzeb Malik, Ghazala, Tasmin Shahzad, Nasim Raouf Cheema and Arbab Sardar Mohammad. In Quetta young artists were doing realistic work and a talented new artist, Jamal Shah, was working in both sculpture and painting. He set up the Department of Fine Arts at Baluchistan University. In Hyderabad, the heart of Sind province, Ali Nawaz painted attractive miniatures, tinged with a local touch, and Mohammad Ali Bhatti specialized in portraiture. A Fine

Arts Department opened at the university headed by a talented artist, A. R. Nagori, who was assisted by Mussarat Mirza and Mohammad Ali. Finally Islamabad, the capital, grew into an art centre with the headquarters of the National Council of the Arts, founded by the Ministry of Culture. Its aim was to promote all forms of the visual and performing arts and to assist artists in their efforts to raise standards and achieve their goals. Prominent figures like Zubeida Agha, Mansour Rahi, Hajra Mansoor, Ghulam Rasul and Misbahudin Qazi moved to the capital, enhancing its artistic scene.

The influence of Khalid Iqbal continued to incite and inspire budding artists all through the seventies and way into the eighties. For three decades this senior consummate painter carried the beacon for landscape painting, portraiture and figurative work; among his most ardent young followers were Ghulam Rasul and Nazir Ahmad.

One of the unfortunate trends of this decade was the tendency of accomplished artists to emigrate. Ahmad Parvez and Anwar Jalal Shemza left for England where they were highly appreciated and Kutub Sheikh went to Germany where he still lives doing pure abstract work.

The secession of Bengal, the eastern part of Pakistan, in 1971 caused the loss of another group of highly gifted and sensitive artists; among them were the late Sultan, Ajmal, Zainul Abedin, Safiuddin Ahmad, Anwarul Huq, Khwaja Shafiq, Qamarul Hassan and Kibria. With the estrangement of this group of artists, Pakistan was deprived of some of its great talent.

The Eighties

The eighties brought with it a more stable political climate in which artists were able to discover fresh forms of expression. All media were explored and graphics developed faster than during all the past three decades put together. Mehr Afroz in Karachi devoted herself exclusively to graphics and won many international awards, while Ghulam Rasul and Ghazanfar Ali in Lahore concentrated on printmaking. In Peshawar, Tasmin Shahzad was the main graphic artist.

Ceramics and sculpture witnessed a rebirth after the slumber of the seventies. Shahid Sajjad, a self-taught artist, demonstrated great talent and strength of expression with his wood and bronze pieces. Masood Kohari is an accomplished figure in three forms of plastic art. Painter, ceramicist and sculptor, this self-taught artist first learned his craft from the traditional potters of the Punjab, before going to France where he spent two years at the Ecole des Beaux Arts and at Savigny perfecting his skill in modern techniques of ceramics. He introduced the ceramic-painting and the ceramic-collage, mixing together different materials like wire and glass, as an extension to the work. His recent abstracts depict a transparency rarely found in ceramics and an innovative style that has won him great acclaim in Paris.

Another artist who works with different forms is Imran Mir. He is a painter and graphic designer who experiments with constructive sculptural arrangements made of plywood cubes that can be arranged singularly and in groups, giving his viewers the chance to wander among the compositions, to shift the blocks and to have the freedom to purchase any part of the arrangement. Other sculptors and ceramicists are Mian Salahuddin, Shezad Alam and Rabia Zubeiri.

One of the most controversial, verbose and topical artists of the eighties is Iqbal Geoffrey. After living twenty years abroad he burst on the art scene like a thunderbolt. A painter with strong initiative and rare originality, he aesthetically harnesses elements of graffiti, accidental mandalas and Japanese calligraphy in his works. He projects his ideas and images with unorthodox symbols such as the pizza and the Rolls Royce causing considerable irritation to the art establishment and shocking the critics and public alike.

A number of artists who were born in the fifties grew up to carve a name for themselves on the art scene of the eighties; they are Lala Rukh, Hajra Mansoor, S. Jalal, Nusrat Ali, Shehbaz Khan, Iqbal Hussein Mustafa, Tasneem Shehzad, Ahmad Zoay, Shirin Pasha, Nayyara Wajid, Jimmy Engineer, Mansoora Hassan, Saba and Bashir.

A growing concern about national and international issues made its way into the list of subjects of the eighties. The collages of Zarina Hashimi and paintings of Zeinul Abdeen deal with hunger and Afghan refugees, social injustice and oppression; while Iqbal Hussein paints the red-light district of Lahore, a subject that would have been taboo in the seventies.

In the eighties, interest was rekindled in miniature painting and some of the new artists, like Sara, started to explore it with today's themes, taking it out of its heyday elitism and treating its content and matter from a new angle.

The revival of calligraphy that had started in the seventies reached a certain degree of maturity in the eighties in a climate of Islamic cultural renaissance. Classical and free form calligraphy, embodying Koranic texts, were integrated into two and three dimensional compositions, although sometimes lacking the desired aesthetic results. As long as the experiment with calligraphy continues, it will certainly bring new developments that might give modern Pakistani art a distinguished character.

Art Criticism

Although art criticism is relatively new, in the eighties it has become more academic and has started to mature. The first serious critic was Jalaludin Ahmad, who in 1954 published his book *Art in Pakistan*, the only record to document the modern art movement of Pakistan. In 1982 Ahmad with his wife Azra started publishing a quarterly magazine in London called *Arts and the Islamic World*. It is the first and only international publication that deals with classical and modern Islamic art inside and outside the Muslim world.

Ayed Amjad Ali, Ijazul Hassan and Miriam Habeeb are relative newcomers to the field of art criticism, yet with their education and insight form a nucleus for this very important aspect in the development of any artistic movement. Their constructive criticism in daily and weekly periodicals is adding a new dimension to artistic activities in Pakistan and to the maturing of its budding talent.

Conclusion

Pakistan is a modern Muslim state whose cultural mainstream reaches back to its Islamic and Indian heritage. In the last two hundred years of its tumultuous history, its people have been subjected to colonization, foreign aggression, war and social and political upheavals. Its visual arts and architecture, more than its literature and music, have completely fallen under the influence of Western culture and there is very little continuity, if any, of the old traditions. The handful of painters who have tried to revive traditional styles have succeeded only momentarily but failed to influence the younger generations of artists and found no proper followers to continue their work.

In spite of the fact that there has not been a distinct Pakistani school, painting, sculpture and ceramics are, in more than one sense, heterogeneous, encompassing what can liberally be called a Western international style, distinctly tinged with local nuances and airs. Be it Gulgee's abstracts or Sadequain's calligraphic paintings, Ali Imam's Impressionistic figures or Kohari's transparent ceramic collages, there is definitely something other than the subject which emerges as an identifiable Pakistani style.

See colour pp. 116–120 for plates of the following artists' work:

MANSOORA HASSAN
ALI IMAM
JAMIL NAQSH
LAILA SHAHZADA
USTAD SHUJAULLAH

ZUBEIDA AGHA
Pakistan, b. 1922
Zubeida Agha had to struggle against many prejudices to become an established artist. She was among the first women artists in Pakistan to exhibit abstract works. Born in Faisalabad, she was educated in Lahore at the Punjab University. In 1944 she joined the studio of B. C. Sanyal for two years to become a painter. She also studied under Mario Perlingieri, a pupil of Picasso. In 1950 she joined St. Martin's School and studied in Paris. Her drawings are simplified and her colours are vibrant reflecting a deliberate and controlled attempt to simplify the structure and achieve a beautiful rhythmic quality. Zubeida is more interested in the essence of things and ideas rather than the reproduction of the apparent forms.

No details available at time of going to press.

ZAHOORUL AKHLAQ
Pakistan, b. 1941
A graduate of the National College of Art, Zahoorul Akhlaq is a painter and sculptor whose disdain for ornamentation drove him to total abstraction. Simple uncluttered lines and plain surfaces distinguish his metal sculptures, with some falling into a minimalist category. He is one of the few artists in his country to tackle international issues concerning the dangers of nuclear weapons and their effect on humanity. He attained maturity in his graphic works which gained recognition in Sweden and New York. He has succeeded in his paintings in reaching a meaningful abstract expression that combines geometry with an abandonment of colour.

Untitled
Mixed media
55 x 75 cm
Undated

COLIN DAVID
Pakistan, b. 1937
David first studied art at the Fine Arts Department, Punjab University, Lahore, and then studied at the Slade School, London. In his early works of crowded cities his canvases are divided into different geometrical shapes, covered with cold blues and greens with one spot of warm colour as the focal point. Gradually he moved to simplified backgrounds with the figure of a woman as his focus. The female figure would more often than not have a nearby splash of bright colour for dramatic effect. David is one of the first Pakistani artists to combine neo-realism with an Eastern reality. His work is distinguished by its precise simplification of the subjects and clarity of vision and brush.

Woman
Oil on carton
90 x 120 cm
Undated

NAZ IKRAMULLAH
Pakistan

Naz Ikramullah was born in London and studied at the Byam Shaw School of Art in Chelsea. She works in acrylics, mixed media, etchings, lithographs and coloured xeroxes to build very personal collages. In whatever media, Naz's 'work evolves from memories of times and places.' Naz is a committed and an innovative artist, passionately involved in her work. She learnt etching at PACC Workshop run by Michael Ponce de Leon. Naz's extensive travels and exposure to other artistic influences and cultures fascinated her, and she distils her experiences into a continuous series of creative processes, enhanced by the physical reality and the invisible reality of the mind.

Reflections through the Mind's Eye
Collage
24 x 18 inches
Undated

GHULAM RASUL
Pakistan, b. 1942

A graduate of the National College of Art in Lahore, Ghulam Rasul is one of Pakistan's better known landscape artists. In his realistic style he has recorded scenes from rural Pakistan in quiet earthy colours. After spending two years in Paris training as a printmaker, he spent some time in London working with his new medium and departing from his conventional style by adopting not only a new art technique but also new abstract motifs.

Landscape 1
Oil on canvas
23.5 x 83.5 cm
Undated

SADEQUAIN
Pakistan, 1930–1987
A highly talented and prolific artist, Sadequain came on the art scene in the mid-fifties with his individual style of thick lines and dark, sombre colours depicting the symbolic cactus to register his social comments on humanitarian themes. His 'Starving Buddha' was another symbolic character that he used in his philosophical and satirical works. He popularized painting among the masses with his illustrations of the Holy Koran and the Prophet's Traditions by combining calligraphy with landscape. His gargantuan calligraphic works show great skill, sound balance, a versatile and audacious hand and a boundless imagination.

Calligraphic Scene
China ink on leather
125 x 175 cm
Undated

SHAHID SAJJAD
Pakistan
Looking at Shahid Sajjad's highly polished and solidly packed bronzes one would never guess that he is a self-taught sculptor. He treats his masses of mutilated figures with a self confidence that only highly developed sculptors possess. In his silent, reclining figures, one detects the sadness and pain that the artist transfers to them and they in turn convey, in a highly expressive manner. Every piece of wood or bronze Sajjad works on carries part of himself in it, his struggle to express himself through a less popular art form and his striving for progress.

Figure
Bronze
40 x 30 x 20 cm
1977

NAJMI SAURA
Pakistan, b. 1951
Najmi Saura's compositions are crowded and dense works depicting earlier traditional trends. The Mughal motifs from miniatures and architecture seem to overlap each other. The impact is fascinating and highly evocative. Born in Karachi, she gained a Bachelor of Arts degree and subsequently studied miniature painting under the famous artist Jamil Naqsh. She has a tremendous skill and precision in translating traditional Mughal subjects in contemporary forms.

Girl with Bird
Oil, acrylic on canvas
92 x 92 cm
1980

HAJI MOHAMMAD SHARIF
Pakistan, 1889–1978
The main propagator of miniature painting and its doyen, Haji Mohammad Sharif is a descendant of Allah Ditta, the court painter of Patiala Raj. He was trained in Mughal painting by his famous father, Basharat Allah. He drew his inspiration from his rich visual heritage and practised his art faithfully according to classical norms. He prepared his own paper, paints and quills and beat his own gold leaf for illumination. Sharif's miniatures depict delicate, intricately detailed scenes from the past, executed with a feathery touch coupled with mastery of the art. Through him Islamic miniatures continued to survive in Pakistan.

Mogul Empress Hunting Tiger
Watercolour
35 x 45 cm
Undated

SHAKEEL SIDDIQUI
Pakistan, b. 1951
Siddiqui's work is precise in detail and imbued with immaculate craftsmanship and a realistic approach. These qualities, combined with a fine sense of colour, make his work significant. After matriculating in 1968 he had the chance to study at the Art Students' League of New York between 1970 and 1972. He returned to Pakistan and continued his studies at the Central Institute of Arts and Crafts in Karachi where he gained his diploma in fine arts in 1975. Siddiqui possesses visual skill, originality and a simple charm.

Untitled
Oil on canvas
55 x 65 cm
1981

HASSAN SHAHNAWAZ ZAIDI
Pakistan, b. 1948
Zaidi is among Pakistan's most promising artists. He graduated with a master's degree in Graphic Design from the University of Punjab in Lahore; he also lectures at the same university in the Fine Arts department. He had the opportunity to travel to Nairobi where he lectured in the department of design at Nairobi University in Kenya. Zaidi's works are sensitive; his pastel drawings of his native Pakistan are delicately executed and simple. He also has distinguished himself in a number of graphic prints. He lives and works in Lahore.

A Wild Flower
Chalk, pencil on board
58 x 61 cm
Undated

ZARINA
Pakistan, b. 1938

Zarina is one of the few modern Islamic artists who has adopted paper as her primary medium of expression. Born in India she studied at Aligarh University and then went on to work in woodcuts, in Bangkok, Europe and then Japan where she studied papermaking itself. Her talents both as an artist and as a lecturer were recognized early in the Western academic world. She has lectured at Princeton University, New York University, Rutgers, Cornell and the American Craft Museum as well as at the National Museum of Pakistan in Karachi. Her prints have attracted worldwide attention from Tokyo to New York. She works with handmade paper because of its connection with the traditions and history of Pakistan.

Homes
Paper sculpture
20 x 60 cm
1981

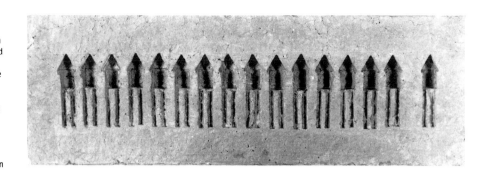

Palestine

Samia Taktak Zaru

Very little has been documented about modern Palestinian art. In his book *The Palestinian Art Movement*, 1985, Mohamad al-Assad describes Palestinian art as a spontaneous growing drive and states that there are no documented sources available yet. ALECSO will soon be publishing a short study on Palestinian art, an attempt which will be complicated by the lack of definition of a Palestinian identity. As a result of the continuous devastation of the Palestinian people and the confiscation of their homeland, they have been scattered around the world, never really belonging to any land they were destined to reside in. Those who were in Palestine prior to 1948 received the nationality of the occupying authorities. While those who are still in the occupied West Bank [of Jordan], 1967, struggle to survive as people. Many of those who lived in other countries were included in the art movement of their new residence. One often wonders, is it birthplace, residency or parenthood that makes the Palestinian ...tist identify with his land?

The Palestinian Arab community was an agricultural one for centuries before World War I. The relationship of the farmers to art was that of visual pleasure and function. They applied decorative designs and patterns to tools and utensils which were crafted and produced mainly for domestic use. Other products which excelled artistically in design were often offered in trade. Primitive drawings by local craftsmen appeared as free sketches on house entrances or carved in stone with patterns of palm trees or abstract plant forms symbolizing life and fertility. There were also calligraphic engraved patterns of Koranic verses for special occasions, as for example the return from the *Haj* (pilgrimage). Even with little consciousness of the so-called religious restrictions of Islam, traditional artists did not use human figure representations. This influence was also felt by local Christian artists who used decorative patterns and designs of floral motifs and animal forms which go back decades in history, thus exposing some basis for culture and civilization in Palestine.

There appears to have been some sort of agreement between art historians that fine arts were not developed in Palestine until 1948; what was considered art then was the tradition of calligraphy, painted icons, engravings on wood, carvings in stone and olive wood, mosaics, mother of pearl work, pottery, weaving and straw work. The local craftsman, considered to be the local artist, was open-minded, modifying his patterns slowly but creatively, keeping his art as the work of the group and family. Those works reflected the culture, values, beliefs and traditions of the different regions in Palestine, the stress being on aesthetic value and function.

One particular art form which expressed the sense of identity was colourful embroidery, mainly done by the women, with a variety of patterns relating to the areas from which they came – a mark of identity by contrast to the men who had nothing in that line. Jewellery in silver and other metals was crafted by men together with the other mentioned crafts.

Pottery and ceramics, the oldest crafts in that part of the world, were revived at the end of Ottoman rule around 1906. In fact, handmade pottery with striking slip-decorations was popular even earlier, and could be traced back to the Bronze Age. By 1937 it had been developed as a fine art which was practised by Palestinians who had studied in Europe, returning on graduation to teach applied arts and designs in local schools. At a much later date, others who studied at art academies in the Arab world, mainly Egypt, Iraq and Syria, as well as in the USA and England, got involved in teaching too rather than in the practice of fine art.

Before the British Mandate (1920–1948) design patterns consisted of abstract geometric elements, and later, due to imported influences, floral designs were introduced and combined with them. This was particularly evident in the art of embroidery which has a strong feeling for colour harmony. Design elements are given due consideration in theme variations and repetitive patterns, yet aesthetic awareness for colour, form and shape expressed the feeling of the group in a decorative rather than a representative manner and involved a great deal of memory.

The creation of a new artistic effect or a new style was very rare indeed; the emphasis was always on adhering to a particular pattern or theme. This conservatism and quietism in artistic expression left no room for the emergence of renowned great artists. Yet the local artist played a similar role: spontaneous and functional with a certain creative style which equalled the continuity of life itself, where parts fade away and new parts emerge taking on new forms, feelings and meanings.

During the British Mandate there was hardly any progress in the arts, despite the intellectually rich background, because education was mainly aimed at the qualification of civil servants who would fulfil the aims and needs of the occupying authorities.

Decorative design was the earliest trend in Palestinian art. The pioneers in that field were the Badran family. Three brothers of that family, namely, Jamal, Abdulrazak and Khairi Badran, went to study applied art and design in Cairo (1922–1927) after the railroad was started between Cairo and Haifa. Later, in 1937, they specialized in weaving, pottery and photography at the Central School of Art and Design in London. In Jerusalem, 'The Badran Brothers' Studio and Workshop' was established. Many contemporary traditional artists were trained there in calligraphy, arabesque design and applied arts. After 1948 Jamal Badran was employed as a UNESCO expert of arts and crafts in Tripoli, Libya. Later, he participated in the renovation of al-Aqsa Mosque in Jerusalem after the fire in 1968. He still maintains his studios in Ramallah and Amman. Abdul Razal Badran is in the Photography Department at the Jordan University in Amman, while the third brother died. It is worth mentioning that in 1947, Prince Abdullah bin al-Hussein of Trans Jordan (later King Abdullah of Jordan) commissioned the Badran studio to produce an art work to be presented to Princess Elizabeth (now Queen Elizabeth II) on her wedding. It was an olivewood chest with painted Islamic motifs and silver inlay.

Artists of this period, prior to 1950, were Expressionistic in character and style with bold nationalistic themes inspired by painful events like the Deir Yasin and Kufr Kasim massacres and the uprooting from their homeland (1948). The sculptural ceramic works of Hanna Mismar are a good example. He still has his pottery factory of functional ceramics in Nazareth. Artists of this period did not only think of techniques but also expressed their experiences and awareness in a historical moment. Art and literary works started portraying a genuine expression which became the character of the Palestinian artist. Artistic expression in painting of the human figure became acceptable and was added to other facets of art such as calligraphy and ornamental design. Works which expressed human suffering, agony and anguish characterized the themes of Mahmoud Wafa Dajani who lived in Damascus after 1948 where he was the art adviser to the Damascus National Museum.

A different trend in arts of the period was landscape painting. Fine arts seemed to attract women who became interested in arts as a hobby rather than a career. Notable amongst them is Sophie Halaby who went to study art in Paris. A pioneer who established a good reputation in the art field, she has excelled in her soft detailed watercolours of wild flowers of Palestine and landscapes. Miss Halaby still lives in Jerusalem. Another woman artist, Lydia Atta from Bethlehem, painted and sketched scenes with domes and churches. Few of her works are in the possession of collectors in Palestine. She left for Australia in 1940.

Many artists became involved in art movements in the Arab world as exemplified by the well-known art critic, writer and artist, Jabra Ibrahim Jabra from Bethlehem, who is one of the pioneers of abstract art. Jabra went to Iraq in 1948 and has been involved in the Iraqi art movement ever since (see the chapter 'Iraq').

The Palestinian art movement after 1948 adopted many theme variations and different dimensions. Some names became prominent, while others faded; some took the identity and nationality of other countries and were included in their movements – as was the case of Jaffa-born Juliana Seraphime and Jerusalem-born Paul Guiragossian. Both were included in the Lebanese art movement as pioneers and actually influenced the Lebanese art scene. Juliana Seraphime's pastels and paintings of fantasy express a unique and different feeling of uprooting, while Guiragossian's figures, subtle, abstract and angry, take you for a long trip in the old city of Jerusalem, the symbol of peace.

From the previous account we can see that the art movement in Palestine actually started around 1940 with the establishment of the Badran studio on Mamilla Street in Jerusalem, the studio which attracted artists, amateurs, collectors and prominent calligraphers such as Yusef Najjar and Muhammad Siam.

The influence of Islamic art and culture is quite obvious in the works of those who were trained in Egypt and Iraq. This influence diminished somewhat after 1948 when artists who were trained in the 1950s moved in the direction of painting impressions of the political crisis. A surprise to the Arab art community was the prominent prize won in London by Fatimah Muheb for her design of a monument to the political prisoner. Fatimah Muheb studied art in Cairo in the early 1950s. She has painted many portraits of distinguished Arab leaders and scenes of Jerusalem and the Dome of the Rock. She still lives in Jericho.

The disaster of 1948 was the turning point; belonging and uprooting became the incentive for creativity. The Palestinian artist joined the individual in summarising the primary elements which justify his existence as a Palestinian dealing with the land, time and conflict. He geared his energy towards the development of a unified character with an attempt to achieve an art that would reflect his experience, sensitive, authentic and genuine, and interpret it sincerely.

Between the years 1950 and 1955 artists who had been studying abroad returned. Afaf Arafat graduated from Bath Academy in England and Ismail Shammout, who had been painting before, acquired an art degree from Cairo and another from Italy. Ismail Shammout, who in the seventies became the official artist of the Palestine Liberation Organization, was strongly inspired by direct contact with events; he reflects the struggle and suffering of his people. In his works there is a close relationship between form and content, though he gives priority to content which is deeply related to his experiences. His symbols express historical events which are indicative of the sensitivity of the impressions he creates. His first exhibition was in Gaza in 1953.

Other works which are direct, strong expressions of conflict and the yearning for a free state are those by artists on the land prior to 1948. Little is known about the art movement between 1948 and 1955, but the work of artists after 1955 is evidence of the presence of a strong stand equivalent to the art revival of Palestinian artists who have studied at art academies in the Arab world, Europe and USA and are now established artists in the occupied territory, Jordan, Kuwait, Lebanon, America and other countries. The nationalistic approach was defined in the works of Abed Abidi from Haifa, Abdullah al-Kara from Dalyat al-Karmel and Faruk Diab from Tamra, and also in the literary works of the prominent Palestinian poets, Mahmoud Darwish, Tawfic Zayyad and Samih al-Qasem.

The return of the Palestinian artists who had been studying abroad in the mid-50s, the introduction of art education in UNRWA schools and training centres, a subject absent in

Jordanian Government Schools, created opportunities for art teachers. Afaf Arafat, whose works were influenced by the British School in tonal, soft colours of still life compositions and landscapes, contributed to the promotion of art education in Jordan. It was not until 1964 that the art movement in this part of the world witnessed a real revival. Together with artists Jamal Badran, Fatimah Muheb, Samia Taktak, Alia Aqil and Afaf Arafat, the Jordan Ministry of Education introduced the first curriculum in art education for the elementary and secondary levels. At a later date government and UNRWA teacher training centres established art education specialization and parallel inservice for art teachers.

On the other hand, the year 1962 marked a general art awareness. Art patrons like Amineh Husseini promoted young artists and helped them establish the first artists' group and crafts' council in Jerusalem. This laid a strong foundation for aspiring artists like Kamal Boullata (b. 1942), Samia Taktak (b. 1938), Vladimir Tamari (b. 1942), Sari Khuri (b. 1942) and Huda Mikheal. Later, between 1964 and 1966, they exhibited in Ramallah, Jerusalem and Amman. The enthusiasm lasted until the untimely political crisis and outbreak of war in 1967. Like many Palestinians, and for reasons beyond their control, artists left their homeland to get established in Amman, Beirut, London, Paris, Washington DC and Tokyo. Also, in 1967, when the Palestinians suffered yet another disaster, Ismail Shammout (b. 1930) and his wife, Tamam al-Akhal (b. 1934), expressed repressed emotions, worry and insecurity in simplified compositions in colour and line with palette knife strokes trying to achieve a balance between expression and the story of a social and a human conflict.

The trend of the art movement became more firmly established after 1967, with the work of the artists who stayed on the land, thus expressing a certain feeling of attachment, while those who were destined to be outside Palestine built up a homeland from memory using symbols and traditional Palestinian motifs related to their country. Such symbols together with legendary features are apparent in the works of Mustafa Hallaj (b. 1938) and Samia Taktak Zaru who use authentic Palestinian patterns of actual embroidery in the construction of their abstract collages and multi-media compositions. 'It is then that the art of pattern and design when used plastically characterizes the Palestinian people,' Mohamad al-Assad states in his book about the Palestinian Art Movement. Hallaj, on the other hand, and Abdul Rahman Mouzzayen (b. 1943) in Lebanon, expressed the suffering of their people. Themes were a summary of events expressed by strong lines and exaggerated symbols. This period also marked the emergence of the political poster. Palestinian artists, graphic designers, poets and writers in Lebanon and the Arab world produced strong bold political statements on posters, book covers and children's books. Artists participated after 1967 in international exhibitions and artists around the world expressed their support of the Palestinian cause by holding exhibitions of their work and that of Palestinian artists jointly. The interaction broadened the art horizon. Palestinian art moved from local to international and from traditional to contemporary modern.

The change is now prominent in the works of Jerusalem-born Kamal Boullata who presently lectures at Georgetown University in Washington. In his recent works he explores the dimensions of Arabic calligraphy in a contemporary approach, using subtle compositions which express authenticity through the medium of silk screen printing, putting Arab art in a contemporary context. While the involvement in the American art movement led artists like Samia Halaby to present herself in Kinetic art as a contrast to her previous vibrant abstracts. Halaby left Jaffa with her family in 1948 hoping to return. She is settled there now and has a teaching post at Yale University. Yet Khuri who lives and lectures in America, continues to remember Jerusalem, his birthplace, and explores the visual and cultural legacy of his past and selects from it constant and spatial energy, presented in geometric shapes and pure colours by the use of the spray gun.

Vladimir Tamari, who left Beirut for Tokyo, carried with him a rich memory of his homeland; bright colours of the landscape, domes and churches, abstract in form, yet mentally recognized to create effective sensitive compositions of eternal melodies.

Paris attracted many Arab artists establishing themselves, each with their own identity. Palestinian art in France is recognised through interesting collages, traditional forms and calligraphy compositions by Samir Salameh (1945) as well as in the soft paintings of Jumana Husseini (1932) which are metaphors for the return, in symbols like the tiger or the horse, women with their embroidered costumes and cities of Palestine.

Again, when the war broke out in Lebanon in 1982, artists had to find a third home. Some went to live in London, others like Leila Shawa move between Gaza and the UK. In London, Palestinian art is very well presented to the British through visiting exhibitions such as the one by artists from occupied Palestine (1976) at the Tattershall Castle boat in London. The group included Nabil Anani (b. 1945) from Latroun, which was demolished in 1967, Ibrahim Hijazi (b. 1945) from Haifa, Khalil Rayan (b. 1946) from Damoun, which was demolished in 1948, Suleiman Mansour (b. 1947) from Ramallah, Bashir Sinwar (b. 1945) from Khan Yunis refugee camp, Gaza, Vera Tamari (b. 1941) from Ramallah, Rihab Nammari (b. 1942) from Jerusalem and Samia Taktak Zaru from Ramallah. Palestinian art has also been represented by the exhibition of artists of the Islamic world (1976), and residents in Britain such as Walid Abu Shakra (b. 1945), whose detailed etchings of Palestinian villages, landscapes, olive trees and stone walls are well recognized.

Although living under adverse conditions, artists in occupied Palestine have continued to produce works of art that reveal their determined struggle to survive as a people. The themes of most of their works reveal a strong and definite attachment to Palestine, and they are joined in this spirit by many other Palestinian artists who are living outside their homeland, scattered to the four winds. Work produced under occupation is bitter, angry and defiant, giving violent artistic expression to the outrage of the Arabs in Israel at the occupation of their land. The art movement in the occupied territory proved its existence in 1970 with exhibitions of the works of artists like Suleiman Mansour, Nabil Anani, Isam Badr, Ibrahim Saba, Tayseer Sharaf and others. The Palestinian Artists' Association had its first meeting in 1972 in Jerusalem. Writers, poets and those interested in culture blessed this move and backed the association, but the occupying authorities disapproved of such a step and halted the association until finally an order was issued by the authorities to close it down and exhibitions and meetings were prohibited. It was a move against art, artists and the national themes they portrayed. Many art works were confiscated and some of their authors were imprisoned. At the same time, the local Palestinian theatre 'Alhakawati', which was established jointly with the co-operation of actors, poets, artists and playwrights from the occupied territory prior to 1948, started an active cultural programme which toured the country, Europe and the USA. Alhakawati worked closely with the Artists' Association by holding regular exhibitions in its hall. Artists like Kamal Boullata were invited to exhibit. Alhakawati Theatre became a Palestinian cultural attraction for Arabs and Jews. It offered a rich programme which included plays, musicals, exhibits, lectures, panel discussions and traditional fashion shows. A similar move was made against the Alhakawati Theatre by the occupying authorities, including threats, censorship restrictions and many other fake claims supposedly on grounds of security. It is now at the mercy of the authorities as to when and how to function. A destiny shared by an organization which voices justice for the Palestinian cause.

The year 1969 marked the creation of the first Palestinian Artists' Association which was located in Amman, later moving to Beirut and then to Kuwait. The constitution names Jerusalem as the head office. The 1970 Association established in Jerusalem and Ramallah was a chapter only.

The Association also established chapters in different parts of the Arab world to accommodate the many scattered artists. This association was actively involved with the Arab Artists' Union in organising touring Palestinian exhibitions in different parts of the world, aiming to assist in the recognition of the rights of the Palestinian people.

It is worth giving a brief picture of Palestinian women artists, who have continuously produced serious and creative works in a variety of media. Women artists started with the emergence of the movement in the 1930s: first Sophie Halaby and later Fatimah Muheb, then Afaf Arafat and Jumana Husseini, Samia Zaru, Rihab Nammari, Vera Tamari, Samira Badran (b. 1954) and Faten Tobbasi (b. 1958).

Afaf Arafat now lives in Nablus, working on the documentation of embroidery motifs. Rihab Nammari, who is a painter, teaches art to children. While Vera Tamari, who is a ceramicist and whose murals reflect a living tradition in the contemporary use of the media, presently occupies neighbourhood children in creative activity in the unpleasant conditions the local community is subjected to because of their 'Intifada' uprising (1988). Samira Badran now lives and works in Spain and moves between Amman, Madrid and Ramallah. Her large, expressionistic, bold canvases convey the suffering of her people in confident lines and brush strokes.

The conflict of 1948 left many Palestinian artists dispersed, but creativity did not stop. Artists such as Ahmad Na'awash (b. 1932), Tawfic el-Sayed (b. 1938) and Yasser Duwaik (b. 1938) studied in France, Spain and Iraq and came back to live in Amman, Jordan. Nawash who has been living in Jordan since 1948 suffers quietly. His thin figures, rather distorted and sad, express the longing of the artist for his roots. Bold and defiant paintings and sculptures summarize the art of Tawfic el-Sayed. Yet the graphic works of Yasser Duwaik, who later studied in England, express symbolically another form of suffering caused by his uprooting from Hebron, his place of birth. Some of the artists who studied in Iraq are rather influenced by the Iraqi art movement, yet their themes stay very Palestinian: agony and pain, the recent massacres and killings of their people such as at Sabra and Shatila in Lebanon (1982). Such themes are apparent in the works of Aziz Ammoura (b. 1942) and Adnan Yehya (b. 1960). The influence of art academies in the Arab world is quite obvious in some of the works of artists like Saleh Abu Shindi (b. 1938), who studied in Cairo. His compositions are built on his memory of Palestinian towns and villages in a decorative traditional style using Arab and Islamic motifs.

In the field of pottery and ceramics, Mahmoud Taha (b. 1942) excelled in wall murals and reliefs, a combination of calligraphy and patterns in subtle Islamic colours and expert mastery of the media. His sculptural ceramic forms are expressive of current events, while his wheel-thrown pots reveal an expert ceramicist and designer. Other ceramicists who are in Jordan include Hazem Zubi and Najwa Annab.

Another important aspect of Palestinian art is that of poster art. It started in Beirut and established itself as an identifiable Palestinian form at international events. It also inspired non-Palestinian artists to contribute, like Dia Azzawi of Iraq and others. Artist and poster designer Dr Kamal Qa'abar is one of the few trained in this field. Sensitive artist-cartoonists have also given support to the cause. Naji al-Ali, a shrewd, highly sensitive artistic cartoonist who moved between Kuwait, Beirut and London, was shot in 1986 in London, so ending the honest statements his sketches portrayed.

As a result of the two wars, 1948 and 1967, many artists live now in Kuwait. A large chapter of the Palestinian Artists' Association is established there and the legal body operates from Kuwait. Watercolourists, graphic artists and well-known painters like Nasir Sumi, Jamal Gharbieh, Ismail Shammout, Mohammad Bushnaq and others participate in exhibitions through the Kuwait office.

Very little has been documented about Palestinian sculpture for the reason expressed previously. Yet stone masons excelled in stone carvings for church decorations with Biblical reliefs and figures and altar pieces. One of those skilled masons is Issa Qa'abor who lives in Amman. He is a talented sculptor and has actually assisted local sculptors in Amman in handcarving and chiselling marble after small models designed by the artist. Carving and sculpture was an art form and a profession mastered by certain families in Palestine, mainly in Bethlehem. At the end of the nineteenth century, Ibrahim Anastas from Bethlehem went to Milan to train under Italian sculptors in the production of pillar crowns for churches. Later most of the stone sculpture was done by this family's descendants. Fawzi, the grandson, went to Italy to study sculpture in 1962 after the style of the classical and Renaissance masters in Milan. He returned in 1972 to work in the Italian tradition on all kinds of marble available in Palestine. He also worked in bronze casting. He has produced a six-metre marble statue of Peace, and one of his sculptures, *The Virgin Mary*, was on exhibition in the Louvre, Paris, in 1975. After the disastrous fire in 1969 at al-Aqsa mosque, he was involved in its restoration and stone carving. Anastas has established a two year academy for teaching sculpture and three-dimensional works.

Sculpture, like painting, is following the contemporary trend. The challenging structural sculptures of Samia Taktak Zaru are metal sheets, hammered and welded. As the work of a woman artist, it is a new medium for this part of the Arab world. It is now finding recognition in the art world and has won her a bronze medal at the International Festival of Creativity held in Cairo in 1984.

Palestinian art and Palestinian artists are creative and spontaneous; they have a strong, growing drive. Their participation in many international exhibitions has proved to be fruitful. Although many live under difficult conditions, their creativity does not seem yet to be exhausted.

See colour pp. 121–124 for plates of the following artists' work:

AFAF ARAFAT
SULEIMAN MANSOUR
SAMIR SALAMEH
SAMIA ZARU

NABIL ANANI
Palestine, b. 1943
Born in Halhul, Anani studied photography at the College of Fine Arts in Alexandria where he graduated in 1969. Anani is a painter and ceramicist as well as an art teacher. He has expressed in a delicate style his vision and dreams of his beloved Palestine in oils, watercolours, pottery or wood. His compositions are filled with symbols and cultural motifs reflecting a deep sense of anxiety and love for his homeland. He works as an art instructor at Ramallah Women's Training Centre and also at Bir Zeit Centre for the development of Palestinian handicrafts. There he maintains his roots while experimenting in different media.

Hebron Villages
Oil on canvas
73 x 53 cm
1980

ISSAM BADR
Palestine, b. 1948

Issam is a ceramicist, a painter and an art instructor. Born in Hebron, he graduated from the Academy of Fine Arts in Baghdad in 1973. He subsequently gained his master's degree in Palestinian ceramics from Tblisi Academy of Fine Arts in the Soviet Union. Pottery inspired Badr at a very early age, and he developed his skills and techniques both in pottery and ceramics, drawing on his Palestinian heritage. Both his ceramics and oil paintings share common colours, designs and meanings. In his paintings there is a tendency towards abstraction, yet nevertheless his canvases reflect a defined series of compositions and gestures.

Jerusalem
Oil on canvas
75 x 100 cm
1986

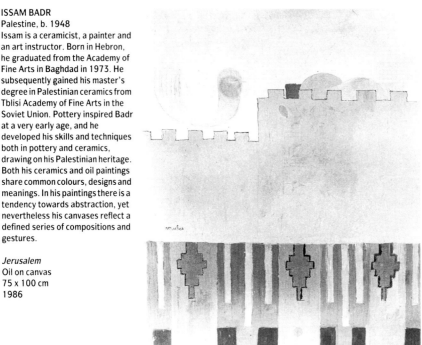

SAMIRA BADRAN
Palestine, b. 1954

Born in Tripoli, Badran studied painting and drawing at the Faculty of Fine Arts at Cairo University in Egypt, then continued her studies in Italy where she studied painting and etching at l'Accademia di Belle Arti in Florence. In 1980 she undertook a mural painting project at Liège University in Belgium where she participated in 'Le Collectif d'Art Public'. Badran works capably in three media: pen and ink, etching and oils. Her works on her native Palestine under occupation are filled with an explosive anger, where shapes are disfigured into a savage psychodrama of paint. Badran displays the inner turmoil behind the superficial masks of human reality.

And We Had a Home
Oil on canvas
186 x 171 cm
1984

TAYSIR BARAKAT
Palestine, b. 1959
Born in Jabalia Refugees' Camp, Barakat studied at the College of Fine Arts in Alexandria where he graduated in 1983. Barakat's subjects have an appeal in their familiar serene landscapes with intimate figures and animal shapes. They are painted with simplicity: unusual shades of yellow, blending into blues and purple, all close in colour value, and interlocking spaces that structure the composition. Shapes in the form of birds and animals and various other symbols are used in his artistic expression. He works as an art instructor at the UNRWA Training Centre, while maintaining his strong roots. Barakat experiments with and paints his own vision of his homeland.

The Birds
Oil on wood
31 x 97 cm
Undated

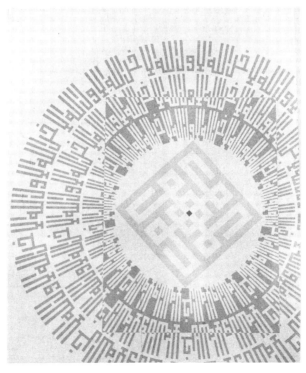

KAMAL BOULLATA
Palestine, b. 1942
An artist as well as a writer, Boullata was born and raised in Jerusalem. He works now at Georgetown University, Washington DC. Boullata graduated from the Fine Arts Academy in Rome and continued at the Corcoran Art Museum School. He creates a colourful network of Arabic letters, in which he lays emphasis on the relationship between language and art. His well constructed compositions are based on methodical study where the linguistic meaning as well as the graphic importance are bound together. His compositions are based on angular Kufic script and Boullata has succeeded in using the Arabic letter as a representational form of art. His sensitive and pure colours intervene subtly and spread to complement the interaction between meaning and form.

The Throne is God's Shadow
Silk screen
59 x 47 cm
1983

MUNIRA NUSSEIBEH
Palestine, b. 1943

Munira Nusseibeh attended school in Jerusalem where her talent was recognised by the French government with the offer of a scholarship. In France she studied first at La Grande Chaumière in Montparnasse and then at l'Ecole des Beaux Arts. Working since between the Gulf, Jordan and New York, her work in both sculpture and paintings exhibits a strength of purpose and a tension of change, with a harsh and a muted dichotomy of light and dark. In her works completed in the Gulf, she employed encrusted tar, sand and gold leaf. Her work is mystical, yet terrestrial and solid. Her sculpture, worked in traditional bronze, contrasts in its strong sense of perspective with her canvases, which have a deliberate absence of perspective.

Four Arab Women
Tar, sand, oil, gold paint
100 x 125 cm
1980

LEILA SHAWA
Palestine, b. 1940

Leila Shawa is a graduate of the School of Fine Arts in Cairo and the Academy of Fine Arts in Rome. She also took painting lessons with Oscar Kokotchka. After pleasant decorative paintings her work duly matured and she started taking up social issues, mostly concerning Arab women. Her paintings, at first glance, can be most misleading by giving an impression of passive submissiveness and pleasant, colourful compositions; however, the artist's quiet rebellion and cold anger starts to show through blind, kohl-laden eyes, the folds of beautifully embroidered restraining veils and manicured hands, tied up by inherited as well as newly acquired social inhibitions and restrictions.

The Impossible Dream
Oil on canvas
100.5 x 75.5 cm
1988

Sudan

Rashid Diab

When the Greeks occupied Egypt, they called all lands south of Egypt 'Ethiopia'. The Romans, who followed the Greeks in Egypt, adopted the same name.

Ethiopia comes from the ancient Egyptian name 'Tanhesu'. When the Arabs conquered Egypt they called our country 'Bilad al-Sudan', the Arabic equivalent of 'Ethiopia', which included the lands extending from the Red Sea to the Atlantic Ocean, in which black, dark skinned people were found. Today the word 'Sudan' refers to the Nilitic Sudan, a region that became a political entity only after the Turkish-Egyptian conquest in 1821, but whose impact in history goes back many thousands of years before the birth of Christ. The Sudan appears on the stage of world history thanks to the cultural and commercial relations that the ancient Egyptian kingdoms maintained with the indigenous civilisations, such as the kingdom of Napta and the Meroitic kingdom. The latter are considered among the most important of African civilisations, based in African soil and developed by the local population. All sorts of influences, from Syria, Persia, India, and even China, have been traced in its art. The Christian and Islamic periods also have great significance for Sudan.

The entry of Arabs into Sudan after the rise of Islam added a new radical element to the races already present, supplied the country with a new religion, the Arabic language, and Islamic culture, connecting it intimately with the rest of the Islamic world.

Perhaps painting is the greatest anomaly in Sudan. Except for the ancient Pharaonic paintings, as well as Islamic, Christian and Coptic art, painting can be considered comparatively new in Sudan as it has only appeared within the last half century. Also painting is thought to be very influenced by Western art styles. This is due to the fact that nomadism of one sort or another was the most common form of life in Sudan, and so the Sudanese were unable to develop an urban culture that would create the conditions required for the practice of the fine arts.

Besides nomadism, the whole ambience blocked the appearance of formative art, on account of the restrictions of Islam on human representation. At the same time the nomads' art (leatherwork, metalwork, containers, weapons, carpets, jewellery) though very modest has its importance as the vehicle of certain motifs which reappear in contemporary fine arts.

Traditionally poetry was the main art of Sudan. It played a crucial role in fostering national sentiments; even during times of extreme political oppression, when speech and the press were stifled, songs were expressions of current emotions.

The conversion of Sudan to Islam was effected by nomadic people who besides the Book could bring with them only such forms of art as could travel: poetry and calligraphy.

The poets who dominated the Sudanese literary world in the 1920s were public orators and performers. The art of poetry had then the original function of delivering a religious message. Many were romantics, longing for the glories of the past, such as Abdalah Abd al-Rahman, Albnna; the romantic mystical school of poetry *El-Fajar* (Dawn), 1932–1934, led by el-Tingali Yousif Bashir, Hamza el-Malk Tambal. . . . They started a certain imagery that fused tradition with the force and drama of life into a new concept of poetry. The creative artist began to respond with visual forms and new ways of expression. The earliest among these artists, being untrained, their work might have remained unknown were it not for the shows of Giha's and Ali-Osman, and the painting and exhibitions of Ahmed Salim and others in the early 40s. The works of the period tend to be figurative, devoted mainly to landscape and different aspects of Sudanese daily life.

The new Sudanese painting and sculpture started only a few decades ago, when Sudanese artists came increasingly into contact with the outside world. The present Khartoum Faculty of Fine and Applied Arts started in 1951 as the School of Design, and produced many interesting artists in the late 1950s, but has produced little significant work since then. This is due to traditional Western art education, which consists mainly in teaching the history created by Europeans and because the purpose of the school was to graduate teachers, drawers and designers for the colonial administration.

The following decade, 1950–60, saw Sudanese new art develop at an accelerated pace. Among the several schools and tendencies in the wide area of painting and sculpture, we can trace three main movements of artistic expression in the country. The most important one is the Khartoum school, composed of a group that includes painters and sculptors, who intend to rediscover their Sudanese identity.

The artist Shibrain explains that it 'married both the African and Islamic visual traditions to Sudanese customs'. The characteristics of expression were so decidedly Sudanese in nature, and successfully executed, that, according to Shibrain, the Jamaican artist, historian and scholar, Denis Williams, was prompted to refer to the indigenous contribution as 'Khartoum school'.

A new syntax was started by poets, composers and plastic artists during the period following independence, in which most of the important modern Sudanese artists began their careers. But in this short time they have produced quantities of marvellous original works.

In Sudan where the Arab culture of the north meets the negro cultures from the south, the Sudanese artist has to combine the essentials and fundamentals of the arts of these disparate groups. This peculiarity characterises and individualises Sudanese art and the Sudanese artist.

Salahi with Shibrain were the principal founders of the old Khartoum school which interprets forms that give a new expression of our society. They usually employ traditional Islamic motives and calligraphy, but Salahi, unlike Shibrain, makes a considerable use of non-Islamic motives. He combines human figures, animals and natural elements with forms of Islamic derivation.

However, the old Khartoum school never had a manifesto. 'We never thought of it, because our work emerges naturally, its logic is to regenerate our heritage and try to inspire and interpret what we really feel about our life.' Shibrain added: 'The manifesto is a Western attitude and we are not in need of it, especially in this case.'

The old Khartoum school is characterised by the use of popular African and Islamic motifs for design rather than for interpretive patterns, the abstraction of calligraphic letters with the symbol of African mask motifs.

In the Afro-Islamic compositions they create visual novels to bring together all the cultural experiences of Sudan so as to form an intermarriage in which no one dominates.

Abd Allah Eteibi, Ibrahim el-Awaam, Kamala Ibrahim, Musa Khalifa, Osman Wagialla, Salih el-Zaki, Gamman, Hassan el-Hadi, Tag Ahmed, and a number of others are also members of the old Khartoum school; they share the mystery of African ritual with the holy text of the Koran, north Nubian civilisation, Islamic civilisation's sufi tradition and the Christian/Coptic churches.

The modern Khartoum school is different from the old one. It shows less influence from Sudan's cultural past and is more Western orientated in its media and technique. Some of these artists, for example Ahmed Almardi, Seif el-Lautta, Isam Abd Alhaliz, are still using Sudanese images; others, Salih el-Zaki, Rabbah, el-Gatim, try to look for new local materials and techniques; the artist Salih el-Zaki tends to combine Sudanese traditional objects (basketwork) with painting and mixed media (collage), while Rabbah developed a 'solar engraving technique' which traditional artists of Sudan use in decorating calabashes and gourds; he also reflects Sudanese themes, and frequently employs both African religious symbolism with Arabic calligraphy in creating new patterns and designs to interpret the contemporary environment.

The critics contend that the Khartoum school actually produces tourist art. At least those who came later, at the beginning of the 70s, were producing a conventional art for the European market, and they have lost the basic intention of the pioneer artists of restoring the cultural heritage in the aftermath of the colonisers.

The Crystallists were the only group who declared a manifesto, very similar to the modern European movements. The well-known painter and head of the painting department at the Faculty of Fine Arts (Khartoum), Kamala Isahag, was identified with the Crystallist group in spite of the inclination in most of her work towards social problems (pertaining to women) in Sudan, and the successful intention to restate an aesthetic of the Sudanese heritage in contemporary expression. The third main tendency has become known as conventional art on account of its formal resemblance to modern European painting and sculpture. It shows little influence from Sudan's cultural past, but it does appeal to part of the public on account of the high quality in its overall expression and composition.

Many other artists remain apart from any classification of style. They do not associate themselves with either movement, the Khartoum school or the Crystallism school.

Ahmed Abd Alaal, Omer Khairy, and Hassan Ali Ahmed have created their own schools. Ahmed Abd Alaal successfully blends influences from several disparate cultures in a highly original sufi vision. Omer Khairy (George Edward) keeps creating the reality of his daily existence in a remarkable sense of composition and unlimited imagination with eternally mysterious logical instinct.

Hassan Ali Ahmed, a young representative of abstract art, hard working and talented, sometimes emotional, is a leader of abstract and modern painting in the country.

Sudanese contemporary art embraces a whole range of styles, each of which is clearly distinguishable and corresponds to a specific decade and generation or groups of artists, although no specific style could be described as more or less Sudanese than any other. It is an example of diversity in unity, or unity in diversity, and proves indirectly that this art has a special character of syncretism.

This study does not claim to describe the whole field of Sudanese plastic art with its various ramifications and to follow its flourishing step by step.

However, all those movements should remain free from the corrupting influence of Western schools and express instead their own qualities; which is what Sudanese art is trying to achieve in spite of the varied approaches that artists adopt.

See colour pp. 125–129 for plates of the following artists' work:

SHAMS EDDIN ADAM
IBRAHIM EL AWAAM
BASTAWI BAGHDADI
KAMALA IBRAHIM
MOHAMED OMER KHALIL

AHMAD IBRAHIM ABDAL AAL
Sudan, b. 1949
Abdal Aal studied first in Sudan and later at the University of Bordeaux, France, where he gained his master's degree. He is a painter as well as a sculptor and a writer. He paints his people and his country with a sensitive approach, while expressing his Sudanese roots through the use of wood and brass. His works reflect a sensitive skill in the use of his material yet at the same time containing many inflections and symbolism. He continuously searches for a balanced identity between the visual experience and the world of symbolism and dreams.

A Body in Space
Wood and bronze
46 x 30 x 50 cm
1980

MUHAMMAD AHMED ABDULLA
Sudan, b. 1935
Abdulla graduated and taught at the School of Fine and Applied Art in Khartoum before coming to England to study ceramics. Training in chemical analysis helped him develop an understanding of ceramic bodies and glazes. In his early period Abdulla produced utiliarian pots with delicate glazes. His success was such that he had 16 entries in the Council of Industrial Design Index from 1968/81. His later phase comprises porcelain and stoneware hand thrown pieces of animals mainly goats, sheep and oxen which vary in glaze, colour and texture. His forms evolve from the expressive to the symbolic, and are evocative of Sudan's spirit, countryside and life. Abdulla is an original ceramicist who expresses his Arabo-African heritage through temporal animal forms.

Bulls
Ceramic
30 x 10 cm
Undated

RASHID DIAB
Sudan, b. 1957
Diab graduated from the faculty of
Fine and Applied Arts in Khartoum.
He is also an art critic and an
illustrator for *Sudanow*. He gained
a scholarship from the Spanish
government to further his studies in
painting. He also gained a diploma
from the Faculty of Fine Arts,
Madrid, and subsequently gained
his master's degree in etching, as
well as painting. He has continued
researching Sudanese
contemporary painting. Diab is a
productive graphic artist; his
etchings come filled with vibrant
colour and sensitive details, whilst
maintaining precision in his work.

Royal Family
Etching
30 x 39 cm
1987

OMER KHAIRY
Sudan, b. 1939
Born in Omdurman, Khairy is a
writer as well as a painter. His
formal art training was at the
Faculty of Fine and Applied Art in
Khartoum. His primary inspiration
is his immediate environment and
culture. His ink and pen drawings on
wood are distinctive and are like a
jigsaw puzzle with an overall
symmetry in which every element is
carefully related. Khairy has also
been occupied writing articles as
well as pursuing his art career. His
works are a direct and natural
response to the contemporary life
that surrounds him.

Nativity
China ink on wood
60 x 95 cm
1976

ABDEL BASIT KHATIM
Sudan, b. 1942

Abdel Basit Khatim's roots belong to the ancient city of Omdurman. His father was an able carpenter who taught his son the skills of the craft. His formal training was at the College of Fine Arts where he graduated in 1967. He subsequently travelled to Europe and returned to involve himself in art. Khatim developed an individual technique and style for himself. Out of wood Khatim has been able to create original works of art which he paints with personal colours. He derives his inspiration from his immediate surroundings and uses calligraphic elements in his works. Khatim is not restricted by any academic style rather his works reflect a free and honest expression of himself.

Untitled
Oil on wood
44 x 44 cm
1981

HUSSEIN HADI MOHAMED NOOR
Sudan, b. 1930

Hussein Hadi Noor was born in the famous city of Omdurman. His formal art training was at the Faculty of Fine Arts in Khartoum and he subsequently travelled to Britain where he furthered his art studies at the Royal College graduating in 1959.
Hussein Noor's paintings combine and distil rich varieties of visual experiences. The store of his imagery is derived from accumulated sources, the intellect which is a source of imagination and inspiration, and dreams. He is exploring his own identity and as far as he is concerned creativity is essentially an intellectual discipline, combined with emotion and sentiment.

Sudanese Tale
Oil on canvas
87 x 87 cm
1987

MOHAMED ABDULLA OTEIBI
Sudan
Oteibi has no preconceived ideas when he paints, because he sees painting as a conflict between ideas and form, expressed in abstract manner for such ideas as he feels. Oteibi is influenced by nature or popular traditions. He believes that art is a language to communicate with. He is a painter, a graphic artist and designs caricature. He was influenced by the Khartoum School and by Ali Othman.

Untitled
Ink on paper
38 x 55 cm
1978

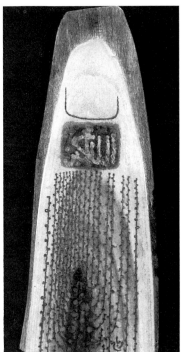

MAJDOUB RABBAH
Sudan, b. 1933
Rabbah's works possesses a distinctive style. He uses natural wood in its original form cut into different shapes and patterns and by different techniques such as burning, carving or printing he expresses his rich visual experiences. In his works he blends calligraphy with other motifs and patterns from his immediate Sudanese culture. His works reflect simplicity and rich intellectual content. Rabbah's early training was at the College of Fine Arts where he graduated in 1954. He completed his art studies at the Central School of Fine Arts in London in 1958. He subsequently travelled to Japan where he mastered techniques in decorative design and printing. He is both innovative and original in his creative processes.

God is Great
Burnt wood
13 x 26 x 66 cm
1975

AHMAD MOHAMED SHIBRAIN
Sudan
Shibrain is an established Sudanese
artist, a painter, graphic artist,
carver and teacher. Because of his
country's unique geographical
position, a crucible of African and
Arabian culture, Shibrain's works
utilise various media, calligraphic
elements, arabesques, Nubian,
Meriotic and African ideas. Shibrain
is also selective about his choice of
colours, black is all colours and a
multiplication of all colours, all
shapes and all hues, with which
Shibrain can identify things vividly
and spaciously. He paints with a
deep response to nature and to all
surrounding echoes. Shibrain
taught and was Dean at the College
of Fine and Applied Arts in
Khartoum; he also was Secretary
General at the Council of Arts and
Letters.

Untitled
Mahgon wood
55 x 56 cm
Undated

Syria
Tareq al-Sharif

Since ancient times, various civilizations have left their imprint on the cultural and artistic background of Syria. The earliest civilization was that of the Akkadians. The fourth millenium witnessed the advent of Hellenistic civilization, followed by the Roman Empire and its legitimate heir, the Byzantine Empire, whose rule lasted until the coming of Islam in the seventh century AD. These varied and diverse cultures managed to create, for the Syrian artist, a background of rich artistic heritage that provides him with the roots for his modern creativity.

Islamic civilization originated in Syria during the Umayyad Dynasty (661–750). The foundation of Islamic art was laid by Syrian Arabs and those from the Arabian Peninsula who founded the Umayyad Dynasty in Damascus, the capital and nucleus, from where Islamic art and culture radiated to reach far off places in Europe, Africa and Asia. After the Umayyads came various dynasties and finally the Ottomans, whose political influence continued until the Arab Revolt in 1917. There followed a short period of Arab rule which ended in 1920 when the country was put under French Mandate until Independence in 1946.

By the end of the nineteenth century new influences started to affect cultural and artistic developments in Syria. The pioneers who were to establish Syrian modern art were inspired largely by Western sources. Although they worked individually, without having a unifying school, collectively they set the example, up to the early twenties, for those who came later. Yet this diversion towards the West does not mean that Islamic art was neglected. On the contrary it continued to flourish in architecture, handicrafts, and calligraphy as well as popular painting inspired by heroic legends, religious stories and shadow theatre, and executed in a two dimensional primitive style reminiscent of Persian miniatures and Christian icons from Eastern churches.

The birth of modern art in Syria, in the twentieth century, fell under various influences, mainly those coming from Europe, carried by the acceleration in communications and the French Mandate. Local influences, guided by circumstantial events, inherited traditions and the political and cultural Arab Awakening, created an interaction between foreign and local influences which, coupled with the personal innovation of the artist, led to the creation of a distinct Syrian art movement with three visible phases: the Traditional Phase that includes the early beginnings and formative years, the Modern Phase that represents the rebellion against old traditional schools, and the Contemporary Phase during which Syrian art was crystalised.

The Traditional Phase

The Ottoman Period

The first Western influences on painting in the Arab countries occurred in the nineteenth century when the Ottoman Sultan Abdul Majeed (1839–1861) opened his country to the West. European artists were invited to reside in the Ottoman court and paint portraits executed in a realistic, classical style. Eventually local governors, in their far flung districts, started emulating the court, and a Western style of copying nature to the last detail, whether in portraiture or landscape painting, became the artistic norm of the day. People liked having their portraits and those of members of their family done to hang in their living room along with imaginary landscapes executed in pastiche, postcard style. Paintings hung on the wall as decoration began to appear for the first time, making local artists adopt Western techniques and aesthetics, and adapt them to their environment and needs. They took up European styles and abandoned their native art forms passed on to them by their Islamic culture. Thus, painting was alienated from its traditional locale of architectural decoration, books and everyday utensils such as lamps, plates, jars, cups, jugs, etc., and turned it into an independently framed piece of art that depicts a scene or a face by imitating nature in a mirror-like fashion. As this style spread, artists started to borrow their subjects from nature, the countryside, and city, and scenes of old houses and popular quarters, all subjects made popular by Orientalist artists visiting the Levant.

The Ottoman period comes to an end with artists like Tawfiq Tariq (1875–1945) who introduced an individual style and approach to the well-known classical school. Tariq's early artistic personality was first influenced by Ottoman painting through his Turkish artist friends and later by the French schools which he encountered during his stay in Paris while studying architecture. Strangely enough, he did not pay much attention to the new revolutionary art movements that were raging in Paris after World War I. His works were confined to portraits of well-known personalities and impersonal classical landscapes. The change in his work occurred when he started depicting contemporary subjects related to his country's background and current circumstances such as episodes taken from Arab historical events, executed in an arduous and meticulous style that recorded every minor detail he saw or imagined; Tariq is considered the pioneer of Syrian modern art. Through his strong personality and skilful technique he was able to impose his imprint on the work of the students, trained in his studio in Damascus, and gain the public's admiration and respect.

Munib al-Naqshabandi (1890–1960), although younger than Tariq, is also considered one of the early pioneers in Syria. His painting, *The Entry of the Arab Army into Aleppo*, depicts King Faysal's armies marching into Aleppo following the Arab Revolt led by Sherrif Hussein of Mecca. It was the first work of the time to deal with a contemporary subject related to an important current national event. It constituted a new trend in subject matter that was soon emulated by his students in Aleppo, where he gave painting lessons. There were other young artists, contemporaries of both Tariq and al-Naqshabandi, who, each on his own, was working in the same classical style. Among them are Abdul Hameed Abd-Rabu, Abdul Wahab Abul Su'ud, Michel Kirsheh, George Khoury, Khalid Maad, and Sa'id Tahseen in Damascus, Nadeem al-Bakhash in Aleppo and Subhi Shu'aib in Homs.

The French Mandate 1920–1946
The period between 1920 and 1946 is distinguished by the influence the French schools of painting exerted on Syrian artists, either through French artists visiting the country or through Syrian students sent to Cairo, Paris and Rome on scholarships, to train in art, and become art teachers.

Two schools were prominent, the Orientalist school recording historical events and the Impressionist school that took the artist out of his studio and into nature.

As a reaction against the French occupation, artists following the classical school painted historical events from their past and commemorated heroic episodes such as the battles of Hittin, al-Qadissya, Yarmouk, the conquest of al-Andalus and other important heroic sequels. Among the best known in this style are Sa'id Tahseen (1904–1986), Abdul Wahab Abul Su'ud (1897–1951), Mahmoud Jalal (1911–1975) and Fathi Mohammad (1917–1958). The last two are also sculptors, who at one time resorted to symbolism in spite of their classical training.

On the other hand, with the expansion of Impressionism, Syrian artists went out to the countryside to paint from nature, presenting a new and fresh outlook that emphasised light and colour and lured the public into acquiring their works. Among the most important Syrian Impressionists are Michel Kirsheh (1900–1973), a prolific artist who, while in Paris, was greatly influenced by the Impressionists. He adopted their style in depicting Damascene streets and environs, while giving art lessons in secondary schools, and leaving his imprint on a generation of young artists. Another artist who propagated Impressionism through his teaching in secondary schools was George Khoury (1916–1975), while Abdul Wahab Abul Su'ud (1897–1951) after visiting Paris, came back to paint stage backdrops and work in the theatre.

During this period, artists became aware of the seriousness of their task. They felt the need for studios where they could work and teach, and for an exhibition space where they could show their work. Consequently they started to organize themselves into groups as well as set up art and literary associations. They held group exhibitions, which spread art appreciation among the educated classes. At the beginning artists joined other clubs instead of forming their own associations. The first such group was 'The House of National Music' which had a branch for fine arts. After a few years it was replaced by the 'Damascus National Club for Sports'; and in 1941 its art subsidiary held the first large group exhibition, in the Institute of Law, which included local and foreign artists. Artist members of the two former clubs soon joined to form an informal group calling themselves the 'Veronese Studio', and took on a paint tube as their emblem. This was the first proper gathering of artists, and later on it was registered under the name 'The Arab Society of Fine Arts', and set up a centre to teach art. In 1944 its members held a large group exhibition in Damascus in which artists from all over the country took part, as well as foreign artists living in Syria. Following 'The Arab Society of Fine Arts' other societies were formed such as 'The Syrian Society of Arts' and 'The Syrian Society of Painting and Sculpture' who, with their predecessor, played a vital role in bringing together intellectuals, writers, poets and artists by holding lectures, discussion groups and seminars where they critically discussed their work and exchanged points of view in a positive climate.

Post-Independence Period 1946–1956

With the end of French rule in 1946 the art movement in Syria witnessed a great development towards self awareness. Individual styles started to evolve marrying Impressionism to local subjects and indigenous aesthetic values, while creating a closer bond between artist and nature.

Consequently, a generation of art lovers developed who came to appreciate the work of local artists, who dealt with native subjects and worked in a local impressionistic style. This new interest encouraged artists and made local 'Impressionism' reach a peak of popularity. Among the most important Impressionist artists of the period are Nazir Shoura (b. 1920), Rashad Quseibati (b. 1911), Noubar Sabbagh (b. 1930) and Abdul Aziz Nashwati (b. 1912). Along with Impressionism, other styles of painting evolved, such as Surrealism and Symbolism, but they never gained the same popularity as Impressionism. There were experiments in Realism, influenced by the Impressionists, carried out by artists like Subhi Shu'aib (1909–1974), Abdul Qadir Al Na'ib (b. 1938), Nazim Al Ja'afari (b. 1918) and others, who emphasised the importance of line and drawing in a painting. On the other hand, Sa'id Tahseen (1904–1986), Mahmoud Jalal (1911– 1975) and Abdul Wahab Abul Su'ud (1897–1951), moved painting from imitation of nature with a simplistic intellectual background to a search for a distinctive individual style and personality.

The Modern Phase 1956–1966

After 1956 new trends in art started to replace old ones and artists began to show an aversion to traditional styles that depicted outside forms without searching for a meaning within the subject. After the Suez War in 1956, Syrian artists looked for new ways and modes to confirm their identity and stop imitating Western schools. They discovered the importance of their Arab-Islamic culture and the role it could play in forming an independent artistic identity through which they could express their political and social views. They also discovered that Modernism could be linked to their own cultural heritage, especially when they realized how this same culture had influenced some Western artists, such as Henri Matisse and Paul Klee, and made them rebel against their own classical art traditions.

The revival of heritage, tying it to modernity and finding a contemporary artistic language for each artist coupled with crucial political developments in Syria, formed several new directions and trends.

The Modern Arab Trend

This movement was based on Arab heritage, such as calligraphy and the arabesque which in most cases developed to correspond with the experience of modern European art. Among those who led this movement were Adham Isma'il (1923–1963), who discovered the importance of calligraphy and employed it in decorative forms through endless variations in a contemporary context, and Naim Isma'il (1930– 1979) who succeeded in finding a new artistic language based on the arabesque, utilizing its forms to express different concepts.

The Social and Political Trend

This movement concentrated on social problems that arose from swift, social changes taking place in Syria's urban and rural life. Among its followers were Mamdouh Qashlan (b. 1929), who painted village women in the city and borrowed some elements from primitive folk art to confirm his artistic identity. Another artist is Burhan Karkoutly (b. 1937), who was inspired by mundane events in the lives of simple people and by folk paintings, and used them to portray social and political subjects.

The Expressionist Trend

The artists of this movement sought inspiration within themselves, expressing their anguish and inner conflict through their art. They used newly discovered forms borrowed from their ancient classical heritage, and reformed them in a fresh style and context. Fateh Mouddarres (b. 1922) and Loua'i Kayali (1934–1978) are the leaders of the expressionist or abstract expressionist movement. Although Mouddarres, painter and novelist, started as a surrealist he soon changed to a naive style, reminiscent of children's drawings, before he turned to Expressionism. Kayali, however, depended on the strength of his elegant lines to define, in depth, his figures. They form well balanced and tightly fitted compositions, that transmit an idea connected with a social or a political concept. Both artists established strong bonds between their inner selves and their artwork and gradually were able to transcend their egos in order to portray social anguish from an objective viewpoint, thus moving from the personal to the universal.

The Abstract Trend

The advocates of this trend move from the national and personal level of interpretation to the neutral ground of abstraction. One of its best established artists was Mahmoud Hammad (1923–1988) who derived his inspiration from Arabic calligraphy. In calligraphy, he discovered the flexibility he needed to constitute an abstract painting that combined logic and sentiment in equal proportions. He was to establish the school of calligraphic painting in Syria.

Slowly, the Abstract movement gained momentum and more artists participated. Nasir Chura (b. 1926), who earlier had been an important impressionist, turned to abstraction and eventually reached a new kind of abstract realism.

The post-independence era witnessed the coming of age of modern art in Syria. It also witnessed many important events that constituted the language of Syrian art. In 1958 the Ministry of Culture was formed and took over from the previous Directorate of Fine Arts, the supervision of all art forms in Syria. In 1959, during Syria's short lived union with Egypt, a College of Fine Arts was established in Damascus. It was based on the College of Fine Arts in Cairo, and had similar departments and curricula; Egyptian teachers formed the bulk of the faculty. In 1972 the Department of Architectural Design moved to the College of Architecture and the College of Fine Arts became part of Damascus University, while Syrian artists replaced Arab and foreign teachers. Consequently, the number of employed artists increased, the patronage of art exhibitions broadened and concerned government agencies took over the supervision of all artistic activities, set the rules for holding important exhibitions, started collecting works of art and set up Fine Art Centres that gave art lessons throughout the country. The number of private and government owned exhibition space increased and this allowed the artist to address a larger segment of the public.

A very important development that took place during this period was the birth of art criticism through daily and weekly publications as well as books. The critics discussed many issues among them Modernism versus Traditionalism. This aroused the curiosity and interest of the general public.

The Contemporary Phase 1968–1988

The Syrian art movement, after much experimentation and research, reached a level of consistency and maturity that crystalised into the present Contemporary Phase. The artist has been able to develop his own clear-cut personality within a broad artistic outline that included original pioneering movements and matched international artistic styles and schools with local heritage and current indigenous realities. A new generation of artists appeared whose boldness pushed the movement forwards. They not only discovered new trends but also developed those trends to take a distinct form and shape, giving the Contemporary Phase a new dimension.

During this period the number of artists graduating from the College of Fine Arts and other Arab and Western art academies increased and artistic activity spread throughout the country. The increase in the number of artists is a distinctive feature of the period that reflected the mushrooming of numerous individual styles within a general framework.

In 1969 the Union of Fine Arts was formed. It included all working artists and undertook the responsibility of organizing the art movement and mediating between the artist and those who employ or commission him to do work. The Ministry of Culture also broadened its activities, and began to mount more official exhibitions. It launched a major exhibition to be held annually at the National Museum in Damascus, in co-operation with the Union of Fine Arts. The number of visiting foreign exhibitions increased with the increase in cultural agreements signed with other countries, while local exhibitions multiplied and a number of new commercial galleries opened, among them Ugarite, Ibla, Ishtar and Urnina. This increased exposure stimulated demand for works of art and individuals began to build their own private collections. Art criticism developed and a new art magazine *Al-Hayat al-Tashkilya* appeared in 1980. It publishes articles on the development of the arts in Syria and other Arab countries.

Increased official and private patronage encouraged artists to work in an open and competitive climate that helped different artistic trends to emerge. Among these, the principal ones were the following:

Individual Trends

These trends do not follow any known Western school but try to show a subjective point of view, through symbols, rendered within a modern concept, of local folk motifs and mythological characters, that are presented within a new realism, sometimes coupled with personal expressionism. Arabic calligraphy is the principal component, and is mixed with other components derived from arabesque patterns, naive drawings, iconographic forms, handicraft designs borrowed from woodcarving and metal work and figures found in Palmyra and Busra, as well as other archeological sites. Among those artists who developed their own personal trend is Elias Zayyat (b. 1935), who borrows from religious icons and local crafts and makes use of patterns applied to wood carvings to come up with works that depict symbols relating to humanitarian and political concepts. Nasha'at Zu'bi (b. 1939), who depicts popular streets and old houses and public baths in a style reminiscent of Arabic miniatures, while building up a painting to represent complex humanitarian concepts in simple language. Ghayath al-Akhras (b. 1937) utilizes popular drawings incised on swords and printed on paper as well as wood decorations in an innovative style. Ahmad al-Siba'i (1935–1988) applied a simple language derived from children's drawings to tackle, in a spontaneous expressive manner, problems related to rural life. Nazir Naba'a (b. 1938) presents a realistic style with female figures on highly decorative backgrounds, using symbolic language and turning woman into a symbol for the people. Ghassan al-Siba'i (b. 1939) presents man in a dramatic manner by breaking the human figure into constructional forms in order to represent social issues, while keeping him the main element in a painting. Khuzaima A'lwani (b. 1934) exploits mythological monsters to represent the powers of evil that fight man and hinder his progress. All these experiences show the arduous efforts on the part of the artist to portray various, and sometimes conflicting, political, social and economic realities which the Arab nation faces, and his endeavour to find some solutions, through a personal symbolic language, so that around his work he can verify his presence in a constructive manner.

The Realist Trend

During the contemporary phase the art movement witnessed a surge of Realism with two distinct schools: the first one records the local environment with its archeological sites in a sensory manner and meticulously portrays the beauty of the country, giving special attention to detail and respecting the outward appearance of scenery and monuments. Among those who follow this school are: George Jaddoura (b. 1930), Ahmad Waleed Izzat (1934–1972), Boutros Khazem (b. 1935), Abdul Mannan Shamma (b. 1937), Izzeddin Hammat (b. 1938), Ali Khalil (b.1950) and Ahmad Ibrahim (b. 1950).

The second group of realists selects national subjects with humanitarian concepts to present a reality different from the sensory one of the first group. To them Realism means finding the connection that exists between the image and reality, rather than the accurate recording of reality itself. Artists who propagate this second school are: Alfred Hatmal (b. 1934), Ghazy Khalidi (b. 1940), Rida Hashas (b. 1939), Fouad Abu Kalam (b. 1945), Khalil Akari (b. 1945), Edward Shahda (b. 1902) and Mahmoud Shikhani (b. 1952).

The Expressionist Trend

Those who follow this trend do so because they are convinced that it is the only way to transmit their inner reactions and feelings about significant events, such as political and social upheavals in Syria and the Middle East. By employing strong colours, and destroying and distorting figuration, they manage to capture the prevailing public mood. They may differ in their choice of subject matter and the style each one follows but they unite in linking their personal suffering to the general climate of their country during a specific time. Among those artists are: Marwan Qassab Bashi (b. 1935), Burhan Karkutly (b. 1932), Labib Raslan (b. 1939), Laila Nasseer (b. 1941), Hind Zulfa (b. 1942), Asma'a Faoumi (b. 1943), Abdullah Murad (b. 1944), George Mahir (b. 1945), Fouad Abu Sa'da (b. 1946), Abdul Qadir A'zouz (b. 1947), Nazir Ismail (b. 1948), Ma'moun al-Himsi (b. 1949), Ghassan Jdid (b. 1946) and Ziad Daloul (b. 1953).

General Arab Trends

Followers of these trends seek inspiration from their Islamic-Arab heritage transmitted through classical calligraphy, the arabesque , Islamic miniatures, local folklore and other designs related to their culture. They interpret them in different forms and styles. The artist discovers the richness of his heritage in forms he can borrow to build up either a decorative or an expressive painting, graphically transmitting a poetic message or a humanitarian problem. Thus some took up the Arabic letter and reintroduced it according to his or her fancy and within a new context, others took up the arabesque design and added it to other matrices. To all, Islamic culture comes alive to become a source of inspiration and experimentation, each according to his need, imagination and mode of interpretation. The most outstanding artists in this group are: Abdul Qadir Arna'ut (b. 1935), Sami Burhan (b. 1932), I'd Ya'aqoubi (b. 1934), Ma'ad Orfali (b. 1934), Sa'id Nasri (b. 1941), Ihsan Abu A'tash (b. 1943), Abdul Rahman Sakhr Farzat (b. 1943), Mohammad Ghannoum (b. 1949) and Walid Agha (b. 1953).

A number of expatriate artists who live abroad have been able to prove themselves in the countries where they reside, building an artistic reputation on a par with others in the West. Among those expatriates are Marwan Qassab Bashi, Burhan Karkutly and Ibrahim Huzaima in Germany, Sami Burhan and Mustapha Yahya in Italy, Ghayath al-Akhras, Sa'ad A'rabi and Sakhr Farzat in France, and Mukhlis al-Hariri and Ali Arna'out in the United States.

The quest of modern Syrian artists has been dramatically intertwined with their nation's social, economic and political life. Their search has culminated in interpreting developments around them with a set of indirect experiences. Their refusal of traditional renditions make them resort to symbolism, abstraction, expressionism and other indirect forms in order to put forth a distinct artistic personality. Today, Syrian artists, while staying within their own reality and culture, have succeeded in combining abstraction and realism in a special equation that introduces their own artistic language. They combine past experience with present introspection to advance towards the future with new aspirations.

See colour pp. 130–133 for plates of the following artists' work:

SAMI BURHAN
FATEH MOUDARRES
NAZIR NABA'A
ELIAS ZAYYAT

NASIR CHURA
Syria, b. 1926

Chura first worked in realistic oils with nature, especially flowers or traditional figures such as the bedouin against the slender lines of their goat hair tents. In all these works, however, he made a conscious effort to shun the third dimension. Gradually his work evolved to stress the colours of the landscape, not its features. He moved to abstract patterns, the delicate tracery of the veins found in plants or the rough edges of rocky crags. These then came to constitute abstract canvas where organic colours, the yellow-brown shades of Syria's rocky plains, piled one upon the other as if cut from construction paper and applied to the surface of canvas.

Town of Maaloula
Acrylic on canvas
77 x 59 cm
1988

MAHMOUD HAMMAD
Syria, 1922–1988

Throughout his artistic career Hammad has always explored new meanings and directions. His academic training in Italy at the Accademia di Belle Arti in Rome and his subsequent travels in Europe and his contacts with the latest trends in the West allowed Hammad to become more appreciative of his rich native land. Upon his return to Syria he immersed himself in painting scenes and subjects of his beloved country. Hammad was a powerful painter, a teacher and a graphic designer. In the sixties Hammad began to use letters from the Arabic alphabet, and was more concerned with their movement and rhythm in space than their actual meaning. Hammad served as dean of the Faculty of Art at the University of Damascus.

Calligraphy
Oil on canvas
60 x 75 cm
1985

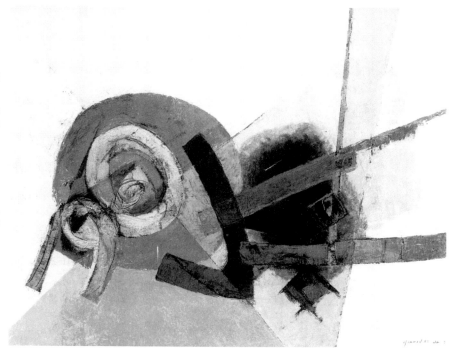

Tunisia

Ali Louati

The Modern Art Movement

The modern art movement in Tunis began to develop on the fringe of traditional culture, under the influence of Western thought and artistic norms. However, Arab Islamic heritage always remained a reference point for Tunisian artists. Even when they worked according to Western aesthetics, many artists borrowed elements from their heritage. As the movement developed, new trends appeared that tried to tie the present with the past and based these experiences on the sum of Islamic artistic expressions.

In the nineteenth century a new form of art appeared in Tunis. Painting on glass, which was already known in some Mediterranean countries, became popular. This marked the first attempt in modern times to open up to neighbouring cultures. This new art form comprises the first step to join Western influences that go back to the Renaissance with elements in calligraphy and arabesque borrowed from Arabic and Islamic traditions. Traditional architecture, Islamic decoration and other traditional arts continued side-by-side with this new development.

Traditions of Islamic art, including painting on glass and decoration, reflect the aesthetic and spiritual beliefs of the community, while modern artistic expressions, in the Western sense, reflect personal taste which makes a painting seem like a window showing a subjective view of the world. The introduction of this new Western outlook started at the beginning of the nineteenth century, in the palaces of princes and the aristocracy, who commissioned European artists to do their portraits. This fad of portraiture came at a time when a gradual change in social life, directed towards the West, began to take place in architecture, modes of dress and furnishings. The first Tunisian artist to follow the newly adopted Western trends and norms, particularly in his portraits, was Ahmed ben Osman who lived in the second half of the nineteenth century. Some of his works still survive in Tunisian museums.

Yet, easel painting and other modern artistic forms would not have developed in Tunis had they been practised only behind closed palace doors, for there must be a relationship between the artist and the public for a modern art movement to grow and develop. In Tunisia, this relationship came about with the emergence of the 'Tunisian Salon' in 1894. The Salon was an annual art exhibition created to satisfy a cultural need felt by the country's foreign inhabitants. It became, nevertheless, the first framework to embrace the birth of the Tunisian modern art movement.

The inauguration of the first exhibition of the Tunisian Salon took place on 12 May 1894, thirteen years after Tunisia was declared a French Protectorate. The organizing of the exhibition was supervised by the 'Carthage Institute', the most important cultural and scientific institution in the country, whose job was to give the French presence a cultural and educational legitimacy that would complement the economic activities of the colonial power. The success of the first exhibition was an initiative to organize others, and eventually the Tunisian Salon became an annual event that continued to be held until 1984, almost twenty years after independence.

During the first two decades, the Tunisian Salon embraced the Orientalist school of art which, having lost ground in Europe through the emergence of new trends such as Impressionism, was going through a revival in North Africa, particularly in Tunisia and Algeria. The spirit that pervaded the Salon was one of narrow, provincial regionalism, maintaining traditional academic pictorial norms; a spirit typical of French colonial mentality that ran contrary to the new trends that were sweeping Parisian artistic and intellectual circles. Just before World War I, new experiments started to find their way into the Salon when a number of works by Albert Gleizes, Marie Laurencin and other members of the 'Salon des Artistes Français' were exhibited in 1913. Up to World War II many foreign artists regularly showed their works in the Salon, among them were Alexandre Fichet who presided over the Salon from 1913 until his death in 1966, Armand Vergeaud who was director of the School of Fine Arts, Abdelkerim Jossot, Alexandre Roubtzoff, Henri Dabadie, Pierre Boucherle, Moses Levy, Antonio Corpora and others.

The Pioneers

The early Tunisian artists took their first steps towards the development of modern art either on the periphery or within the framework of the annual French exhibitions. The late Hedi Khayachi (1882–1948) was the second artist after Ahmed ben Osman to follow Western norms and the first professional artist in the modern sense of the word. Although he managed to live off his art, he never held personal exhibitions which made him lack the fundamental dimension that is provided to the artist through interaction with the public. After Khayachi came Abdulwahab Jilani (1890–1961), who in 1912 started exhibiting in the 'Tunisian Salon' and stopped just before World War I. He went to France and took part in the activities of the Paris School, worked next to Modigliani, Picasso, Soutine, Chagall, Zatkin and others. He started his art training at the beginning of the century, in the Atelier Pinchart, which belonged to a French artist, and was popular among art students before the creation of the School of Fine Arts in 1923. Jilani was the first Tunisian Muslim artist to join the Salon, yet, because of his long sojourn in France, where he died in 1961, his style adhered to Western norms. In his few remaining works there is nothing that indicates any ties with his local cultural environment.

Next to Hedi Khayachi, who is known as a portrait artist for the elite, and Jilani, whose vision developed outside the Tunisian environment, Yahia Turki (1901–1968) stands out as the most important among the pioneer artists who influenced the formation and development of modern Tunisian art. Turki succeeded in creating a new artistic vision that was based on a spontaneous relationship with the reality of the Tunisian environment, in a simple expressive modernistic language, far from the academic methods and techniques that were popular among the colonial settlers.

Yahia Turki was born in Tunis in 1901; ill health forced him to cut short his education and join the civil service. He took part in the 'Salon d'Automne' in 1922 and in the 'Tunisian Salon' in 1923, where the founding director of the School of Fine Arts noticed him and offered him a scholarship. He accepted and resigned from his job at the Directorate of Finance. Yet after a few months he left the school, preferring the freedom of dealing spontaneously with forms and colours taken from his environment to the restraints of academic training.

The road in front of Yahia Turki was not an easy one. Taking up art as a profession in the twenties was a difficult and arduous task for foreign artists let alone for a native artist. Tunisians could never be treated with respect equal to that given to the French settlers. Nevertheless, Turki persevered to achieve his ambitions and realize his dreams by setting new guidelines for artists to follow regarding the relationship between a painting and its surroundings. A direct and genuine relationship evolved between Turki's works and the Tunisian way of life. He had a great love for the old city of Tunis and its people whom he portrayed in their busy, everyday life, going about their tasks, in their homes, gathering places and souks. He used direct cheerful colours, and paid little attention to detail, focusing on expressing, in a free and sometimes abrupt manner, a simple feeling of happiness. He opened vistas for those who followed him and gave painting a new indigenous meaning.

Among artists emulating Turki's artistic concept were Abdelaziz ben Rais, Ali ben Salem, Hatem Mekki, Amara Debbech and Ammar Farhat. They formed the vanguard who built the modern art movement in Tunisia and won Turki the title 'Father of Tunisian Painting'.

Each of the pioneer artists had his own independent personality that distinguished his works and set the broad outline for successive developments in the art movement. Abdelaziz ben Rais (1903–1962) tried to express a peaceful world of landscapes and sceneries shrouded by silence where the richness of limited colours seem to be the main element in the formation of the painting. Ali ben Salem worked hard at finding elements of traditional folk culture to employ in compositions reminiscent of miniatures and paintings on glass. Hatem Mekki (b. 1918) has a strong and mercurial personality; he could not decide on any one style but instead practised different styles and techniques, jumping from light watercolours to heavy calligraphy, from realism to expressionism, to superrealism and primitive art, while in the process, practising graphic design such as designing posters, postage stamps and currency.

Ammar Farhat (b. 1911) is considered if not the most outstanding figure in the history of modern art in Tunis then certainly one of its important leaders. A self-taught artist who did menial jobs at the beginning of his life, he endured poverty, and yet remained faithful to high aesthetic values. He used to depict social realities. Farhat's experience grew out of a life full of strife and human suffering. From a simple member of the poor classes he became one of the great artists of the country. His world wavered between a realistic outlook of things and spontaneous dreamy images overwhelmed by metaphor and symbolism. His realism is connected to his direct experience with urban surroundings and his relationships with people from different social levels, in particular with labourers, small shopkeepers, and negro musicians. On the other hand, Farhat sometimes expressed general ideas and symbolic concepts such as the significance of the family, youth and the beauty of rural life.

The mature and free drawings of the late Amara Debbech (b. 1918) won him a special position in the history of Tunisian modern art. He started showing at the Tunisian Salon in 1937, and continued to do so until after World War II when he emigrated to France and stayed until the early sixties. In 1967 he held a massive exhibition of more than two hundred of his drawings and paintings at the Municipal Hall for Arts in Tunis, summing up more than a quarter of a century of his artistic life. At the end of the sixties he went back to France, a hopeless and disturbed man and put an end to his life.

The Second Generation

Most of the second generation artists belong to the Tunis School which was the first artistic group that accepted Tunisian artists as members, although its founder, Pierre Boucherles, was a French artist. From the pioneers there were Yahia Turki and Ammar Farhat. From the second generation there were Jellal ben Abdallah (b. 1921), Abdelaziz Gorgi (b. 1928), Ali Bellagha (b. 1925), Safia Farhat (b. 1924), Zoubeir Turki (b. 1924), and Hedi Turki (b. 1922). From the third generation that came about after independence there were Hassan Soufi (b. 1937) and Abdelkadir Gorji (b. 1940). Each member of the Tunis School had his or her own personal trend but the majority agreed on a number of aesthetic values and standpoints and enjoyed a great deal of discipline and solidarity. Thus they are active up to the present, unlike many other groups which appeared but did not last long because of their lack of organization and cohesion.

Although the Tunis School does not have defined and common aims that unite its members, yet they are able, through practice, to represent a common and general idea of reality based on a special feeling in interpreting that reality. This feeling is best translated through holding onto aesthetic and sentimental values related to the traditional way of life, to folk culture and the validity of artistic heritage. Those who best represent this trend are Yahia Turki, Ammar Farhat, Zoubeir Turki, Abdelaziz Gorgi, Ali Bellagha and Safia Farhat.

The influence of traditional artistic values is visually interpreted in the works of Abdelaziz Gorgi and Bellagha. The former tried to rediscover the aesthetics of Islamic miniatures and, during a later period, tried to portray the afflictions of the common man's life, while the latter tried to make use of painting on glass, Arabic calligraphy and the different forms and techniques of handicrafts. As for Zoubeir Turki, his vast popularity is built mainly on his ability to interpret the real, diverse world of mankind with the cynical outlook of a folk philosopher, using mainly lines devoid of colour.

Jellal ben Abdallah borrows different elements from his traditional environment: artistic forms and architectural components, pieces of furniture and textiles, utensils and tools, clothing and jewellery, with which he embellishes an imaginative world where beautiful women live. He opens his intimate world to the infinity of the sea and the blue of the sky, beyond Buqarnain mountain in the Tunisian Gulf.

The Tunis School played an integral part in the introduction and development of Tunisian modern art. In the mid-fifties, after independence, and until the early sixties, its traditions and values became synonymous with what art should express in terms of national, spiritual and material values.

The Generation of Change

Some artists like Hatem el-Mekki and Hedi Turki (though he belonged to the Tunis School) opted to divert from the shared belief of their contemporaries that belonging to one's culture means transforming folk values to either a symbolic or a thematic painting. Their attitude, which contradicts the basic technical and aesthetic tenets of the Tunis School, was an indicator for the emergence of new ideas among young artists in the early sixties. The artists of the sixties believed that in order to assert their national and cultural identity, they must get away from the harmonious ambience of local environments, beyond the thematic content of everyday life, and benefit from the experience of international art, by cutting loose their provincial restraints. Many artists turned towards Abstraction, Expressionism, Surrealism and other contemporary trends of the international scene, while some focused on searching into the significance of symbols derived from their artistic heritage. The desire for change and experimentation overpowered the old trends, emphasising the necessity of change as a basic quality of the work of art.

Abstract Painting

Tunisian abstract artists had a fundamental mission in the history of the Tunisian art movement. They stood up to old attitudes, raised new questions about the aims and means of visual arts and helped awaken the educated public to modern aesthetic forms. By raising new questions, Abstraction managed to activate the whole artistic milieu. It directly influenced figurative artists who, though they did not give up their original subjects, began to pay more attention to problems of a purely visual nature as well as to the means of executing a work of art and its constructional techniques. Although the Abstract trend in Tunisia conformed to Western norms, nevertheless, it helped bring forth many significant artists, among them Hedi Turki who started his artistic career under the influence of Jackson Pollock's expressive abstraction and then Mark Rothko's contemplative aura. Turki then developed his own distinctive identity. It is based on the artist, trying to express a mysterious relationship between the world of reality and abstraction, through employing colour in a symbolic sense that verges on Sufism.

Among the Tunisian abstract artists are Habib Chebil (b. 1939) whose abstraction is in its purest form, and Ridha Bettaieb (b. 1939) who belongs to the same generation and implements in his compositions constructive elements that radiate strength and stability. Others are Amor ben Mahmoud (b. 1938), Habib Bouabana (b. 1942), Ismail ben Fredj (b. 1938), Mahmoud Tounsi (b. 1944) and Rafik el-Kamel (b. 1944) whose works carry a special significance in the Tunisian abstract trend, for their own merit as well as their influence on some of the young artists who studied with el-Kamel in the School of Fine Arts. In the late seventies he moved to a new style in his abstraction based on strict lines and colours and firmer compositions than his earlier floating shapes, while making use of collage techniques.

Besides artists like Hedi Turki, Habib Chebil and others who are totally dedicated to abstract painting, there are those who practised it at some time during their artistic careers; among them are Khelifa Cheltout (b. 1939), Amor ben Mahmoud (b. 1938) and Adel Megdiche (b. 1949). By the end of the seventies the tide of abstraction began to wane under the influence of figuration which resurged in different styles of expressionism, neo-realism and primitive art. By the early eighties a number of artists such as Hassan Soufi and Rafik el-Kamel, gave up abstract painting and el-Kamel moved to Pop Art and painted mundane daily scenes while making full use of photography.

The Authenticating Trends

Simultaneously with the Abstract trend, there was a new attempt in the early sixties, led by Nejib Belkhodja, to give Abstraction a local flair by tying it to traditional culture. Following this trend, many artists experimented with the Arabic script and calligraphy and elements of arabesque decoration. Those trends were meant to authenticate the modern fashions that were pervading the Tunisian art scene. They recalled the similarity between the two dimensional space in modern art and the space in Arab Islamic art. This trend is divided into two sets: one led by Nejib Belkhodja, based on constructivism, and another propagated by Nja Mahdaoui, dependent on calligraphy and the elasticity of Arabic writing.

Nejib Belkhodja's (b. 1933) experience is founded on his belief in the necessity of tying up with international art experiences through a critical attitude towards Abstraction, which in Tunisia, totally conformed to Western norms. He believed that artists should try and make use of traditional elements from the Arabic script and architecture, and encompass them in a two-dimensional aesthetic space. Belkhodja builds his painting based on the architectural construction of a city, tied up to applications of cursive and angular writings that recall the rhythm of the geometrical Kufic script and Islamic architecture.

Nja Mahdaoui (b. 1937) started his abstract experience with relief paintings, then in the early seventies moved to calligraphic painting under the influence of the Iranian painter Hossayn Zenderoudi (see the chapter 'Iran'). Mehdaoui is careful not to emphasize the content of words, but stresses instead the visual effect of compositions. He occasionally creates new marks and a modernistic script, but remains faithful to the traditions of Arabic calligraphy and Islamic decoration. On the whole, he abides by the laws of traditional space, filling it in completely, while paying great attention to its decorative appearance as a modernistic calligrapher. Other artists like Mohamed Sammoud (b. 1942) and Mohamed Zwawi joined the calligraphic trend, while numerous others like Ali Bellagha, Khelifa Cheltout, Hedi Labban and others tried it at some point in their careers.

There is a group of adherents to the authenticating trends who started with Abstraction and ended up by combining the freedom of abstract construction with symbols and signs taken from Islamic decorative traditions and folk handicrafts. To these belong a number of young artists, among them Ali Zenaidi (b. 1950), Noureddine el-Heni (b. 1954) and Habib Bida (b. 1953).

Modern Figurative Experiences

Although abstract art was the most significant experience of the sixties' generation, many other modern figurative trends appeared to confront and challenge the Tunis School. These dealt with figuration in original and different styles. Artists like Mahmoud Sehili (b. 1931), Habib Sidi and Bechir Lakhdar, like the abstract painters, believe that a free plastic experience should be the main concern of the artist. They refuse, however, to break down the elements of realism and totally submerge them in colour. They throw a new insight into objects, sometimes abbreviating them to near abstraction. It is obvious that the neo-figurative artists refuse the abstractionist's disregard for realism as much as they refuse the classical superficial rendition of the world. Through Expressionism, Surrealism, Neo-realism and primitive painting, they fragment reality then reconstruct it according to their personal likes and dislikes, mixing figurative depiction of the outside world with the world of the subconscious.

Sometimes this figuration sways towards current social issues as seen in one of the stages of Sadok Gmach (b. 1940). Others who contributed to the new figurative trends came from former generations who were known for their conservatism, among them Hatem el-Mekki, who in his latest phase, tried modern figuration beyond realism, and Abdelaziz Gorgi, who gave up his meticulous style derived from Islamic miniatures for the abandonment of free experience that portrays a cynical folk spirit related to primitive art and children's drawings; thus alienating himself from the seriousness of his generation. Among the new figurative artists are Adel Megdiche (b. 1949), with his cubist world floating in a translucent atmosphere, Abderrahmane Medjaouli (b. 1936), Teher Megdemini, both influenced by Francis Bacon, Moncef Menci (b. 1949) with his sickly wrapped corpses and Moncef ben Amor (b. 1943), who links fantasy to biting social criticism.

Another group of figurative artists follow a personal vision that is cut off from reality; it expands outside the limit of time, like the spacious world of Bechir Lakhdar. Fathi ben Zakour's (b. 1947) environment is reminiscent of the German poet Rilke's verses; Fouad Zaouche's drawings swing between illusion and a photographic rendition of realistic scenes; Ahmad Hajari's distinctive works combine the fantasy of creativity, scattered elements of his daily reality and fragments from childhood events. The significance of Hajari in the development of Tunisian modern art lies in his ability to join the spontaneous expression of a world filled with imagination and a mature restraint in handling his media that put him among the gifted artists of Tunisia and the Arab world.

Primitive Painting

Primitive painting represents a trend that grew on the fringes of common artistic styles. Works by primitive artists reflect diverse aspects such as personal dreams and images of social reality, a yearning for the old city and a celebration of family life. The most outstanding artists among this group are Baghdadi Chniter (b. 1938), Ali Guermassi (b. 1923), Mehrezia Ghaddab (b. 1934) and Ali Jtita.

Sculpture, Ceramics and Weaving

Painting is the most common form of art practised in Tunisia while other forms like sculpture, ceramics, designing and weaving thrive on the periphery of the modern art movement. The slow development of sculpture has historical, social and cultural causes. Before independence in 1956, sculpture occupied a minor part in the exhibitions of the Tunisian Salon. Sculpture is alien to Islamic cultural traditions. Moreover, the cost of executing sculpted work is relatively high and is prohibitively expensive for many artists. Nearly all of the larger statues in Tunisia have been commissioned by the government for public places. Among the outstanding Tunisian sculptors are Hedi Selmi (b. 1934) and Heshmi Marzouk (b. 1940). Some painters have also turned sculptor like Amor ben Mahmoud and Zoubeir Turki.

Although Tunis enjoys a rich cultural and artistic heritage of ceramics, yet this form of art has undergone no development in the modern period equal to its historical importance. This equally applies to weaving. The reason for the limited number of ceramicists and weavers may be the artists' inability to supersede their rich heritage where the traditions and standards of folk handicrafts are still very high. Among the major ceramicists are Khalid ben Suleiman, Heshmi Jamal and Mohamed Yangi, while the weavers include Safia Farhat (b. 1924) and Mohamed Njah (b. 1948).

Graphics and Printmaking

Interest in graphics started with Brahim Dahak's (b. 1931) exhibition of woodcuts held in 1966. A limited number of Tunisian artists are interested in graphics and studied it. Among Tunisia's graphic artists are Khelifa Cheltout, Mohamed ben Meftah (b. 1946), Gouider Triki (b. 1949) and Hedi Labban (b. 1946). Some like Fawzia el-Hichri (b. 1946) studied graphics and printmaking in short sporadic courses, and trained intermittently between 1962 and 1976.

In spite of the importance of Tunisian graphic artists in the development of the Tunisian modern art movement and their continuous efforts to introduce printmaking, the public has not come to accept it as a major art form, because the work is produced in numerous editions instead of a unique piece. The use of graphics in a variety of forms has also been limited. The only artist to make use of the versatility of this art form is Brahim Dahak, who has published two books which include his etchings. Dahak is inspired by a spontaneous folk spirit which he transmits through primitive and rough drawings. Ben Meftah's world is poised between the freedom of the medium in its reaction to acids and a tight and balanced space. Gouider Triki is impulsive in his spontaneous world of childhood dreams, while silence and dark environments form the background on which Hedi Labban's characters of the human tragedy move.

Conclusion

After approximately one century since the beginning of the modern art movement in Tunisia, creativity in the visual arts has become an integral part of the country's cultural development. The ever growing number of artists and numerous art exhibitions held every year confirm the solid but dynamic growth of the visual arts. The modern artist in Tunisia finds himself within a stimulating, supportive working environment. The government over the years has also helped young artists by offering them free exhibition halls, allocating budgets for acquiring art works and by establishing the Centre for Living Arts for the City of Tunis at the Belvedere Gardens. This includes the Museum of Modern Art that houses the state's art collection. It is also here that important international and national exhibitions have been held for the last ten years.

On the training level, the Institute of Technology for Arts and Architecture prepares specialists to teach fine arts and trains students in the different plastic arts. The Institute was founded in 1973 and is a continuity to the School of Fine Arts founded in 1923.

Modern Tunisian artists have had long experience with the visual arts and their works enrich the cultural life of Tunisia. The only way to cherish and develop this achievement is by continuing a critical dialogue to evaluate the sum of this new cultural tradition, and try to move it outside the normal circuit and make it play a new role. This role means a new definition of the artist's part in the development of the community which would make him an active and integral element in planning and building the Tunisian society of the future.

See colour pp. 134–139 for plates of the following artists' work:

KHALID ASRAM
IBRAHIM DAHAK
ALI GUERMASSI
NJA MAHDAOUI
GOUIDER TRIKI
HEDI TURKI

BRAHIM AZZABI
Tunisia, b. 1949
Growing up in Tunis among the monuments of Carthage may well have created in Azzabi a fascination not only with the monumental but also with ancient wall paintings. Trained at the School of Fine Arts in Tunis, Azzabi went through a period of copying European artists like Delacroix, Ronault and Klee and later in Paris at the Cité des Arts of discovering the work of Dubuffet and Fautrier. Thereafter his own style took shape where ochre yellows, like stretches of coastal beach, are constructed on the canvas from sand mixed with oil. These abstract works have the calming effect of desert expanses illuminated by shafts of light and silent rock intrusions.

Twilight at Magrada
Mixed media on canvas
70 x 58 cm
1982

MOHAMED BEN MEFTAH
Tunisia, b. 1946
Ben Meftah is a distinguished engraver of the second generation of Tunisian artists. An outstanding student at the School of Fine Arts in Tunis, Ben Meftah soon recognized that he was drawn to graphic design. He studied engraving techniques in Paris with Robert Cane, and also lithography. In 1974 he became professor of graphic design at the Technical Institute of Art and Architecture and City Planning, Tunis. Ben Meftah uses both the traditional techniques of engraving and new inventions of his own. His abstracts show technical accomplishment and imagination where an onlooker scans a timeless range of pyramids and globes. His human figures caught in the maelstrom of earthy struggle is equally arresting.

The Tent
Etching
50 x 75 cm
1979

KHALID BEN SLIMAN
Tunisia, b. 1951
Ben Sliman is both a ceramicist and a painter who has worked with fellow artists like Rachid Koraichi to produce monumental murals. But his own individuality gained international recognition from his first days as a student in Tunis and then in Barcelona. He takes geometric symbols, some very bold and even crude, then overlays them on the most delicate Arabic calligraphy. This contradiction between the everyday ciphers and the sublime expression of mankind's most noble sentiments is nevertheless visually attractive. It awakens the mind of the viewer and satisfies his senses with a skilful use of colour: dark green, brilliant blues and then the black charcoal smudges of graffiti smeared across the fine white penmanship of the manuscript itself.

Untitled
Acrylic
92 x 61 cm
1987

RAFIK KAMEL
Tunisia, b. 1944

Rafik Kamel belongs to the second generation of Tunisian painters. He had the opportunity of studying under the Tunisian Master, Hedi Turki, when he was still in secondary school. His athletic abilities however, took him into national and international football until his fascination with drawing brought him back to the School of Fine Arts in Tunis, and then to Paris. He is an abstract painter, who moves with ease between figuration and abstraction, and shows that there is no inherent contradiction, or real separation between the two. He uses biological or molecular forms in subtle colours that suggest an inner reality not visible to the naked eye.

Transfiguration
Oil on canvas
145 x 111 cm
1985

HEDI LABBAN
Tunisia, b. 1946

Labban is a distinguished graphic artist as well as a painter. His formal art training was at the School of Fine Arts in Tunis specializing in painting where he graduated in 1971. Subsequently he continued his art studies in France where he specialized in graphic art. He graduated from the Higher School of Fine Arts in Paris in 1975. Labban has studied different techniques and has expressed himself freely. He is among the new generation of artists who have freed themselves from social obligations and they express themselves naturally and truly.

The Wounded Bird
Etching
49 x 36 cm
1987

Turkey

Leila T. Bisharat

Turkey has no rival in the Middle East and North Africa to its claim to be the region's earliest leader in Western art forms and the first country in the region to found an academy of fine arts along European lines. This is not surprising. Modern Turkey is heir to the heartland of the Ottoman Empire and its cultural traditions. The Empire's capital, Istanbul, long monopolised the region's contact with the West before the nineteenth century.

Training in the Beaux Arts before the Turkish Republic

The school background of Turkey's first painters in the Western style at first glance bears no resemblance to training in the fine arts. The biographies of Turkey's prominent nineteenth century painters make curious reading: 'he was a graduate of the Imperial War College' or 'the Imperial College of Engineering' or 'the Palace Pages School'. This spans the century from 1794, when the Imperial War College was founded, to 1883 when the school that would become the Istanbul Academy of Fine Arts was opened.

None of these schools was a direct colonial imposition. The decision to form the schools, open courses in drawing and even the subjects included in the classes came from the Ottoman ruling elite. If they turned to foreign instructors to staff these programmes, all elements remained very much under the State's thumb; they were neo-colonialist perhaps, but nevertheless Ottoman in conception and execution.

The Palace School of Miniature Painters began to incorporate Western art forms in the eighteenth century. Despite an early incorporation of changing social values, the Palace School failed to make the transition; it refused to take seriously the new world of the nineteenth century. More importantly, the ruling elite was looking elsewhere for its entertainment. The Palace School had lost its patrons.

The Academy of Fine Arts

Founded in 1883, the Academy of Fine Arts today is only one among many institutions in Turkey where students may study the fine arts. Yet only this Academy is referred to, even today, as 'the Academy'. From 1883 until today it has had no rival in Turkey, but has spawned many provincial academies, associations, and institutes, the most important of which is the Gazi Institute founded in Ankara in 1930.

Behind the Academy's development was a remarkable Ottoman artist, museum curator and archaeologist, Osman Hamdi Bey (1842–1910). Osman Hamdi stayed in Europe long enough, twelve years, to become thoroughly Westernised not only in his painting technique but also in his views. He drew up the founding regulations of the Academy of Fine Arts and became its first director in 1883. It flourished under his leadership, but in a visual world that centred almost exclusively around the Bosphorus, with occasional infusions from Paris. The teaching staff was European, and Istanbul society during the first years of the century adopted French mannerisms.

An Academy for Women

In 1914, in response to repeated parental demands, the Ottoman government opened an Academy of Fine Arts for Women. This well preceded later claims of the Atatürk Revolution during the 1920s to have championed the cause of women's equality. There was an Academy for men, why not for women? Co-education was yet unheard of in Ottoman society, but painting for women was not. Young Muslim women had taken up painting as part of the finishing school arts that they ought to bring to marriage.

The new academy had a woman as its director who was every bit as remarkable as Osman Hamdi Bey. Her name was Mihri Müşfik Hanım. She was already a strong painter, whose work moved between the world of the veiled Istanbul ladies and the Levantine fashions of Paris. She was determined to offer her students the same opportunities that men had at the Academy. She is one of a number of Turkish women painters, such as Hale Asaf, whose work deserves careful research.

In 1926 the Women's Academy merged with the Academy of Fine Arts. Two years later men and women students shared the same studios. Equal education opportunities for girls and boys, including integrated classrooms from primary school through university, were a basic tenet of the Republic. The separate, secluded studios for women, so romantically painted by Ömer Adil, were now a relic of the past. Today Turkey has four generations of determined, recognized women painters.

Teaching the New Forms to Children

The early introduction of Western style drawing into the curricula of the teachers' training schools is clear evidence that the new forms were not restricted to the few, nor to a single group that fell under influential changes introduced by the 'New Order' in the military during the early nineteenth century. These training schools included drawing lessons as an integral part of the curriculum from the mid-nineteenth century onwards. These introductions all antedate the founding of the Academy of Fine Arts. By the time the Academy was founded, there was already one generation of young men, outside the military, who had Western art forms as part of their regular school education from the earliest classes. More importantly, they became the foundation for the active art training that goes on today through the teachers' training schools in Turkey. One of them, the Gazi Institute of Education in Ankara, has produced some of Turkey's major painters of today and has come to rival the Academy in Istanbul.

Istanbul: A World Unto Itself

As the Empire waged wars on multiple fronts in the Balkans and North Africa, and grew hopelessly indebted to European bankers, painters of the Çallı group painted serene, misty landscapes along the shores of the Bosphorus, mastered the impressionistic reflections of sunlight dancing on the sea's surface and executed both still life and female figures surrounded by lush drapery. There is no hint, not a single suggestion, of a society under siege. Istanbul was a world unto itself.

Çallı (1882–1960) was a graduate of the Academy of Fine Arts and spent the years immediately before the First World War in Paris studying under Cormon. He returned to teach at the Academy just as war erupted, bringing with him an independence of approach and a freshness of vision that moved him beyond imitative skill.

All the Çallı group became teachers at the Academy and trained the next generation of painters who went to Europe during the 1920s. The Çallı group not only continued to paint during these war years but also formed the first Arts Association, put out the first periodicals of art news and criticism, and exhibited in the galleries of Galata, the European quarter of the city.

Turkish Independence: The Creation of a National Identity

The first generation of the Academy's graduates replaced their European professors during the First World War. They looked back upon their Turkish teachers of the older generation as imitators of European styles, restricted by forms and incapable of freeing themselves in order to express their own Turkish personalities and heritage. Once having returned to Istanbul from their studies abroad they basked in the glories of the Bosphorus and developed a new, freer more abstract style that came to characterize many Turkish painters until the mid 1930s. But they did not look inward. Each student who returned from Europe was eagerly debriefed to learn the latest news of the Paris art world.

The Turkish War of Independence, which followed the Ottoman defeat at the end of World War I, turned to Anatolia for the strength to resist invasion. The Anatolian peasant, once ridiculed by the urban elite of Istanbul, was now idealized as the symbol of unadulterated Turkish culture, simplicity and perseverance. Turkish artists turned to Anatolia for their subjects. Although most of them were from well-off Istanbul families, they adopted the new symbols of the Republic. Many of the paintings bear the same clichés as the 'Soviet realism' of the 1930s: brawny peasants, ploughshares and later tractors.

The first years of the Turkish Republic which followed the Treaty of Lausanne (1923) later became known as the Atatürk Revolution. Mustafa Kemal Atatürk led the new Republic. The revolutionary 'reforms' he introduced included the banning of the Arabic script for writing Turkish in 1928 and its replacement with a new hybrid Latin alphabet. Introduced as a measure to speed literacy, the reform drove a final wedge between modern Turkey and the culture of the Ottoman Empire, between traditional art forms where the calligraphy of the Koran played a predominant role and the Western art forms espoused by the Republic's leaders. Mustafa Kemal Atatürk and his Kemalist entourage openly supported the arts in their new form. Painters, poets, archaeologists, writers and musicians enjoyed the limelight at the new, rugged court that Atatürk had opened in his rough, spartan capital, Ankara, in the centre of Anatolia.

Suddenly the subject matter shifts. The languorous waters of Küçüksu at the 'Sweet Waters of Asia' on the Bosphorus are replaced by barren hillsides, soldiers marching in tattered but proud disarray and martial portraits of Turkey's new leaders. Gone are the sumptuous brocades of Istanbul, replaced by rough great coats and the *kalpak*, astrakhan headgear of the frontier generals.

Peasants playing the traditional *saz*, longhaired Angora goats and village women at work followed the years of martial, epic paintings of the 1920s. Namık Ismail made the transition from the Bosphorus to the village, and late in his life painted Anatolian peasants riding behind oxen on the traditional threshing sleds of the harvest season. Muhittin Sebatı (1901–1935) has left some of the most sensitive scenes of the new capital, Ankara; the smoke of a train merges with the low hanging clouds that stretch over the vast steppe behind the simple railway buildings of the city. Cemal Tollu (1899–1968) and Refik Epikman (1902–1974) brought abstract cubism to the subject of Anatolia.

The 'D Group' and the Etatist Period of the 1930s

The best of this generation called themselves the 'D Group', and among them were the first professors at the Academy under the Turkish Republic. Most of them had had their own first training from teachers of the Çallı group, but now they thought they had been liberated by their exposure in Europe to Fauvism, Cubism and Expressionism. They were looking for a new national identity. Both Tollu and Epikman were among the founders of the 'D Group' in 1933. Others included Nurullah Berk (1906–1982), Bedri Rahmi Eyöboğlu (1913–1975), Eşref Üren (1897–1984), Elif Naci (b. 1898) and Arif Kaptan (b. 1906). They called themselves the 'D Group' to set apart what they saw as their own stage in the development of contemporary Turkish art. In their mind 'A' identified the Association of Ottoman Painters (the 1916 Istanbul-Galatasaray School), 'B' The Association of Fine Arts and 'C' The Association of Independent Painters (the 1929 first painters of the Republic such as Ibrahim Çallı, Mahmud Cuda (b. 1904), Hale Asaf (1905–1938) and Şeref Akdik). The 'D Group' was also joined by other painters, among them Fahrelnissa Zeid (b. 1901).

All the founding members shared a common rejection of the Turkish Impressionism of the Istanbul School, practised by Çallı and their other teachers at the Academy. They looked to the studios of practising artists for guidance, not to 'art academies' that lagged a generation behind new developments in expression. With support from Atatürk himself they turned to Anatolia for their subjects, but their experiments in Cubism and Expressionism were even more radical for Turkey than their subject matter. Most had worked with Lhote, Grommaire or Hoffman at some point. They replaced the soft, shimmering impressionist surfaces of their teachers with hard, architectonic, geometrical lines. Among them only Bedri Rahmi Eyöboğlu spent time in Raoul Dufy's studio. Dufy's influence is easily detected in the fluid lines of Eyöboğlu's compositions. Eyöboğlu's work and that of his wife, Eren Eyöboğlu (b. 1913), stand out among their contemporaries for their freedom, strength and diversity of expression. Bedri Rahmi addressed a broad public with new forms, such as textile design, which could be mass produced.

The 'D Group' used Cubism to abstract form from detail, and members like Nurullah Berk turned the delicate tracework of Turkish embroidery into abstract, cubist forms, much akin to the motifs of the Turkish kilim, or flatwoven rug. There is a freedom and individuality of expression, where the works, for the first time, can clearly be identified as Turkish.

The State sponsored artists to travel through the steppe country of Anatolia and paint. The first trip was conducted in 1937, and others followed each year until 1944. Bedri Rahmi wrote that he could never have painted the green of Bursa without being immersed in its layers of colour. Nurullah Berk during the same period comes forward with strong, designer-like statements of oriental colour, motif and subject that reject the third dimension. Berk also established himself as the spokesman and art critic of the group. Bedri Rahmi moved confidently into colourful mosaics that in subject and technique make the Istanbul paysage paintings of the preceding generation look imitative and drab by contrast.

During these State-sponsored annual trips artists worked together in Anatolia with all the material they needed provided by the State. These tours over eight years covered 63 of Turkey's 67 provinces. Nearly as many artists, 53 in all, benefited from the opportunity and made direct contributions to the State of 675 canvases they had executed as a result of the tours. This exposure to the Turkish countryside had a lasting effect on the inclusion of Anatolian motifs and subject matter in Turkish art over the next decades.

Behind this Etatist support for the arts was a remarkably broad-minded and creative Minister of Education, Hasan Ali Yücel. In 1940, when Turkey was already readying itself for long years of military preparedness and economic scarcity, Yücel promoted the annual State Exhibition of Fine Arts, first launched in 1938, and added a competition to select each year by jury, those artists that were most outstanding and promising. His granddaughter, Su Yücel (b. 1961), is one of Turkey's promising artists of the mid-1980s. In 1986 she held an exhibition of oils in Istanbul at the Baraz

Gallery where the subject was the frock coats of her grandfather and the evening gowns of her grandmother. This personal and talented commentary in the semi-abstract on the change in fashions showed the same kind of iconoclastic but loving integration with the past that her grandfather had used.

In 1938 at the first State sponsored national exhibition which opened in Ankara, the teachers of the 'D Group', including Çallı himself, gave up their places so that the new generation could receive all the awards. The Ankara exhibitions were to become regular events, with large if less than sleek spaces designated just for this purpose. Paintings of Anatolia, and those of Ankara, best exemplified by the work of Eşref Üren, settled down to become an integral part of the painters' regular expression, not simply a brief, commissioned trip.

Studied Folk or Naive Art

Most distinctive of all the painters who dedicated themselves to Anatolia was Turgut Zaim (1906–1974). He created a unique, deceptively naive style to present the children and women of rural Anatolia. The figures are lovingly moulded with warm curves, and the dark, almond-shaped eyes in each small face are outlined with black. At the centre of the painting are often placid, fluffy goats whose sharp little horns form the only counterpoint to the round childish faces, melons and water pots.

A graduate of the Istanbul Academy of Fine Arts and a participant in the 'D Group', Zaim was sent to study in Paris. He stayed only a few months claiming that there was nothing for him to learn there, no reason for him to even try to relate to the West. Influenced during his short stay by the Mexican painter, Diego Rivera, Zaim is an early example of the 'South' rejecting the 'North'. Once he moved to Anatolian subjects Zaim found himself and grew progressively apart from the Istanbul coterie with his unique style and orientation. It is the quiet Anatolian peasant, especially the central Asian eyes of the Turcoman villager and nomad, that rivet the viewer.

Zaim's daughter, Oya Katoğlu (b. 1940), is the only contemporary Turkish artist who is clearly imprinted with his style, so much so that they seem to go hand in hand. Painting largely since the late 1960s, her canvases have none of the depth of feeling, the mournful quiet of Zaim's monumental works. Instead they are full of cheerful, idealized images of small town, traditional festivities: the colourful headkerchieves of women, their abundant balloon-like trousers (*shalvar*) imprinted with gay flowers, chubby children on the run and well fattened sheep docilely awaiting slaughter. They belong to a more comfortable Turkey, one where a commercial market for paintings of this sort was already well established. Even the tiled roofs of Bursa look plump and prosperous in her paintings.

Other contemporary Turkish painters have continued, however, Zaim's search for forms that would link Anatolian subjects with simplified miniatures, or folk representations. None of these artists is, in fact, an autodidact folk artist. Nearly all are of the intellectual elite, and some have had the same kind of advanced training in the fine arts that Zaim enjoyed. Turkish art critics occasionally group them together as 'Naive Painters'.

It is their 'naive', childlike or optimistically simplistic approach to life that sets them apart. Fahir Aksoy (b. 1917), who has also written about art in Turkey, is an example of the studied naivete of those who chose this form of expression. He fills his canvases with boats, city people out on a stroll, a horsedrawn carriage or phaeton of the past promenading by the shops in a small town. Hüseyin Yüce (b. 1928), on the other hand, had no training whatsoever. His work rarely includes human figures and instead there is a nostalgic repetition of rural landscapes from the Kütahya area which he left to become a factory worker. Mehmet Peşen is a younger painter who has also chosen to present village life in a naive form. Among Turkey's current generation of promising young artists, Yalçın Gökçebağ, a graduate of the Gazi Educational Institute and a television producer, is a recognized interpreter of Anatolia in naive forms. His canvases have the perspective of the television camera's eye that views village activity and the countryside from a wide angle, overlooking a site from above. Activity is frozen in each scene as if a 'take' had been stopped. Others that may be included in this school are Ruzin Gerçin (b. 1930) and Neşe Erdok (b. 1940). More commercial in his 'folk' orientation is Mustafa Pilvneli, who has succeeded in moving from miniaturesque scenes of simple hunting figures to mass produced textile designs. Cihat Burak, about whom we will have more to say later, has occasionally been included among these 'pseudofolk' or 'naive' painters. His work, we feel, is distinctive and transcends such a classification.

The New Group: 1940 and Onwards

Although Turkey did not enter the Second World War, the 1940s were lean years. Turkey closed its borders during the 1930s to the outside world, isolated itself as far as possible from the international marketplace of the Depression, and did a bootstrap operation to build local heavy industry, encourage light industries and develop the country's rich agricultural resources. The harvest of the 1930s had to be channelled to national defence during the 1940s. It was a grey, cold period of bread lines, food scarcity and malnourished children. Paintings of the period reflect these scarcities.

Artists over the war years watched the fishermen of Istanbul strain the Bosphorus in a valiant effort to find fish for the protein-starved people of the city. Everyone was out on the waterfront. The fisherman, ragged but hardy, became the centre-piece of their paintings. The working man, not the salon, was the subject. Nuri Iyem (b. 1915), Ferruh Başağa (b. 1915), Avni Arbaş (b. 1919), Haşmet Akal, Selim Turan (b. 1915), Agop Arad and Abidin Dino called themselves now the 'New Group'. They dispersed after 1951, but nevertheless initiated a deeper commitment to expressing social problems in art.

With the Turkish Revolution of 1960, a military government briefly cleansed away what it viewed as the corruption of the multiparty regime of the 1950s and laid the constitutional basis in 1961 for what was hoped would be greater individual freedom. The new freedom of expression opened the way for the explicit representation in art of class oppression. Ibrahim Balaban (b. 1921), a peasant from a village near Bursa, allied himself with the Turkish Labour Party and openly depicted the subdued anger of the labouring peasants. His graphic art, from 1953 onwards, developed strong, hard lines that make peasant figures a corporal part of the oxen they press forward behind the plough or absorb working women into the branches of the trees where they pluck fruit. His explicit portrayal of the uprooted villager, huddled on the city streets in search of a day's wages, so enraged some spectators that a number of his exhibitions were stoned. Powerful artistic expression in league with a highly controversial social reality aroused unexpected anger. Art had come a long way from the salons of the privileged and the 'social realism' of one-party rule under Atatürk.

Other artists who continued the social commentary of the 'New Group' included Neşet Günal (b. 1922), another villager dedicated to the graphic portrayal of misery in the countryside, Nedim Günsür (b. 1924) and Kayihan Keskinok (b. 1923). All of them children of the Atatürk Etatist period of the 1930s, each of them has tried to project the life of the common man in an expressionist, or pseudo-folk art form. Keskinok paints the festivities of village life on the Black Sea, the 'Village Bride' being conveyed triumphantly in a dory, surrounded by oarsmen and chanting, drumbeating sailors, their women and children accompanying them across the sea to the bridegroom and his village.

Two other painters carved out a unique position for themselves during the 1950s. One was Cihat Burak (b. 1923). an architect, and the other was Sabri Berkel (b. 1909), a teacher from 1935 onwards at the Academy of Fine Arts. Their work is dramatically opposed. Burak is fanciful, suffused with fairytale colour and a prankish sense of humour. Burak's architectural training of the 1940s and project work of the early 1950s moved into full-time painting by 1953 when he studied art in Paris for two years. Suggestions of his architectural bent remain in the detailed arches of the covered market or palatial backdrops that provide the setting for his colour-bedazzled, often dwarfed, figures that promenade through a fantasy cityscape.

Berkel, on the other hand, produces works that are abstract, dark and cold in their discipline. Already a professor at the Academy when Burak was a student next door at the Faculty of Architecture, Berkel (b. 1909) was born in Üsküp, now a part of Yugoslavia but then part of 'Turkey-in-Europe'. He studied art in Belgrade as well as at the Academy in Florence under Carena (1929–1935). A student also of Chini and Celestini, Berkel taught at the Istanbul Academy from 1935 onwards. A founding member of the 'D Group', he abandoned naturalism after 1947 for semi and then pure abstraction. With time his incessant productivity has spawned a ceaseless set of harsh, abstract canvases with perfectionist balance in composition. A luminous, bright ellipse and line may contrast with projecting dark diagonals and a sombre background. His work has remained strangely isolated, pure in its forms and determination, from the social commitments and free form expressions of younger artists of the same period.

During the 1950s Turkish artists had their works exposed for the first time, on a large scale, to foreign critics on their home shores. In 1954 the International Association of Art Critics held its meeting in Istanbul and a Turkish bank took the opportunity to enlist these eminent art critics a jury the bank formed to judge a set of works submitted by contemporary Turkish artists. The first award, much to the surprise of many of the participants, went to Aliye Berger (1903–1974), an engraver, the sister of Fahrelnissa Zeid and aunt of Füreya Koral, the ceramicist, but not someone the leading artists such as Cemal Tollu and Bedri Rahmi Eyöboğlu saw as real competition. They had to revise their opinions, and look at the work around them with a new eye. For despite the spate of argumentative articles, all saw the event as a very positive contribution to the art movement. Turkish art was now reaching out to begin the kind of mature development of the next two decades, in which artists would take their places abroad as well as in Turkey.

Among the 'New Group' Nuri Iyem (b. 1915) has shown the most consistent growth with time. He moved from abstract canvases in the 1940s and 1950s to stylized portraits of Anatolian women from 1960 onwards. Their eyes stare in mute, proud silence, from below the smooth circumference of their kerchiefs. There is a stolid beauty in their subjugation. Trained at the Academy under both Çallı and Leopold Levy, he participated in all the Group's exhibitions from 1941 through 1951, but unlike the others continued to work exclusively in Turkey with an occasional exhibition abroad. A ceramicist as well as a painter, Iyem's paintings make a bold statement about Turkey's social order. They incorporate beauty and optimism in an appeal for the recognition of injustice.

By the mid-1960s travel to Europe was no longer the monopoly of the upper classes and the educated. Turkish villagers were moving in droves to Western Europe as labourers. Concern for their well-being also became part of the artists' expression. Orhan Peker (1927–1978) made a special, almost childlike effort to incorporate these new dimensions into his art in a fashion that might start a dialogue with the new, uprooted class of villagers, especially their children. They were isolated in Europe not only from their village orchards and fields but also from their own language, neighbours, animals and culture. A graduate of the Istanbul Academy and a student of Bedri Rahmi Eyöboğlu, Orhan Peker had all the makings of an artist who could choose his audience, to his own profit. Instead, he whiled away hours in his Ankara studio sketching animals, his own cat or a hobbyhorse mule he had himself created to serve as a model. Many of his watercolours and oils were intended to become children's stories. Only a few ever did. One that he finished was called *The Kite that Got Caught in a Tree*, 1974. It was published for the children of Turkish workers in Germany. Sadly many other stories, illustrations all in serial order, were dispersed among art dealers upon his untimely death. There is a sensitive, innocent tranquillity and concern in all his work.

The Absence of Calligraphy in Modern Turkish Art

Few modern Turkish painters used calligraphy in the nineteenth century, even before the Atatürk 'language reform' closed the book on expression with the Arabic script. Western art forms and those who used them, set themselves apart from traditional forms of expression. Among the Çallı group Feyhaman Duran (1886–1970) was singled out as something of an oddball because he was so interested in the calligraphic arts and privately collected works of the *hattat* calligraphers. Şeref Akdik's portrait of his father, the noted calligrapher Hattat Kâmil Akdik, relegates calligraphy to the past. He painted Akdik as an old man, seated pensively next to his traditional Ottoman scribe's writing case with an example of his calligraphic art in black and grey hanging in the musty shade of the wall behind him. There is no light or energy in the portrait. By contrast Feyhaman Duran's portrait of Hattat Şeref Akdik portrays an elegant, confident gentleman whose calligraphic art is symbolized by a delicately rolled tube of white paper that shines at the very centre of the painting.

With the exception of Bedri Rahmi Eyöboğlu, few of Turkey's modern painters who have used calligraphy are among its most prominent artists. Elif Naci (b. 1898) is one of the few artists who has used calligraphy and classical Turkish motifs on canvas. But both Naci and Eyöboğlu went to school when Arabic was still the script every schoolboy learned to write Turkish (then called Ottoman). Naci was already thirty years old when the language reform took place; Bedri Rahmi was only fifteen. Naci is best remembered as an art critic and a museum director. His years at the Museum of Turkish and Islamic Art were spent with the most remarkable examples of Seljuk and Ottoman tiles, ceramics and carpets. When he introduced these motifs into his paintings he nevertheless felt obliged to point out that Matisse also had done so.

Where the art of the calligrapher has persisted in Turkey, it has been in the hands of a small group of devout specialists. Adnan Turani (b. 1925) saw the potential of calligraphy in abstract art, but the calligraphic forms in his canvases are stilted, an artificial introduction to the composition. Their shapes are devoid of symbolism or reference. He belongs to the first generation which was never exposed to the Arabic alphabet in primary school.

While the art of calligraphy has failed to merge with modern art forms in Turkey as it has in other Islamic countries, there are some master practitioners of the calligraphic arts. Without the cultural development that comes with an integrated secular and religious culture that combines the language of daily expression (Ottoman in Arabic and Persian characters) with the holy word of the Koran (Arabic), this atrophy in calligraphic development is likely to persist.

Those today who learn Arabic are for the most part those who attend religious schools. Western art forms have not been part of the curricula in these schools. Turkey's young painters are occasionally fascinated with the rich possibilities of Arabic calligraphy, but they are unable to use the characters except in an amateurish, superficial manner. They have become strangers to this part of their own cultural heritage.

Turkish Painters Abroad

Links with Europe have woven a tapestry in the development of modern art in Turkey. The United States from 1950 onwards has played a role, although a more peripheral one, and after worker migration to Germany, Austria, Sweden and the Netherlands became part of Turkey's national experience in the 1970s, a number of cities in Europe, Berlin in particular, have played formative roles in the lives of Turkish artists.

With few exceptions, until the 1970s, Turkish artists had lived abroad for only short periods, either as students or as established artists. Return to the 'fatherland', *vatan*, has exerted a powerful force as does 'longing for home', *vatan hasreti*. Dedication to promoting art in Turkey formed the creed accepted by many generations of Turkish painters. To remain abroad meant shirking one's responsibilities. Turkish artists comment on the irony that today their works gain value with the new middle class when reimported from abroad. While patriotism has strengthened Turkey's art movement, the absence of colonies of expatriate Turkish painters abroad has also meant that their art is not as universally recognized as it deserves to be.

To this simplistic generalization, there are two remarkable exceptions. One is Fikret Mualla (1903–1967), the other is Fahrelnissa Zeid (b. 1901). For many years both were overlooked or rejected at home because they 'jumped ship'. Both artists worked abroad for most of their lives, and each has achieved a universality of expression that transcends classification into a movement or a group. For this reason as well, some critics continue to exclude them from a review of modern Turkish art. All their paintings bear the indisputable mark of individuality, of genius. Mualla's work is inward looking, sometimes caustic and melancholic, but always brilliant in its colours and graceful, simplistic lines: the Paris bistros and bars, hungry workmen on the Istanbul-Munich train. Fahrelnissa Zeid's work is of monumental proportions, cosmic whirlwinds, 'I see the world from a higher plane', and searching portraits that bare the inner soul: scenes of Baghdad, Loch Lomond, the Day of Judgement, portraits of European intellectuals, beautiful women of society, and her own family.

Two people could not have led more different lives. Born on the Asian shore of the Bosphorus in 1902, Mualla grew up in the household of a modest Ottoman civil servant. He attended Galatasaray, but was only seventeen when his mother died. He became estranged from his father after his mother's death, and rarely mentioned his family again.

Between 1920 and 1926 he spent six years in Berlin studying graphic art. Upon his return to Turkey he could barely eke out a living and at the encouragement of friends turned to teaching. Unable to keep a teacher's job in Turkey, then confined to the Istanbul insane asylum at Bakırköy, Mualla fled from his native country. But Mualla's departure was a quiet one; he simply boarded the Orient Express in 1938 with a small inheritance from his father. Later when friends urged him to return he had a stock response: 'I cannot live in a country where trials have no jury'.

He died in a farmhouse in France on the slopes of the Alps, an impoverished alcoholic tended only by a softhearted, hardworking farmwoman. She had little idea of the treasures he produced, but Picasso, who had suggested he come to live with him in the south of France, and a number of European collectors already had recognized the strength of his talents. Only after his death has his work become so appreciated that canvases change hands for vast sums both abroad and in Turkey.

Mualla's gouache and watercolour paintings are filled with the seamy and extravagant sides of Paris nightlife. His drawings are a humorous, sometimes tortured, commentary on human behaviour. None of his work falls within the 'groups' of modern Turkish painters, and as such has been rejected by some as alien. The universality of his expression, his mastery of colour and his widespread popularity today in Turkey are the best evidence of native eyes identifying with and appreciating his art.

The other Turkish painter of the same generation who defies any classification into a Turkish 'group' or 'school' is Fahrelnissa Zeid. Born into a distinguished Turkish family of statesmen, intellectuals and nonconformists, Fahrelnissa Zeid was surrounded from early childhood with family warmth and supportive creativity. Long before the Atatürk Revolution 'liberated Turkish women' there were headstrong, creative and very independent women in her family. She spent her childhood in the luxury of Büyükada's mansions during the summer and the wealthy European quarters of Istanbul during the winter.

She began her formal education in the fine arts at the Istanbul Academy of Fine Arts (1920) and continued in Paris. Upon her return to Turkey she was among the founders of the 'D Group'. After 1935 she left Turkey as the wife of the Emir Zeid bin Hussein, to return only for an occasional exhibition or holiday, and a colossal one-woman show at Ankara's Hittite Museum in 1964 (see the chapter 'Jordan').

Since the 1970s more Turkish artists have remained abroad and succeeded in the competitive art world of New York and Paris. In 1977 leaders of this group mounted a joint exhibition in Istanbul, thus taking their work home to the Turkish public. Among them Avni Arbaş, Abidin Dino, Selim Turan, Hakkı Anlı, Adnan Varınca, Fahrelnissa Zeid's son from her first marriage, Nejat Melih Devrim (b. 1923), whose work is exhibited at the Museum of Modern Art in Paris, Yüksel Arslan, Sarkis Zabunyan, Gürkan Coşkun and Utku Varlık. Recognized for their work in New York are Erol Akyavas and Burhan Doğançay. Akyavaş, an architect by training, creates on canvas abstract studies of spatial relations or semi-abstractions of Ottoman miniature subjects, Kerbala, fortress walls as spatial elements or campaign tents pitched in a geometrically dissected campground. Doğançay is known for his 'Shadow Sculpture'. These are three-dimensional transformations of his 'Wall Paintings', published by the Centre Pompidou in their catalogue, *Les murs murmures, ils crient, ils chantent*. As the Turkish government has encouraged private sector enterprises since the 1980s to enter the international export market, artists have been able to move more freely back and forth between art capitals of the West and Turkey, without the old stigma of abandoning the national cause.

Modern Art Museums in Turkey

The opportunity for the general public, those who cannot afford to purchase paintings and are reticent to enter the more exclusive atmosphere of private galleries, to look at and learn about contemporary art, marks a major development in a country's progress in the arts. This did not happen early, nor did it develop in harmony with the extraordinary productivity of artists in Turkey.

Museum space was designated in 1937, more than half a century after the Academy of Fine Arts had opened in Istanbul. The space was a dramatic one, the crown prince's wing of the Dolmabahçe Palace. Its two storey windows look directly down on the sweep of the Bosphorus and across to the hills of Asia. Its growth as a museum has been sadly disappointing. The palace wing was quite unsuited to be a museum, without vast expenditure on renovation and climate control. That has never happened, and for long periods the collection remained shut, its collections dusty and mouldy, its staff not appointed or underpaid.

Efforts to open a museum date to Osman Hamdi himself. He well understood the role a museum could also play in the development of young painters, giving them the opportunity to open their visual horizons as well as to have a venue for exhibiting. This would not happen until the 1940s, where the impact of the newly opened museum is evident on the young generation of painters who followed the 'D' group. During subsequent long periods when the museum remained shut, students entered and graduated from the Academy without ever seeing the inside of the collection.

Not until the 1980s would a real museum of modern Turkish painting and sculpture open, this time in Ankara. Ankara had not only a handsome structure to house modern art, but also the means to restore, manage and build a healthy, growing collection in an interactive environment open to school children, artists and connoisseurs. Its founders acquired the former 'Turkish Hearth' (*Türk Ocağı*) meeting place, a neo-Ottoman structure designed by Arif Koyunoğlu (1888–1982) in the 1930s, situated appropriately enough between the old, traditional centre of the city and the planned government centre laid out during the 1930s.

The building has been totally revamped and is well suited to its new function. Today it houses restoration workshops, lecture halls and temporary exhibition space as well as the museum's growing permanent collection. When the museum first opened, the Istanbul Museum of Painting and Sculpture as well as Turkey's Labour Bank (*İş Bankası*) had to send early pioneering works of the nineteenth century on loan from their own collections so that the museum might have a comprehensive display of all stages in the development of contemporary Turkish art. As the museum acquires new work, especially from the young generation of painters, its own collection may come to equal the superior quality of its display space.

Banks as Custodians and Patrons of the Arts

The banks of Turkey have played a prominent role as custodians and patrons of the arts. Turkey's first national bank of the Republican period, the Labour Bank (*İş Bankası*), began to collect paintings from contemporary artists as far back as the late 1920s. Bank managers looked upon acquisition as a cultural responsibility. Today the Labour Bank has one of the nation's richest collections of modern art in its vaults. It also is a well-known donor to and publisher of books on the visual arts in Turkey. Consistently in the early period it played the role in publication, education and advocacy for the arts that one might expect of a national endowment for the arts. Major contributions to the public's understanding of modern art, such as Mustafa Cezar's book on *Osman Hamdi and Turkish Art Looking Westward*, Giray's book on *Mahmud Cuda*, Ataöv's book on *Eşref Üren* and *Atatürk, Painting and Sculpture*, are all publications of this bank. It has also provided exhibition space in many locations throughout Turkey.

Other banks that were founded somewhat later, such as Akbank, have tried to emulate the Labour Bank's prominence. They put out publications and also provide exhibition space at central locations in Turkish cities, giving a large public the opportunity to see new work and offering artists a wide selection of display space. Bank presidents and chairmen, among them some of Turkey's prominent elite, grasped the notion at a very early stage that new art forms were an important form of expression that not only deserved support but that also, in the long run, would repay early recognition of promise with high returns on the investment. They have proven themselves correct many times over.

Public Appreciation and the Market for Modern Art

How conducive an environment is to sustained artistic production may be gauged, in part, by market demand as well as by attendance at museums, private galleries and lectures and by articles in journals. The wider the spread or circulation, the greater the market or interest that the artist may count on to support his work.

Turkey has seen the interest in and demand for modern art spread to wider and wider zones emanating from Istanbul. In 1916 the first regular exhibitions began at Galatasaray in Istanbul, earlier ones of the 'First Istanbul Salon' were organized on an individual basis by the painter Şeker Ahmet Pasha from 1900 onwards at Pera Palace. By 1909 there was an 'Association of Ottoman Artists' and by 1914 critical reviews appeared regularly in the Association's periodical and the Istanbul papers. Artists, however, painted out of a sense of national duty and did not intend to sell. Paintings were usually given away, not sold. Making a living as an artist usually meant employment as a teacher, at best in a school of art. Few artists could think of living from their work and until the 1980s there was no real market. Subsequently, there was rapid expansion and after the 1970s private galleries opened in abundance.

Today a young painter has the choice not only of a wide selection of government and private exhibition spaces in Istanbul, but also of other locations elsewhere in Turkey such as Ankara, Izmir and even intermediate regional centres like Antalya. The small Aegean port of Bodrum has become a favourite painting and exhibition location for many of Turkey's prominent artists since the late 1960s. Here painters like Turan Erol and Cemil Eren, and architects, such as Turgut Cansever and Nail Çakırhan, both of them Aga Khan Award winners, ceramicists and sculptors have worked next to writers, such as Azra Erhat and Fatma Mansour or film producers and even popular singers like Zeki Müren. All of it is disorganized; there is no one atelier or festival to bring them together. Most of the production is seasonal, the results of a summer retreat, and finds its way to the exhibition spaces and galleries of the international market or the market of the largest Turkish cities in the winter. But some artists stay on to produce through the winter, and many more exhibit as well as sell in Bodrum during the summer. The town's fort, built by the Knights of Rhodes and handsomely restored by the Turkish Government, offers a dramatic exhibition space at the very entrance to the harbour. The town itself is littered with coffee shops and galleries, most of them effervescent, which offer display space to artists.

Moving from the centre, still Istanbul, to the periphery along the coast and eastwards into Anatolia shows how pervasive the interest in modern art has become. After the 1950s an industrial and interior design market opened to give many artists a means of livelihood between exhibitions. The graphic arts have so developed that commissions to artists for the design of book covers, television advertisements, posters, cartoons, theatre sets and even postage stamps are a standard part of the market's operation. Ceramicists, like Füreya Koral, are asked to do large-scale panels in public buildings, such as the ones she executed for the Patisserie Divan or the Hilton Hotel in Istanbul, as well as design items for mass production such as the work of Atilla Galatalı at the Eczacıbaşı Ceramic Factory. A few artists, like Cemil Eren, have worked in all the decorative architectural forms, including theatre sets, stained glass and mosaics in order to support themselves on their art alone and paint. Nevertheless, supporting oneself on art alone is no easy task. There is no government support that might provide studio space, materials and an income.

By contrast, however, artists in Turkey today have the freedom to express themselves as individuals, to display their works to a broad public and to sell. The Turkish artist today is faced with much the same circumstances as one working in New York or London. He must enter a highly competitive, if somewhat less discriminating market, via the major dealers or patrons of the arts, both public and private. He must compete with and ultimately dislodge older artists who have established such wide reputations that whatever they produce is reserved in advance. The artist must also find his or her own way into the market place, because the ability to sell at a profit depends in part on having received a foreign cachet of acceptance. On the other hand, he can turn to many means to promote his work. Turkey now has a variety of regular publications on the arts, some of them, like *Milliyet Sanat Dergisi* (The Nation's Art Journal), are devoted exclusively to the arts.

Art has become an established investment item. The market may at times seem fickle to the young artist, but in a country where galloping inflation has become endemic, works of art, no matter how unrecognized, have taken on an unusual security as well as pleasure value. Turkey's expanding industrial and modern service economy as well as the wealth of the new class of private and public entrepreneurs have created the main buying public.

Modern art is firmly rooted in Turkey. After more than one century of formation along Western lines, it has achieved a clear identity of its own.

See colour pp. 140–144 for plates of the following artists' work:

NURI ABAÇ
AVNI ARBAŞ
BEDRI RAHMI EYÖBOĞLU
YALÇIN GÖKÇEBAĞ
FIKRET MUALLA

ABIDIN DINO
Turkey, b. 1913
Dino was one of the original founders of the 'D Group' in 1933 and then 'The New Group' in the early 1940s. By 1938 he felt Turkey lagged fifty years behind Europe and made an about face to establish himself in Paris, first with illustrations then sketches and particularly abstracts. Abidin Dino has used watercolours, as well as other media, to create 'flower' paintings that float with a light wash and simplicity of abstract form. He was an important friend of Fikret Mualla. Among his striking works are those where he has created a luminescent surface of oils on whose dark surface float incandescent islands of striped colour.

Untitled
Oil on canvas
25 x 40 cm
Undated

DEVRIM ERBIL
Turkey, b. 1937
Erbil studied at the Academy of Fine Arts in Istanbul where he now teaches. The etched detail of his paintings, often combining oils and acrylics, move into a rhythmic whole. Turkish miniatures inspire many of his recent compositions. The cartographic images of the sixteenth century miniaturist, Matrakci Nasuh, have shaped his bird's-eye views over the cityscape of Istanbul to capture the city's complex details. Erbil's figurative paintings also include delicate variations on trees etched in long, knife-edge strokes that give the impression of an engraving. Erbil once reduced his work to two-dimensional trees and an abstract lyricism of the sea, only to return once again to a figurative, if flat, composition of trees and houses.

Migrating Birds
Oil on canvas
100 x 100 cm
1982

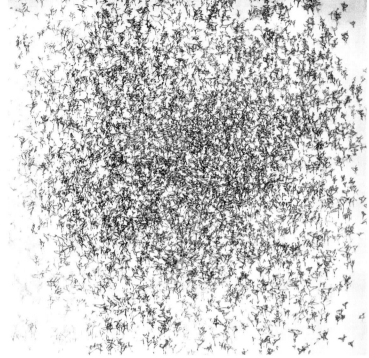

Cemil Eren
Turkey, b. 1917
Eren is one of Turkey's few self-taught artists. Born in Merzifon in central Anatolia, Eren trained as an officer. He has worked as a set designer and as a mosaicist in Ankara. His work has spanned many media, including stained glass for public buildings as well as ceramic panels. For a considerable period he focused on abstraction alone, and still today combines it with increasing experimentation in figuration. Today he is best known for his mastery of white, that has developed with his affection for Bodrum, a small town on the Aegean filled with white houses and fishing boats. His fascination with the smooth, silent cubism of Bodrum houses is an extension of his work in the abstract.

Bodrum
Oil on canvas
115 x 145 cm
1982

Turan Erol
Turkey, b. 1927
Born on Turkey's Aegean coast, Erol's mature work often returns to themes of his native region. He first studied in Istanbul under Bedri Rahmi Eyöboğlu, and then went on to Paris to study etching. Anatolia, village life and the wide, open fields form a special theme in his works, where monochromatic sensitivity throws into relief the day to day objects of life. These he produces with a technique which initially gives the impression of naivete compared to the polychromatic excitement of an earlier generation. He is bound to nature, without imitating it. It is the essence of nature, not what is taken in by the eye, that comes forth in bold patches of colour on his canvases.

Snowy Road
Oil on canvas
80 x 100 cm
1981

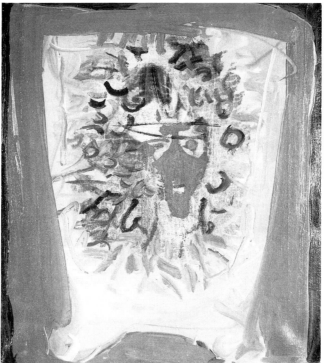

ADNAN TURANI
Turkey, b. 1925
Turani's work has been described as lyrical abstraction. He both pioneered and adhered to abstraction in a variety of forms. Born in Istanbul, Turani moved to Ankara to study and teach at the Gazi Institute before going on to teach at Hacettepe University. Most noted for his sweeping calligraphic expressions, Turani is one of the very few contemporary Turkish painters working seriously to integrate calligraphy into modern abstract expression. Colour never restricts his work; Turani moves through the firm, confident use of colour in all its shades and tones. He also has broken away to produce almost comic, cheerful canvases where the abstract openly suggests a bridal figure bedecked with streamers and the gay pastels of a marriage celebration.

Abstraction
Oil on canvas
55 x 50 cm
1980

BURHAN UYGUR
Turkey, b. 1940
Uygur shocks with intensely
intellectual, figurative paintings
whose subjects are often disturbed,
unbalanced or introverted, in sharp
contrast to the carefully balanced
layout of his composition. An
Academy of Fine Arts graduate and
a student of Bedri Rahmi Eyöboğlu,
Uygur also worked in Austria and
Holland before settling in Istanbul
to live by his art. The loneliness of
the individual in contemporary
society, figures frozen in dejected
contemplation, promise the viewer
a story behind the image. Uygur's
paintings have been used as
illustrations by a number of Turkish
writers and poets, and upon
occasion he himself has worked
with a poet to put together the
illustrations for a book. Critics have
frequently noted the poetic nature
and hypersensitivity of his
paintings.

Untitled
Mixed media/canvas
47 x 33 cm
1978

Yemen

Wijdan Ali

The birth of the modern art movement in North Yemen can be traced to the mid-seventies. The limited number of early artists, none of them with any formal art training, and the occasional group exhibition made the beginnings very simple. The government realized the need to train artists and started sending students on art scholarships to Arab and foreign art schools. With the advent of the eighties, those who had gone to study abroad started coming back, thus increasing the number of professional artists and the number of exhibitions, including one-person shows and an annual group exhibition.

In 1986 artist Fuad al-Futaih opened the first exhibition hall in Yemen. It was meant to be the nucleus for an arts centre.

In 1987 the Yemeni Artists' Society was established with thirty-five members – twelve of them artists and the rest gifted students and amateurs. Its aim was to help artists solve their problems, expose their work to the public and assist them in every way possible. With the increase in the number of exhibitions the public became interested in paintings and started to buy art works.

Among the pioneer artists were Hashim Ali, Fuad al-Futaih, Abdul Jabar Nu'man, Jamila Kamim, Abdou Hutheifi, Abdul Jalil Srouri, Abdul Aziz al-Zubeiri, al-Jarmouzi and al-Youssefi. Most of them paint local landscapes and subjects pertaining to local customs in a realistic manner.

In the Ministry of Information there is a Department of Plastic Arts which is concerned with artistic affairs and the promotion of arts and artists. Although there is no formal art teaching in the country, the number of government art scholarships to Arab countries, the Eastern Bloc and the West is ever increasing. Recently, the government commissioned al-Futaih to do the first modern sculpture in Yemen, entitled *Power and Peace*, for the new Sana' International Airport, showing an early sign of official art patronage.

FUAD AL-FUTAIH
Yemen, b. 1948
Trained in art in the Federal
Republic of Germany, Fuad al-
Futaih is the foremost North
Yemeni artist. He has represented
his country in the United States,
Europe and Asia. His illustrative,
highly detailed, stylized paintings
recall scenes from *A Thousand and
One Nights* in monochromatic
prints and silkscreens reminiscent
of Medieval woodcuts. A hardworking and diligent artist, al-
Futaih is the one to establish a
modern art movement in his
country.

Heaven and Earth 3
Silk screen
54 x 39 cm
1972